KU-298-027

DOMESDAY BOOK

Buckinghamshire

History from the Sources

DOMESDAY BOOK

A Survey of the Counties of England

LIBER DE WINTONIA

Compiled by direction of

KING WILLIAM I

Winchester
1086

DOMESDAY BOOK

text and translation edited by

JOHN MORRIS

13

Buckinghamshire

edited from a draft translation prepared by

Elizabeth Teague and Veronica Sankaran

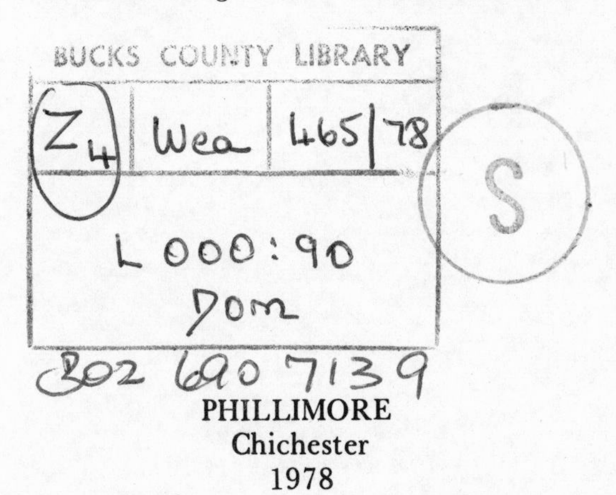

PHILLIMORE
Chichester
1978

1978
Published by
PHILLIMORE & CO. LTD.,
London and Chichester
Head Office: Shopwyke Hall,
Chichester, Sussex, England

© John Morris, 1978

ISBN 0 85033 167 6 (case)
ISBN 0 85033 168 4 (limp)

2.9. 7.P

Printed in Great Britain by
Titus Wilson & Son Ltd.,
Kendal

BUCKINGHAMSHIRE

Introduction

The Domesday Survey of Buckinghamshire

Notes on Text and Translation

Index of Persons

Index of Places

Maps and Map Keys

Systems of Reference

Technical Terms

History from the Sources
General Editor: John Morris

The series aims to publish history written directly from the sources for all interested readers, both specialists and others. The first priority is to publish important texts which should be widely available, but are not.

DOMESDAY BOOK

The contents, with the folio on which each county begins, are:

Domesday Book is termed *Liber de Wintonia* (The Book of Winchester) in column 332c

INTRODUCTION

The Domesday Survey

In 1066 Duke William of Normandy conquered England. He was crowned King, and most of the lands of the English nobility were soon granted to his followers. Domesday Book was compiled 20 years later. The Saxon Chronicle records that in 1085

> at Gloucester at midwinter ... the King had deep speech with his counsellors ... and sent men all over England to each shire ... to find out ... what or how much each landholder held ... in land and livestock, and what it was worth ... The returns were brought to him.[1]

William was thorough. One of his Counsellors reports that he also sent a second set of Commissioners 'to shires they did not know, where they were themselves unknown, to check their predecessors' survey, and report culprits to the King.'[2]

The information was collected at Winchester, corrected, abridged, chiefly by omission of livestock and the 1066 population, and fair-copied by one writer into a single volume. Norfolk, Suffolk and Essex were copied, by several writers, into a second volume, unabridged, which states that 'the Survey was made in 1086'. The surveys of Durham and Northumberland, and of several towns, including London, were not transcribed, and most of Cumberland and Westmorland, not yet in England, was not surveyed. The whole undertaking was completed at speed, in less than 12 months, though the fair-copying of the main volume may have taken a little longer. Both volumes are now preserved at the Public Record Office. Some versions of regional returns also survive. One of them, from Ely Abbey,[3] copies out the Commissioners' brief. They were to ask

> The name of the place. Who held it, before 1066, and now?
> How many *hides*?[4] How many ploughs, both those in lordship and the men's?
> How many villagers, cottagers and slaves, how many free men and Freemen?[5]
> How much woodland, meadow and pasture? How many mills and fishponds?
> How much has been added or taken away? What the total value was and is?
> How much each free man or Freeman had or has? All threefold, before 1066, when King William gave it, and now; and if more can be had than at present?

The Ely volume also describes the procedure. The Commissioners took evidence on oath 'from the Sheriff; from all the barons and their Frenchmen; and from the whole Hundred, the priests, the reeves and six villagers from each village'. It also names four Frenchmen and four Englishmen from each Hundred, who were sworn to verify the detail.

The King wanted to know what he had, and who held it. The Commissioners therefore listed lands in dispute, for Domesday Book was not only a tax-assessment. To the King's grandson, Bishop Henry of Winchester, its purpose was that every 'man should know his right and not usurp another's'; and because it was the final authoritative register of rightful possession 'the natives called it Domesday Book, by analogy

[1] Before he left England for the last time, late in 1086. [2] Robert Losinga, Bishop of Hereford 1079-1095 (see *E.H.R.* 22, 1907, 74). [3] *Inquisitio Eliensis,* first paragraph. [4] A land unit, reckoned as 120 acres. [5] *Quot Sochemani.*

from the Day of Judgement'; that was why it was carefully arranged by Counties, and by landholders within Counties, 'numbered consecutively ... for easy reference'.[6]

Domesday Book describes Old English society under new management, in minute statistical detail. Foreign lords had taken over, but little else had yet changed. The chief landholders and those who held from them are named, and the rest of the population was counted. Most of them lived in villages, whose houses might be clustered together, or dispersed among their fields. Villages were grouped in administrative districts called Hundreds, which formed regions within Shires, or Counties, which survive today with minor boundary changes; the recent deformation of some ancient county identities is here disregarded, as are various short-lived modern changes. The local assemblies, though overshadowed by lords great and small, gave men a voice, which the Commissioners heeded. Very many holdings were described by the Norman term *manerium* (manor), greatly varied in size and structure, from tiny farmsteads to vast holdings; and many lords exercised their own jurisdiction and other rights, termed *soca*, whose meaning still eludes exact definition.

The Survey was unmatched in Europe for many centuries, the product of a sophisticated and experienced English administration, fully exploited by the Conqueror's commanding energy. But its unique assemblage of facts and figures has been hard to study, because the text has not been easily available, and abounds in technicalities. Investigation has therefore been chiefly confined to specialists; many questions cannot be tackled adequately without a cheap text and uniform translation available to a wider range of students, including local historians.

Previous Editions

The text has been printed once, in 1783, in an edition by Abraham Farley, probably of 1250 copies, at Government expense, said to have been £38,000; its preparation took 16 years. It was set in a specially designed type, here reproduced photographically, which was destroyed by fire in 1808. In 1811 and 1816 the Records Commissioners added an introduction, indices, and associated texts, edited by Sir Henry Ellis; and in 1861-1863 the Ordnance Survey issued zincograph facsimiles of the whole. Texts of individual counties have appeared since 1673, separate translations in the Victoria County Histories and elsewhere.

This Edition

Farley's text is used, because of its excellence, and because any worthy alternative would prove astronomically expensive. His text has been checked against the facsimile, and discrepancies observed have been verified against the manuscript, by the kindness of Miss Daphne Gifford of the Public Record Office. Farley's few errors are indicated in the notes.

[6] *Dialogus de Scaccario* 1,16.

The editor is responsible for the translation and lay-out. It aims at what the compiler would have written if his language had been modern English; though no translation can be exact, for even a simple word like 'free' nowadays means freedom from different restrictions. Bishop Henry emphasized that his grandfather preferred 'ordinary words'; the nearest ordinary modern English is therefore chosen whenever possible. Words that are now obsolete, or have changed their meaning, are avoided, but measurements have to be transliterated, since their extent is often unknown or arguable, and varied regionally. The terse inventory form of the original has been retained, as have the ambiguities of the Latin.

Modern English commands two main devices unknown to 11th century Latin, standardised punctuation and paragraphs; in the Latin, *ibi* ('there are') often does duty for a modern full stop, *et* ('and') for a comma or semi-colon. The entries normally answer the Commissioners' questions, arranged in five main groups, (i) the place and its holder, its hides, ploughs and lordship; (ii) people; (iii) resources; (iv) value; and (v) additional notes. The groups are usually given as separate paragraphs.

King William numbered chapters 'for easy reference', and sections within chapters are commonly marked, usually by initial capitals, often edged in red. They are here numbered. Maps, indices and an explanation of technical terms are also given. Later, it is hoped to publish analytical and explanatory volumes, and associated texts.

The editor is deeply indebted to the advice of many scholars, too numerous to name, and especially to the Public Record Office, and to the publisher's patience. The draft translations are the work of a team; they have been co-ordinated and corrected by the editor, and each has been checked by several people. It is therefore hoped that mistakes may be fewer than in versions published by single fallible individuals. But it would be Utopian to hope that the translation is altogether free from error; the editor would like to be informed of mistakes observed.

The maps are the work of Jim Hardy.

The preparation of this volume has been greatly assisted by a generous grant from the Leverhulme Trust Fund.

Conventions

* refers to a note to the Latin text

[ ] enclose words omitted in the MS.

( ) enclose editorial explanations.

BOCHINGHSCIRE.

143 a

BOCHINGHEHĀ cū Bortone Pro una hida se defđ. T.R.E. & modo similit facit. Tra. ē. viii. carucarū. In dñio sunt. ii. 7 uitti hnt. iii. car 7 dim. 7 adhuc ii. 7 dim poss fieri. Ibi sunt xxvi. burgenses. 7 xi. borđ. 7 ii. serui. Ibi. i. molin de. xiiii. sot. Ptū. viii. car. Pasta ad pecuniā uillæ. In totis ualentijs. T.R.E. reddeb. x. lib ad numerū. Modo reddit. xvi. lib de albo argento.

Æcclam huj burgi ten Remigi eps. 7 trā. iiii. car quæ ad eā ptin. Ibi sunt. iiii. car. 7 iii. uitti. 7 iii. borđ. 7 x. cot. 7 i. molin. x. solidoꝝ. Ptū. ii. car. Nem ad sepes. Valet 7 ualuit. vi. lib. T.R.E. vii. lib. Hanc æcclam tenuit Wluui eps de rege. E.

BUCKINGHAMSHIRE

B

1 BUCKINGHAM with BOURTON answered for 1 hide before 1066 and does the same now. Land for 8 ploughs; in lordship 2. The villagers have 3½ ploughs; a further 2½ possible. — 143 a

26 burgesses, 11 smallholders and 2 slaves.

1 mill at 14s; meadow for 8 ploughs; pasture for the village livestock.

In total value it paid £10 at face value before 1066; now it pays £16 in white silver.

2 Bishop Remigius holds the church of this Borough. Land for 4 ploughs, which belong to it. 4 ploughs there.

3 villagers, 3 smallholders and 10 cottagers.

1 mill, 10s; meadow for 2 ploughs; wood for fencing.

The value is and was £6; before 1066 £7.

Bishop Wulfwy held this church from King Edward.

In hoc burgo eps constantiensis ht . III . burgses. quos tenuit Wluuard fili Eddeuæ . Hi reddunt VI . sol 7 VI . den . p annu . 7 regi reddt . XI . den.

Hugo comes ht . I . burgsem . q fuit ho Burcardi de senelai. Hic reddit . XXVI . den . p annu . 7 regi . V . denar.

Robt de Olgi ht . I . burg . qui fuit ho Azor . f . Toti. Hic reddit . XVI . den . 7 regi . V . denar.

Rogeri de Juri ht . IIII . burg . qui fuer hoes ejd Azor. Hi reddt . VII . sol 7 VI . den . 7 regi XIII . denar.

Hugo de bolebec ht . IIII . burg . qui fuer hoes Alrici. Hi reddt . XXVIII . den . 7 regi . XII . denar.

Manno brito ht . IIII . burg . qui fuer hoes Eddeue femine Syred . Hi reddt . XXIX . den . regi nil deb.

Hascoius musart ht . I . burg . qui fuit ho Azor f . Toti. Hic reddit . XVI . den . 7 regi . II os . denar.

Ernulf de Hesding ht . I . burg . qui fuit Wilaf. Hic reddit p annu . II . sol . 7 regi . III . den.

Wills de castellon de feudo epi baiocensis ht II . burg . qui fuer hoes Leuuini comitis . Hi reddt . XVI . den . 7 regi m nichil . sed T.R.E . reddeb . III . den. De feudo Alberici com . I . burg . redd regi . II . den.

Leuuin de Neuueha ht . V . burg . 7 T.R.E . habuit. Hi reddt ei . IIII or . sol p annu . 7 regi . XII . den.

3 In this Borough the Bishop of Coutances has 3 burgesses, whom Wulfward son of Edeva held. They pay 6s 6d a year, and pay the King 11d.

4 Earl Hugh has 1 burgess who was Burghard of Shenley's man. He pays 26d a year, and 5d to the King.

5 Robert d'Oilly has 1 burgess who was Azor son of Toti's man. He pays 16d, and 5d to the King.

6 Roger of Ivry has 4 burgesses who were also Azor's men. They pay 7s 6d, and 13d to the King.

7 Hugh of Bolbec has 4 burgesses who were Alric's men. They pay 28d, and 12d to the King.

8 Mainou the Breton has 4 burgesses who were men of Edeva, wife of Sired. They pay 29d; they owe nothing to the King.

9 Hascoit Musard has 1 burgess who was Azor son of Toti's man. He pays 16d, and 2d to the King.

10 Arnulf of Hesdin has 1 burgess who was Wiglaf's. He pays 2s a year, and 3d to the King.

11 William of Castellion has 2 burgesses, of the holding of the Bishop of Bayeux, who were Earl Leofwin's men. They pay 16d, and now nothing to the King; but before 1066 they paid 3d.

12 From Earl Aubrey's holding, 1 burgess pays 2d to the King.

13 Leofwin of Nuneham has 5 burgesses, and had them before 1066. They pay him 4s a year, and 12d to the King.

.I.REX WILLELMVS.

.II.Archieps cantuariens.

.III.Eps Wintonienſis.

.IIII Eps Lincolienſis.

.V.Eps Baiocenſis.

.VI.Eps Conſtantienſis.

.VII Eps Liſiacenſis.

.VIII Abb Weſtmonaſt.

.IX.Abb de S Albano.

.X.Abbatiſſa de berching.

.XI.Canonici de Oxeneford.

.XII Rainbaldꝰ pbr.

.XIII Comes moritonienſis.

.XIIII.Comes Hugo de ceſtre.

.XV.Walterius gifard.

.XVI.Wiłłs de Warenna.

.XVII.Wiłłs peurel.

.XVIII.Wiłłs filius Anſculfi.

.XIX Robtꝰ de Todeni.

.XX.Robtꝰ de Oilgi.

.XXI.Robtꝰ gernon.

.XXII.Goisfridꝰ de manneuile.

.XXIII Giſlebtus de gand.

.XXIIII.Milo criſpin.

.XXV.Eduuard de Sariſberie.

.XXVI.Hugo de belcamp.

.XXVII Hugo de bolebech.

XXVIII.Henricus de ferrarijs.

.XXIX Walterius de vernon.

.XXX.Walterius filiꝰ Other.

.XXXI.Walterius flandrenſis.

.XXXII.Wiłłs de felgeres.

.XXXIII.Wiłłs camerarius.

XXXIIII.Wiłłs filius conſtantini.

.XXXV.Wiłłs filius magni.

.XXXVI.Turſtinꝰ filius Rolfi.

.XXXVII.Turſtinꝰ mantel.

.XXXVIII Radulfꝰ de felgeres.

.XL.Bertrannꝰ de Verduno.

.XLI.Nigellꝰ de Albinio.

.XLII.Nigellꝰ de bereuille.

.XLIII.Rogerius de Jueri.

.XLIIII.Ricardus Ingania.

.XLV.Manno brito.

.XLVI.Gozelinus brito.

.XLVII.Vrſo de berſeres.

.XLVIII.Winemarus.

.XLIX.Martinus.

.L.Herueus Legatus.

.LI.Haſcoitus muſart.

.LII.Gunfridꝰ de cioches.

.LIII.Gilo fr Anſculfi.

.LIIII.Mathildis regina.

.LV.Judita comitiſſa.

.LVI.Azelina uxor tailgeboſch.

.LVII Taini regis 7 elemoſinarij.

[LIST OF LANDHOLDERS IN BUCKINGHAMSHIRE]

1 King William
2 The Archbishop of Canterbury
3 The Bishop of Winchester
3a The Bishop of Lincoln
4 The Bishop of Bayeux
5 The Bishop of Coûtances
6 The Bishop of Lisieux
7 The Abbot of Westminster
8 The Abbot of St. Albans
9 The Abbess of Barking
10 The Canons of Oxford
11 Reinbald the Priest
12 The Count of Mortain
13 Earl Hugh of Chester
14 Walter Giffard
15 William of Warenne
16 William Peverel
17 William son of Ansculf
18 Robert of Tosny
19 Robert d'Oilly
20 Robert Gernon
21 Geoffrey de Mandeville
22 Gilbert of Ghent
23 Miles Crispin
24 Edward of Salisbury
25 Hugh of Beauchamp
26 Hugh of Bolbec
27 Henry of Ferrers
28 Walter of Vernon
29 Walter son of Othere
30 Walter the Fleming
31 William of Feugeres
32 William the Chamberlain
33 William son of Constantine
34 William son of Mann
35 Thurstan son of Rolf
36 Thurstan Mantle
37 Ralph of Feugeres
38 Bertram of Verdun
39 Nigel of Aubigny
40 Nigel of Berville
41 Roger of Ivry
42 Richard the Artificer
43 Mainou the Breton
44 Jocelyn the Breton
45 Urso of Bercheres
46 Winemar [the Fleming]
47 Martin
48 Hervey the Commissioner
49 Hascoit Musard
50 Gunfrid of Chocques
51 Giles brother of Ansculf
52 Queen Matilda
53 Countess Judith
54 Azelina wife of [Ralph] Tallboys
[55 Alric Cook]
[56 Alfsi]
57 [Leofwin of Nuneham and] the King's thanes and almsmen.

TERRA REGIS.

EILESBERIA dnicū maneriū regis. p xvi.
hid se desd sēp. Tra. ē. xvi. car. In dnio
sunt. ii. Ibi xx. uilli cū. xiiii. bord. hnt. x. car.
7 adhuc. iiii. poss fieri. Ibi. ii. serui. 7 ii. molini
de. xxiii. sol. Ptū. viii. car. 7 de remanenti. xx. sol.
In totis ualentijs reddit. lvi. lib arsas 7 pensatas.
7 de Theloneo. x. lib ad numerū. T.R.E. reddeb
xxv. lib ad numerū

In hoc M fuit 7 est. unus sochs habens. i. uirg træ
quā potuit dare l uende cui uoluit. 7 tam seruit
sēp uicecomiti regis. Æcclam huj M ten eps Lincoliensis.

143 c

M WENDOVRE. p xxiiii. hid se desd sēp. Tra. ē
xxvi. car. In dnio sunt. iii. car. Ibi xxvi. uilli
cū. vi. bord. hnt. xvii. car. 7 vi. adhuc poss fieri.
Ibi. ii. molini de. x. sol. ptū. iii. car. 7 de rema
nenti. xx. sol. Silua. ii. mil porc. In totis ualent
reddit p annū. xxxviii. lib Arsas 7 pensatas. T.R.E.
reddeb. xxv. lib ad numerū. In hoc M sunt. ii. sochi.
unā hid 7 dim tenent. non jacuer ibi T.R.E.

M RISEBERGE. fuit uilla Heraldi com. p. xxx. hid se
desd sēp. Tra. ē. xxiiii. car. In dnio. xx. hidæ. 7 ibi
sunt. iiii. car. Ibi xxx. uilli cū. xii. bord. hnt xx.
car. Ibi. iii. serui. 7 ii. molini de. xiiii. sol 7 viii. den.
ptū. vii. car. Silua. mille porc. Int tot reddit
p annū. xl.vii. lib de albo argento. xvi. den min.
T.R.E. reddeb. x. lib ad numerum. In hoc M jacet
7 jacuit qdā burgensis de Oxeneford redd. ii. sol.
Adhuc un salinarius de Wicg. redd sūmas salis.
7 in eod M fuit 7 est qdā sochs. iii. uirg tenens.
uende qdem potuit. sed tam uicecomiti seruiu.

[1] LAND OF THE KING

[In AYLESBURY Hundred]

1 AYLESBURY, a household manor of the King, always answered for 16 hides. Land for 16 ploughs; in lordship 2.
20 villagers with 14 smallholders have 10 ploughs; a further 4 possible
2 slaves; 2 mills at 23s; meadow for 8 ploughs; from the remainder, 20s.
In total value it pays £56 assayed and weighed and from tolls £10 at face value; before 1066 it paid £25 at face value.
In this manor there was and is one Freeman who has 1 virgate of land which he could grant or sell to whom he would; however he always serves the King's Sheriff. The Bishop of Lincoln holds the church of this manor.

2 M. WENDOVER always answered for 24 hides. 143 c
Land for 26 ploughs; in lordship 3 ploughs.
26 villagers with 6 smallholders have 17 ploughs; a further 6 possible
2 mills at 10s; meadow for 3 ploughs; from the remainder, 20s; woodland, 2,000 pigs.
In total value it pays £38 a year, assayed and weighed; before 1066 it paid £25 at face value.
In this manor are 2 Freemen who hold 1½ hides; they did not lie there before 1066.

[In RISBOROUGH Hundred]

3 M. (Princes) RISBOROUGH was a village of Earl Harold. It always answered for 30 hides. Land for 24 ploughs; in lordship 20 hides; 4 ploughs there.
30 villagers with 12 smallholders have 20 ploughs.
3 slaves; 2 mills at 14s 8d; meadow for 7 ploughs; woodland, 1,000 pigs.
In total it pays £47 a year in white silver less 16d; before 1066 it paid £10 at face value.
In this manor there lie and lay (the dues of) a burgess of Oxford who pays 2s; further a salt-boiler of Droitwich pays... packloads of salt; in the same manor was and is a Freeman who holds 3 virgates; although he could sell, he nevertheless served the Sheriff.

ɱ Sveneborne . uilla fuit Heraldi com̃. p̱ IIII . hid̃
7 dim̃ se defd̃ . Tra . ẽ . IIII . car̃ . In dñio . III . hidæ
7 III . uirg̃ . 7 ibi . ẽ una car̃ . 7 alia pot̃ fieri . Ibi . III .
uitti hñt . I . car̃ 7 dim̃ . 7 tot poss̃ fieri adhuc . Ibi
un̄ seruus . 7 p̃tũ . v . car̃ . Int̃ totũ redd̃ p̱ annũ
xxx . sol̃ de albo argento . T.R.E. xxx . sol̃ ad num̃.
ɱ Opetone fuit uilla Heraldi com̃. p̱ XVIII . hid̃
se defd̃ . Tra . ẽ . x . car̃ . In dñio . II . hidæ 7 dim̃.
7 ibi sunt . II . car̃ . Ibi . XIX . uitti cũ . v . bord̃ . hñt
xv . car̃ . Ibi . II . serui . 7 I . molin̄ de . IIII . sol̃ . De
piscar̃ . mitt anguitt . p̃tũ . II . car̃ . Silua . cc . porc̃.
Int̃ tot̃ redd̃ p̱ annũ XXI . lib̃ arsas 7 pensatas.
T.R.E. reddeb̃ . xv . lib̃ ad numerum.
ɱ Brvnhelle fuit ɱ . R . E . p̱ . xx . hid̃ se defd̃
sep̱ . Tra . ẽ . xxv . car̃ . In dñio sunt . III . Ibi . XIX .
uitti cũ . XIII . bord̃ . hñt . XVII . car̃ . 7 adhuc . v .
poss̃ fieri . Ibi . II . serui . 7 I . molin̄ de . x . sol̃ . p̃tũ . xx .
car̃ . Silua . cc . porc̃ . Int̃ tot̃ reddit p̱ annũ . XXXVIII .
lib̃ de albo argento . 7 pro foresta . XII . lib̃ arsas
7 pensatas . T . R . E . reddeb̃ . XVIII . lib̃ ad numerũ.
ɱ Bechesdene ten̄ Rex . W. *In Stofald hvnd̃.*
Alberic̃ com habuit de eo . Ibi . IIII . hidæ 7 I . uirg̃.
Tra . ẽ . VIII . car̃ . In dñio . II . hide . 7 ibi . ẽ una car̃.
7 II . plus poss̃ fieri . Ibi . IIII . uitti 7 v . bord̃ . hñt
II . car̃ . 7 III . poss̃ fieri adhuc . Ibi . IIII . serui . 7 II .
molini de . XXVIII . den̄ . p̃tũ . I . car̃ . Silua . cc . porc̃.
Val̃ . xxx . sol̃ . Q̃do recep̃ . IIII . lib̃ . T.R.E. XL . sol̃.
Hoc ɱ tenuit Azor filius Tored . teign̄ . R . E.

[In MURSLEY Hundred]

4 M. SWANBOURNE was a village of Earl Harold. It answers for 4½ hides. Land for 4 ploughs; in lordship 3 hides and 3 virgates; 1 plough there, another possible.

3 villagers have 1½ ploughs; as many again possible.

1 slave; meadow for 5 ploughs.

In total it pays 30s a year in white silver; before 1066, 30s at face value.

[In STONE Hundred]

5 M. UPTON was a village of Earl Harold. It answers for 18 hides. Land for 10 ploughs; in lordship 2½ hides; 2 ploughs there.

19 villagers with 5 smallholders have 15 ploughs.

2 slaves; 1 mill at 4s; from the fishery 1,000 eels; meadow for 2 ploughs; woodland, 200 pigs.

In total it pays £21 a year assayed and weighed; before 1066 it paid £15 at face value.

[In IXHILL Hundred]

6 M. BRILL was a manor of King Edward's. It always answered for 20 hides. Land for 25 ploughs; in lordship 3.

19 villagers with 13 smallholders have 17 ploughs; a further 5 possible.

2 slaves; 1 mill at 10s; meadow for 20 ploughs; woodland, 200 pigs.

In total it pays £38 a year in white silver, and for the Forest £12 assayed and weighed; before 1066 it paid £18 at face value.

In STOTFOLD Hundred

7 M. King William holds BIDDLESDEN. Earl Aubrey had it from him. 4 hides and 1 virgate. Land for 8 ploughs; in lordship 2 hides; 1 plough there, 2 more possible.

4 villagers and 5 smallholders have 2 ploughs; a further 3 possible.

4 slaves; 2 mills at 28d; meadow for 1 plough; woodland, 200 pigs.

Value 30s; when acquired £4; before 1066, 40s.

Azor son of Thored, a thane of King Edward's, held this manor.

.II. TERRA LANFRANCI ARCH̄. *IN STANES HVND̄.*

M̄ ARCHIEPS LANFRANCVS ten̄ *NEDREHAM.*

p̄. XL. hid̄ se defd̄. Tra. ē. XXX. car̄. In dn̄io XVIII. hidæ. 7 ibi sunt. VI. car̄. Ibi. XL. uitt̄i cū. XVI. bord̄ hn̄t. XIIII. car̄. 7 x. poss̄ fieri adhuc. Ibi. XV. serui. 7 II. molini de. XX. sol̄. P̄tū. VI. car̄. Pasta ad pecun̄. 7 ad firmā archiepi p̄ VIII. dies fenū. In totis ualentijs uat. XL. lib̄. Q̄do recep̄: XX. lib̄. T.R.E: XL. lib̄. De hac tra ten̄ Gisleb̄t p̄b̄r de Arch̄. III. hid̄ 7 I. æccl̄am cū decim̄. Tra. ē. I. car̄. 7 ibi. ē cū uno uitt̄o 7 III. bord̄. Vat 7 ualuit sēp. LX. sol̄. Hoc M̄ tenuit Tosti comes.

M̄ Ipse Archieps ten̄ *HALTONE*. p̄ V. hid̄ se defd̄. Tra. ē VII. car̄. In dn̄io. II. hide 7 dim̄. 7 ibi sunt. II. car̄. Ibi X. uitt̄i cū. XV. bord̄. hn̄t. V. car̄. Ibi. I. molin̄ de. XV. sol̄. p̄tū. II. car̄. Silua. C. porc̄. 7 II. sol̄. In totis ualent̄ uat. VIII. lib̄. 7 ualuit sēp. Hoc M̄ tenuit Leuuin̄ com̄.

M̄ Ipse Archieps ten̄ *RISEBERGE.* *IN RISEBERG HVND̄.*

p̄. XXX. hid̄ se defd̄. Tra. ē. XIIII. car̄. In dn̄io. XVI. hidæ. 7 ibi sunt. II. car̄. Ibi XXXII. uitt̄i cū. VIII. bord̄ hn̄t. XII. car̄. Ibi. IIII. serui. P̄tū. VI. car̄. Silua. CCC. porc̄. In totis ualent̄ uat. XVI. lib̄. Q̄do recep̄: C. sol̄. T.R.E: XVI. lib̄. Hoc M̄ tenuit Asgar stalre de æccl̄a xp̄i cantuar̄. ita qd̄ n̄ poterat separari ab æccl̄a T.R.E.

.III. TERRA WINTONIENSIS EP̄I.

M̄ WALCHELINVS eps Winton̄ ten̄ *WICVMBE.*

p̄ XIX. hid̄ se defd̄. Tra. ē. XXIII. car̄. In dn̄io. V. hidæ. 7 ibi sunt. III. car̄. Ibi. XXVII. uitt̄i cū. VIII. bord̄ hn̄t XIX. car̄. Ibi. VII. serui. 7 III. molini de. XX. solid̄. 7 I. piscar̄ de mitt Anguitt̄. P̄tū. VII. car̄. Silua. mille porc̄. In totis ualent̄ uat. XV. lib̄. Q̄do recep̄: X. lib̄. T.R.E:

2 LAND OF ARCHBISHOP LANFRANC

143 d

In STONE Hundred

1 M. Archbishop Lanfranc holds HADDENHAM. It answers for 40 hides.
Land for 30 ploughs; in lordship 18 hides; 6 ploughs there.
40 villagers with 16 smallholders have 14 ploughs; a further 10 possible.
15 slaves; 2 mills at 20s; meadow for 6 ploughs.
Pasture for the livestock; eight days' hay for the Archbishop's revenue.
Total value £40; when acquired £20; before 1066 £40.
Gilbert the priest holds 3 hides of this land from the Archbishop, and 1 church with tithes. Land for 1 plough; it is there, with
1 villager and 3 smallholders.
The value is and always was 60s.
Earl Tosti held this manor.

[In AYLESBURY Hundred]

2 M. The Archbishop holds HALTON himself. It answers for 5 hides.
Land for 7 ploughs; in lordship 2½ hides; 2 ploughs there.
10 villagers with 15 smallholders have 5 ploughs.
1 mill at 15s; meadow for 2 ploughs; woodland, 100 pigs and 2s too.
The total value is and always was £8.
Earl Leofwin held this manor.

In RISBOROUGH Hundred

3 M. The Archbishop holds (Monks) RISBOROUGH himself.
It answers for 30 hides. Land for 14 ploughs;
in lordship 16 hides; 2 ploughs there.
32 villagers with 8 smallholders have 12 ploughs.
4 slaves; meadow for 6 ploughs; woodland, 300 pigs.
Total value £16; when acquired 100s; before 1066 £16.
Asgar the Constable held this manor from Christ Church, Canterbury, before 1066, on condition that it could not be separated from the church.

3 LAND OF THE BISHOP OF WINCHESTER

[In DESBOROUGH Hundred]

1 M. WALKELIN, Bishop of Winchester holds (West) WYCOMBE. It answers for 19 hides. Land for 23 ploughs; in lordship 5 hides; 3 ploughs there.
27 villagers with 8 smallholders have 19 ploughs.
7 slaves; 3 mills at 20s; 1 fishery at 1,000 eels; meadow for 7 ploughs; woodland, 1,000 pigs.
Total value £15; when acquired £10; before 1066 £12.

xii. lib. Hoc M̄ fuit 7 est de uictu monachoꝝ æcclæ Winton. Stigand tenuit. T.R.E. *In Erlai hvnd.*

M̄ Ipse eps Winton ten *Evinghehov*. p xx. hid se defd. Tra. ē. xxv. car. In dnio. v. hidæ. 7 ibi sunt. iii. car. 7 iiii. pot fieri. Ibi xxviii. uitti. cū. iiii. bord hnt xx. car. 7 adhuc pot. i. fieri. Ibi. vi. serui. ptū. v. car. Silua sexcent porc. 7 x. sol. In totis ualent uat. xviii. lib. Qdo recep: x. lib. T.R.E: xv. lib. Hoc M̄ jacuit 7 jacet in dnio æcclæ S Petri Wintoniensis.

TERRA EPI LINCOLIENSIS. *In Elesberie hd*

M̄ Remigius eps Lincoliæ ten *Stoches*. p viii. hid se defd. Tra. ē. xxi. car. In dnio. iii. hidæ. 7 ibi sunt vi. car. Ibi. xx. uitti cū. iiii. bord hnt. xv. car. Ibi. iii. serui. 7 i. molin de. x. sol. Silua. xxx. porc. Ptū. iii. car. Hoc M̄ jacet ad æcclam de Elesberie. Ibi. xviii. bord qui reddunt p annū. xx. sol. In totis ualent uat. xx. lib. Qdo recep: xii. lib. T.R.E: xviii. lib. Hoc M̄ cū æccla tenuit Wluui eps T.R.E. De. viii. hund q jacent in circuitu Elesberie. unusqisq, sochs qui ht. i. hidā aut plus: redd unā sumā annonæ huic æcclæ. Adhuc etiā de unoqq, socho. i. ac annonæ aut. iiii. denarij soluebant huic æcclæ T.R.E. sed post aduentū regis. W. redditū non fuit.

144 a

M̄ *Bocheland* ten Walter de Remigio epo. p. x. hid se defd. Tra. ē. viii. car. In dnio sunt. ii. 7 7 xiiii. uitti cū. vi. bord. hnt. vi. car. ptū. ii. car. Silua. ccc. porc. Int totū uat. viii. lib. Qdo recep: iii. lib. T.R.E: x. lib. Hoc M̄ tenuit Godric fr Wluui epi. n potuit dare t uende pter ej licentiā. *In Bvrneha hvnd.*

Isdē Walter ten de eod epo dim hidā. Tra. ē dim car. Vat 7 ualuit sēp. v. sol. Hanc terrā

This manor was and is for the supplies of the monks of the Church of Winchester. Stigand held it before 1066.

In YARDLEY Hundred

2 M. The Bishop of Winchester holds IVINGHOE himself. It answers for 20 hides. Land for 25 ploughs; in lordship 5 hides; 3 ploughs there; a fourth possible.
28 villagers with 4 smallholders have 20 ploughs; a further 1 possible.
6 slaves; meadow for 5 ploughs; woodland, 600 pigs and 10s too.
Total value £18; when acquired £10; before 1066 £15.
This manor lay and lies in the lordship of St. Peter's Church of Winchester.

[3a] LAND OF THE BISHOP OF LINCOLN

In AYLESBURY Hundred

1 M. REMIGIUS Bishop of Lincoln holds STOKE (Mandeville). It answers for 8 hides. Land for 21 ploughs; in lordship 3 hides; 6 ploughs there.
20 villagers with 4 smallholders have 15 ploughs.
3 slaves; 1 mill at 10s; woodland, 30 pigs; meadow for 3 ploughs.
This manor lies with the (lands of) Aylesbury Church.
18 smallholders who pay 20s a year.
Total value £20; when acquired £12; before 1066 £18.
Bishop Wulfwy held this manor with the church before 1066.
From the eight hundreds which lie in the circuit of Aylesbury, each Freeman who has 1 hide or more pays one load of corn to this church. Furthermore from each Freeman 1 acre of corn or 4d was paid over to this church before 1066, but after the coming of King William it was not paid.

2 M. Walter holds BUCKLAND from Bishop Remigius. It answers for 10 hides. Land for 8 ploughs; in lordship 2. 144 a
14 villagers with 6 smallholders have 6 ploughs.
Meadow for 2 ploughs; woodland, 300 pigs.
In total, value £8; when acquired £3; before 1066 £10.
Godric brother of Bishop Wulfwy held this manor; he could not grant or sell except with his permission.

In BURNHAM Hundred

3 Walter also holds ½ hide from the Bishop. Land for ½ plough. The value is and always was 5s.

tenuit Leuric' hō Heraldi comit'. 7 uende potuit.

M Ipse Walteri' ten' de eod' epo *WABORNE*. *IN DVSTEBGE*
p VIII. hid' 7 dim' se defd'. Tra. ē. IX. car'. *HVND.*
In dn̄io sunt. II. 7 XII. uilli cū XIII. bord'. hn̄t. X. car'.
Ibi. I. seruus. 7 VIII. molini. de. C 7 IIII. sol. ptū. VI. car'.
7 ad eqs. De piscar'. CCC. Anguill. Silua. CC. porc'. 7 VII.
sol 7 IIII. den'. In totis ualent' ual'. XV. lib. Qdo recep'.
C. sol. T.R.E. XII. lib. Hoc M tenuit Herald' comes.
In Lede ten' Walt' de eod' epo. I. hid' 7 dim'. Tra. ē
II. car'. Ibi. ē una 7 dim'. 7 dim' pot' fieri. Ibi. II. uilli
cu. I. bord'. Ibi. I. seruus. 7 III. molini de. XIIII. sol.
Val' 7 ualuit sep. XXX. sol. Hoc M tenuit Leuric'
hō Heraldi comit'. 7 uende potuit. *IN ROVELAI HVND.*
Ipse eps ten' Chauescote. quæ jacet in æccla de
bochingehā. Ibi. ē. I. hida. Tra. I. car' 7 dim'. 7 ibi sunt
cū. II. bord' 7 uno seruo. Ptū dim' car'. Val' 7 ualuit
XXX. sol. T.R.E. XL. sol. Hanc trā tenuit Wluui eps.

.IIII. TERRA EPI BAIOCENSIS. *IN STANES HVND.*

M Eps Baiocensis tenet in Stanes. VII. hid'. Helto ten'
de eo. Tra. ē. VII. car'. In dn̄io sunt. III. 7 un' uills cū
XV. bord' hn̄t. I. car'. 7 adhuc. II. poss fieri. Ibi. VII. serui.
Ptū car'. In totis ualentijs ual' 7 ualuit. C. sol. T.R.E.
VI. lib. Hoc M tenuer'. II. frs. un' hō Vlf. 7 alt' hō Eddeuæ.
potuer' dare t' uende cui uoluer'.

M Isdē Helto ten' de eod' epo *DANITONE*. p XV. hid' se
defd'. Tra. ē. XIII. car'. In dn̄io sunt. III. 7 XXXV. uilli
cū. VII. bord' hn̄t. X. car'. Ibi. VIII. serui. ptū. XIII. car'.
7 I. molin' de. IIII. sol. In totis ualentijs ual' XV. lib.
7 ualuit sep. Hoc M tenuit Auelin teign'. R.E.

Leofric, Earl Harold's man, held this land; he could sell.

In DESBOROUGH Hundred

4 M. Walter holds WOOBURN himself from the Bishop. It answers for 8½ hides. Land for 9 ploughs; in lordship 2.
12 villagers with 13 smallholders have 10 ploughs.
1 slave; 8 mills at 104s; meadow for 6 ploughs, and for the horses. From the fishery 300 eels; woodland, 200 pigs and 7s 4d too.
Total value £15; when acquired 100s; before 1066 £12.
Earl Harold held this manor.

5 In LUDE Walter holds 1½ hides from the Bishop.
Land for 2 ploughs; 1½ there; [another] ½ possible.
2 villagers with 1 smallholder.
1 slave; 3 mills at 14s.
The value is and always was 30s.
Leofric, Earl Harold's man, held this manor; he could sell.

In ROWLEY Hundred

6 The Bishop holds GAWCOTT himself; it lies in the church (lands) of Buckingham. 1 hide; land for 1½ ploughs; they are there, with 2 smallholders and 1 slave.
Meadow for ½ plough.
The value is and was 30s; before 1066, 40s.
Bishop Wulfwy held this land.

4 LAND OF THE BISHOP OF BAYEUX

In STONE Hundred

1 M. The Bishop of Bayeux holds 7 hides in STONE; Helto holds from him. Land for 7 ploughs; in lordship 3.
1 villager with 15 smallholders have 1 plough; a further 2 possible.
7 slaves; meadow for a plough.
The total value is and was 100s; before 1066 £6.
Two brothers held this manor; one of them a man of Ulf's, the other a man of Edeva's; they could grant or sell to whom they would.

2 M. Helto also holds DINTON from the Bishop. It answers for 15 hides.
Land for 13 ploughs; in lordship 3.
35 villagers with 7 smallholders have 10 ploughs.
8 slaves; meadow for 13 ploughs; 1 mill at 4s.
The total value is and always was £15.
Avelin, a thane of King Edward's, held this manor.

In Herdeuuelle ten Helto de epo . III . hid . Tra . ē . III . car.
7 ibi sunt . cū . I . uillo 7 VII . bord . 7 I . mol de . VIII . sol.
Int tot uat 7 ualuit sēp . L . sol . Hanc trā tenuer . III . sochi.
Vn hō . S . Arch . Alt hō Leuuini com . tcius hō Auelini.
7 uende 7 dare potuer.
In ead uilla ten Robt de epo . I . hid . Tra . ē . II . car.
Ibi . ē una . 7 alia pot fieri . Ibi un uills 7 IIII . serui.
Vat 7 ualuit . XX . sol . T . R . E . XL . sol . Hanc trā tenuit
Auelin teign . R . E . 7 uende potuit.
Ⓜ Rogeri ten de epo WESTONE . p XX . hid se desd.
Tra . ē . XVII . car . In dnio sunt . III . 7 IIII . pot fieri.
Ibi . XII . uilli hnt . XII . car . 7 adhuc una pot fieri.
Ibi XII . serui . 7 IIII . mol de . XXXIII . sol . 7 IIII . den.
ptū X . car . 7 VI . sol . Silua . C . porc . In totis ualent
uat . XV . lib . Qdo recep . VIII . lib . T . R . E . XV . lib.

144 b

De tra huj Ⓜ tenuit Leuuin . IX . hid 7 dim . 7 Godric
III . hid 7 dim p uno Ⓜ . 7 II . hoēs ejd Godrici . III . hid
7 dim . 7 un hō Tosti com . II . hid . 7 II . hoēs Leuuini com
. I . hid 7 dimid . Oms ū uende potuer . De his hid unā ht
eps Lisiacsis de epo baiocensi . Tra . ē . I . car . s; n est ibi car.
Vat 7 ualuit sēp . V . solid . Hos hoēs quos Roger ten
in Westone . n ptinuer comiti Leuuino . T . R . E.
Ⓜ Ipse Roger ten Begraue . p . II . hid se desd.
Tra . ē . III . car . In dnio . ē una . 7 V . uilli cū . V . bord hnt
II . car . Ptū . I . car . Vat XXX . sol . Qdo recep . X . sol.
T . R . E . XL . sol . Hoc Ⓜ tenuit Suen hō Aluuini uari.
7 uende potuit.
In Bortone ten isd Roger de epo . I . hid 7 III . uirg.
Tra . ē . I . car 7 dim . 7 ibi sunt cū . III . bord . Vat 7 ualuit XX.
sol . T . R . E . L . sol . Hanc trā tenuer . II . sochi . Vn hō
Aluuini uari . 7 alt hō Leuuini com . 7 uende potuer.

3 In HARTWELL Helto holds 3 hides from the Bishop. Land for 3 ploughs; they are there, with
1 villager and 7 smallholders.
1 mill at 8s.
In total, the value is and always was 50s.
3 Freemen held this land, one, Archbishop Stigand's man, ½ hide, the second, Earl Leofwin's man, 2 hides, the third, Avelin's man, ½ hide; and they could sell and grant.

4 In the same village Robert holds 1 hide from the Bishop. Land for 2 ploughs; 1 there; another possible.
1 villager and 4 slaves.
The value is and was 20s; before 1066, 40s.
Avelin, a thane of King Edward's, held this land; he could sell.

[In AYLESBURY Hundred]

5 M. Roger holds WESTON (Turville) from the Bishop. It answers for 20 hides. Land for 17 ploughs; in lordship 3; a fourth possible.
12 villagers have 12 ploughs; a further 1 possible.
12 slaves; 4 mills at 33s 4d; meadow for 10 ploughs and 6s too; woodland, 100 pigs.
Total value £15; when acquired £8; before 1066 £15.
Of the land of this manor Earl Leofwin held 9½ hides; Godric the Sheriff, 3½ hides, as one manor; also two of Godric's men, 3½ hides; a man of Earl Tosti's, 2 hides; two of Earl Leofwin's men, 1½ hides; all could sell. 144 b
The Bishop of Lisieux has 1 of these hides from the Bishop of Bayeux. Land for 1 plough; but no plough there.
The value is and always was 5s.
The men whom Roger holds in Weston did not belong to Earl Leofwin before 1066.

6 M. Roger holds BEDGROVE himself. It answers for 2 hides. Land for 3 ploughs; in lordship 1.
5 villagers with 5 smallholders have 2 ploughs.
Meadow for 1 plough.
Value 30s; when acquired 10s; before 1066, 40s.
Swein, Alwin Varus' man, held this manor; he could sell.

7 In BIERTON Roger also holds 1 hide and 3 virgates from the Bishop. Land for 1½ ploughs; they are there, with
3 smallholders.
The value is and was 20s; before 1066, 50s.
Two Freemen held this land; one was Alwin Varus' man, the other Earl Leofwin's man; they could sell.

In HORSEDENE ten Rog de epo IN RISBERGE HVND.
dim hid. Tra. ē dim car. 7 ibi. ē cū uno bord. Vat 7 ua
luit. III. sol. T.R.E. v. sol. Hanc trā tenuit hō Leuuini com
7 uendere potuit.
In ead uilla ten Robt de epo dim hid. Tra. ē dim car.
sed n̄ ē ibi car. Vat 7 ualuit. II. sol. T.R.E. v. sol. Hanc trā
tenuit Goduin hō Leuuini com. 7 uende potuit.
M In Celfunde ten Roger de epo IN BERNEHĀ HD.
IIII. hid 7 III. uirg. Tra. ē. xv. car. In dnio. ē una. 7 XIIII.
uilli cū. IIII. bord hnt. XIIII. car. Ibi. II. serui. 7 I. molin
de. VI. sol. ptū. II. car. Silua sexcent porc. 7 una area
accipitris. In totis ualent uat. cx. sol. Qdo recep. LX.
sol. T.R.E. cx. sol. Hoc M tenuit Leuuinus com.
In Elmodeshā ten Rogeri de epo dim hid. Tra. ē. I. car.
7 ibi. ē. cū. III. bord. 7 I. molin de. IIII. sol. ptū. I. car.
H tra uat 7 ualuit sēp. xx. sol. Hanc tenuit trā Aluuin
hō reginæ Eddid. 7 uendere potuit.
In Cestrehā ten Rogeri dim hid. Tra. ē. II. car. In dnio
. I. car. 7 un uills cū. II. bord hnt. I. car. Silua. L. porc.
Vat 7 ualuit sēp. xx. sol.
In Cestrehā ten ipse eps baiocsis. I. hid 7 dim. Tra. ē. III.
car. In dnio. ē. I. hida. 7 ibi una car. 7 II. uilli cū. III. bord
hnt. II. car. Ibi. II. serui. 7 II. molin de. III. sol. ptū. III. car.
Vat 7 ualuit sēp. LX. sol. Hoc M tenuer. II. sochi. un hō
Leuuini com. alt hō Heraldi com. 7 uendere potuer.
M GISLEBERT eps Lisiacsis ten de epo Baiocsi DILEHERST.
p x. hid se defd. Tra. ē. x. car. In dnio sunt. II. 7 III.
potest fieri. Ibi. XIIII. uilli cū uno bord hnt. VI. car.
7 VII. pot fieri. Ibi. I. seruus. 7 I. molin de. III. sol. ptū
II. car. Silua. ccc. porc. In totis ualent uat. VI. lib.

In RISBOROUGH Hundred

8 In HORSENDEN Roger holds ½ hide from the Bishop.
Land for ½ plough; it is there, with
1 smallholder.
The value is and was 3s; before 1066, 5s.
A man of Earl Leofwin's held this land; he could sell.

9 In the same village Robert holds ½ hide from the Bishop.
Land for ½ plough; but no plough there.
The value is and was 2s; before 1066, 5s.
Godwin, Earl Leofwin's man, held this land; he could sell.

In BURNHAM Hundred

10 M. In CHALFONT (St. Peter) Roger holds 4 hides and 3 virgates from the Bishop. Land for 15 ploughs; in lordship 1.
14 villagers with 4 smallholders have 14 ploughs.
2 slaves; 1 mill at 6s; meadow for 2 ploughs; woodland, 600 pigs; a hawk's eyrie.
Total value 110s; when acquired 60s; before 1066, 110s.
Earl Leofwin held this manor.

11 In AMERSHAM Roger holds ½ hide from the Bishop.
Land for 1 plough; it is there, with
3 smallholders.
1 mill at 4s; meadow for 1 plough.
The value of this land is and always was 20s.
Alwin, Queen Edith's man, held this land; he could sell.

12 In CHESHAM Roger holds ½ hide. Land for 2 ploughs; in lordship 1 plough.
1 villager with 2 smallholders have 1 plough.
Woodland, 50 pigs.
The value is and always was 20s.

13 In CHESHAM the Bishop of Bayeux holds 1½ hides himself.
Land for 3 ploughs; in lordship 1 hide; 1 plough there.
2 villagers with 3 smallholders have 2 ploughs.
2 slaves; 2 mills at 3s; meadow for 3 ploughs.
The value is and always was 60s.
Two Freemen held this manor; one was Earl Leofwin's man, the other Earl Harold's man; they could sell.

14 M. Gilbert Bishop of Lisieux holds 'DILEHURST' from the Bishop of Bayeux. It answers for 10 hides. Land for 10 ploughs; in lordship 2; a third possible.
14 villagers with 1 smallholder have 6 ploughs; a seventh possible.
1 slave; 1 mill at 3s; meadow for 2 ploughs; woodland, 300 pigs.

Q̃do recep̃: XL. sol. T.R.E: VI. lib. Hoc m̃ tenuit Leuuin com in dnio.

m̃ Rogeri ten de epo THAPESLAV. p VIII. hid 7 I. uirg se desd. Tra. ẽ XVI. car. In dnio. ẽ una. 7 XVIII. uitti cũ. IIII. bord hñt XV. car. Ibi. II. serui. De piscar. mille anguitt. p̃tũ. I. car. Silua septingent porc. In totis ualent uat. VIII. lib. Q̃do recep̃: LX. sol. T.R.E: IX. lib. Hoc m̃ tenuit Asgot hõ Heraldi com. 7 ibid habuit. I. hõ. S. archiepi una hid. 7 uende pot.

144 c

m̃ Witts filius Ogeri. ten de epo IN DVSTENBERG. HD. HVCHEDENE. p X. hid se desd. Tra. ẽ X. car. In dnio sunt. II. 7 XV. uitti cũ. III. bord hñt. VIII. car. Ibi. V. serui. p̃tũ. II. car. Silua sexcent porc. In totis ualent uat. X. lib. Q̃do recep̃: VI. lib. T.R.E: VII. lib. Hoc m̃ tenuit Eddid regina.

In Wicũbe. ten Roger de epo dim hid. Tra. ẽ. I. car. 7 ibi est cũ uno bord. Vat 7 ualuit. VII. sol. T.R.E: X. sol. Hanc trã tenuit un hõ. S. archiepi. ñ potuit uende nec dare ext Wicũbe. m̃ suũ. testante Hund.

In BERLAVE ten Tedald de epo. V. hid. Tra. ẽ. IIII. car. In dnio. I. hida 7 dim. 7 ibi. ẽ una car 7 dim. Ibi VI. uitti cũ. IIII. bord hñt. II. car 7 dim. Ibi un seruus. 7 I. molin. XX. sol. De piscar. qngent Anguitt. p̃tũ II. car. Silua. L. porc. In totis ualent uat. VII. lib. Q̃do recep̃: IIII. lib. T.R.E: tntd. Hoc m̃ tenuit Eddid regina.

In Santesdone ten Roger de epo. V. hid. Tra. ẽ. V. car. In dnio sunt. II. 7 XIII. uitti cũ. III. bord hñt. III. car. Ibi. II. serui. 7 I. molin. p̃tũ. I. car. Silua. L. porc. Vat 7 ualuit. C. sol. T.R.E: VI. lib. Hoc m̃ tenuit un hõ Leuuini com. 7 uende potuit.

Total value £6; when acquired 40s; before 1066 £6.
Earl Leofwin held this manor in lordship.

5 M. Roger holds TAPLOW from the Bishop. It answers for 8 hides and 1 virgate. Land for 16 ploughs; in lordship 1.
18 villagers with 4 smallholders have 15 ploughs.
2 slaves; from the fishery 1,000 eels; meadow for 1 plough; woodland, 700 pigs.
Total value £8; when acquired 60s; before 1066 £9.
Asgot, Earl Harold's man, held this manor;
there a man of Archbishop Stigand's also had 1 hide; he could sell.

In DESBOROUGH Hundred — 144 c

6 M. William son of Oger holds HUGHENDEN from the Bishop. It answers for 10 hides. Land for 10 ploughs; in lordship 2.
15 villagers with 3 smallholders have 8 ploughs.
5 slaves; meadow for 2 ploughs; woodland, 600 pigs.
Total value £10; when acquired £6; before 1066 £7.
Queen Edith held this manor.

7 In (West) WYCOMBE Roger holds ½ hide from the Bishop.
Land for 1 plough; it is there, with
1 smallholder.
The value is and was 7s; before 1066, 10s.
A man of Archbishop Stigand's held this land; he could not sell or grant outside his manor of Wycombe as the Hundred testifies.

8 In MARLOW Theodwald holds 5 hides from the Bishop.
Land for 4 ploughs; in lordship 1½ hides; 1½ ploughs there.
6 villagers with 4 smallholders have 2½ ploughs.
1 slave; 1 mill, 20s; from the fishery 500 eels; meadow for 2 ploughs; woodland, 50 pigs.
Total value £7; when acquired £4; before 1066 as much.
Queen Edith held this manor.

9 In SAUNDERTON Roger holds 5 hides from the Bishop.
Land for 5 ploughs; in lordship 2.
13 villagers with 3 smallholders have 3 ploughs.
2 slaves; 1 mill; meadow for 1 plough; woodland, 50 pigs.
The value is and was 100s; before 1066 £6.
A man of Earl Leofwin's held this manor; he could sell.

In Hanechedene tenuit Tædald de epo. III. hid. Nc
est ad firmā regis. Tra. ē. VII. car. In dnio dim hid.
7 ibi sunt. II. car. Ibi. VI. uitti cū. III. bord. 7 V. serui. hnt. V. car.
In totis ualent uat 7 ualuit. C. sol. T.R.E. IIII. lib.
De hoc M tenuit Fridebt hō Leuuini com. II. hid 7 dim.
7 Alric gangemere 7 soror ej' tenuer dim hid. quæ. T.R.E
eis injuste ablata est. *IN TICHESELA HUND.*
In Wadruge ten Helto de epo. II. hid 7 I. uirg.
Tra. ē. II. car. In dnio. ē una. 7 II. uitti hnt. I. car.
Ibi un seruus. 7 ptū. II. car. Vat 7 ualuit. XX. sol.
T.R.E. XL. sol. Hanc trā. II. sochi tenuer. un hō
Auelini. 7 alt hō Alueue soror Heraldi com. uende pot.
In Imere ten Robt de epo. IIII. hid. Tra. ē. V. car.
In dnio sunt. II. 7 VIII. uitti cū. I. bord hnt. III. car.
Ibi. IIII. serui. 7 I. molin de. X. sol. Ptū. V. car.
Vat. IIII. lib. Qdo recep: C. sol. 7 tntd T.R.E. Hoc
M tenuit Goduin hō Leuuini comit. 7 uende potuit.
Isd Robt ten de epo Estone. p. II. hid. Tra. ē. V. car.
In dnio sunt. II. 7 VII. uitti hnt. III. car. Ibi. IIII. serui.
ptū. V. car. Vat. IIII. lib. Qdo recep: C. sol 7 tntd
T.R.E. Hoc M tenuit Auelin teign regis. E.
In Bichedone ten. II. Angli de epo *IN ESSEDENE HD.*
. I. uirg. Tra. ē Vat 7 ualuit sēp. V. sol. Istimet
tenuer. T.R.E. un hō Brictric 7 alt hō Azori. pot uende.
In Merstone ten Robt. I. hid de epo. *IN VOTESDONE HD.*
Tra. ē. I. car. 7 ibi. ē. ptū. I. car. Vat 7 ualuit sēp. XX.
sol. Hanc trā tenuit un homo Azor filij Toti. 7 uende pot.

20 In *HANECHEDENE* Theodwald held 3 hides from the Bishop. Now it is in the King's revenue. Land for 7 ploughs; in lordship ½ hide; 2 ploughs there.

6 villagers with 3 smallholders and 5 slaves have 5 ploughs.

The total value is and was 100s; before 1066 £4.

Fridbert, Earl Leofwin's man, held 2½ hides of this manor; Alric Gangemere and his sister held ½ hide, which was wrongfully taken from them before 1066.

In IXHILL Hundred

21 In WALDRIDGE Helto holds 2 hides and 1 virgate from the Bishop. Land for 2 ploughs; in lordship 1.

2 villagers have 1 plough.

1 slave; meadow for 2 ploughs.

The value is and was 20s; before 1066, 40s.

Two Freemen held this land; one was Avelin's man, the other Aelfeva's, Earl Harold's sister; they could sell.

22 In ILMER Robert holds 4 hides from the Bishop. Land for 5 ploughs; in lordship 2.

8 villagers with 1 smallholder have 3 ploughs.

4 slaves; 1 mill at 10s; meadow for 5 ploughs.

Value £4; when acquired 100s; before 1066 as much.

Godwin, Earl Leofwin's man, held this manor; he could sell.

23 Robert also holds ASTON (Sandford) from the Bishop for 2 hides. Land for 5 ploughs; in lordship 2.

7 villagers have 3 ploughs.

4 slaves; meadow for 5 ploughs.

Value £4; when acquired, 100s; before 1066 as much.

Avelin, a thane of King Edward's, held this manor.

In ASHENDON Hundred

24 In BEACHENDON two Englishmen hold 1 virgate from the Bishop. Land for....

The value is and always was 5s.

They held it themselves before 1066; one was Brictric's man, the other Azor's; they could sell.

In WADDESDON Hundred

25 In (? North) MARSTON Robert holds 1 hide from the Bishop. Land for 1 plough; it is there.

Meadow for 1 plough.

The value is and always was 20s.

A man of Azor son of Toti held this land; he could sell.

In Wadone ten Roger . III . uirg de epo. *IN ERLAI HD.*
Tra . e dim car . 7 ibi . e . cu . I . uillo . ptu dim car . Val.
7 ualuit . v . sol . T.R.E. x . sol . Hanc tra tenuit un ho.
uende pot.

144 d

M Tvrstin de Giron ten de epo *IN MVRSALAI HD.*
DODINTONE . p . x . hid se defd . Tra . e . VIII . car.
In dnio sunt . II . 7 tcia III . pot fieri . Ibi . VI . bord
hnt . III . car . 7 adhuc duæ poss fieri . Ibi . IIII . serui.
ptu . VIII . car . Int totu uat 7 ualuit sep . c . sol.
Hoc M tenuit Leuuin comes.
In Draitone ten Roger de epo . III . uirg . Tra . e . III.
car . 7 ibi sunt cu . II . uillis . 7 III . bord . ptu car . Val
7 ualuit . xx.v . sol . T.R.E. xxx . sol . Hanc tra tenuer
II . frs hoes Aluuardi cilt . 7 uende potuer. *IN STODFALD*
In Westberie ten Rogeri de epo . II . hid 7 dim. *HD.*
p uno M . Tra . e . VII . car . In dnio sunt . II . 7 VIII . uilli
cu . III . bord hnt . v . car . Ibi un seru . ptu . v . car.
Silua . CCL . porc . Val . III . lib . Qdo recep . L . sol.
T.R.E. LX . sol . Hoc M tenuit Alnod cilt teign . R . E.
Ipse eps ten *CELDESTANE* . v . hid p uno M . Tra . e
. v . car . In dnio sunt . II æ . 7 IIII . uilli cu . I . bord hnt
II . car . 7 tcia III . pot fieri . Ibi . III . serui . Silua . L . porc.
Val . xxx . sol . Qdo recep . xx . sol . T.R.E. IIII . lib.
Hoc M tenuer . II . teigni p . II . maner . Godricus III . hid
7 Wilaus II . hid . 7 cui uoluer uende potuer.
Rolgi otbt 7 Rogeri juri ten de epo *STOV* . p . v . hid se defd.
Tra . e . v . car . In dnio . e una . 7 II . adhuc poss fieri.
Ibi . III . bord hnt dim car . 7 I . 7 dim fieri possunt.
ptu . VI . car . Silua . L . porc . Val . XL . sol . Vasta
recep . T.R.E. LX . sol . Hoc M tenuit Turgisus ho
Balduini filij Herluini . 7 uende pot.

In YARDLEY Hundred

In WHADDON Roger holds 3 virgates from the Bishop.
Land for ½ plough; it is there, with
1 villager.
Meadow for ½ plough.
The value is and was 5s; before 1066, 10s.
A man[of...] held this land; he could sell.

In MURSLEY Hundred 144 d

M. Thurstan of Giron holds DUNTON from the Bishop. It answers for 10 hides. Land for 8 ploughs; in lordship 2; a third possible.
6 smallholders have 3 ploughs; a further 2 possible.
4 slaves; meadow for 8 ploughs.
In total, the value is and always was 100s.
Earl Leofwin held this manor.

In DRAYTON (Parslow) Roger holds 3 virgates from the Bishop.
Land for 3 ploughs; they are there, with
2 villagers and 3 smallholders.
Meadow for.... ploughs.
The value is and was 25s; before 1066, 30s.
Two brothers, Young Alfward's men, held this land; they could sell.

In STOTFOLD Hundred

In WESTBURY Roger holds 2½ hides from the Bishop as one manor.
Land for 7 ploughs; in lordship 2.
8 villagers with 3 smallholders have 5 ploughs.
1 slave; meadow for 5 ploughs; woodland, 250 pigs.
Value £3; when acquired 50s; before 1066, 60s.
Young Alnoth, a thane of King Edward's, held this manor.

The Bishop holds SHALSTONE himself, 5 hides, as one manor.
Land for 5 ploughs; in lordship 2.
4 villagers with 1 smallholder have 2 ploughs; a third possible.
3 slaves; woodland, 50 pigs.
Value 30s; when acquired 20s; before 1066 £4.
Two thanes held this manor as two manors; Godric 3 hides and Wiglaf 2 hides; they could sell to whom they would.

Robert d'Oilly and Roger of Ivry hold STOWE from the Bishop. It answers for 5 hides. Land for 5 ploughs; in lordship 1; a further 2 possible.
3 smallholders have ½ plough; [another] 1½ possible.
Meadow for 6 ploughs; woodland, 50 pigs.
Value 40s; when acquired waste; before 1066, 60s.
Thorgils, Baldwin son of Herlwin's man, held this manor; he could sell.

Turstin ten de epo Foxescote . p . vi . hid se defd.
Tra . e . iiii . car . In dnio . ii . sun . 7 un uills cu . ii . bord
hnt . ii . car . Ibi . i . seru . 7 ptu . iiii . car . Silua . xxx.
porc . Val 7 ualuit sep . iii . lib . Hoc m tenuit Leit
teign . R . E . 7 uende potuit.

Gisleb maminot ten de epo *LECHASTEDE*.
p . xviii . se defd . Tra . e . xii . car . In dnio sunt . iii.
7 iiii . pot fieri . Ibi . xviii . uitti cu . vi . bord hnt . iiii.
car . 7 aliae . iiii . fieri poss . Ibi . ii . serui . ptu . xii . car.
Silua . cccc . porc . In totis ualent uat 7 ualuit . vi . lib.
T.R.E . viii . lib . Hoc m tenuit Leuuin comes.

Ernulf de hesding ten de epo *IN ROVELAI HVND*.
in Ledingberge . vii . hid p uno m . Tra . e . v . car.
In dnio sunt . ii . 7 un uills cu . vi . bord hnt . i . car.
7 . ii . adhuc poss fieri . Ibi . iii . serui . ptu . v . car . De silua
iiii . sol p annu . Val 7 ualuit . lx . sol . T.R.E . iiii . lib.
Hoc m tenuit Wilaf ho comit Leuuini . 7 potuit uende.

Ansgot de Ros ten de epo prestone . p xv . hid
se defd . Tra . e . viii . car . In dnio sunt . iii . 7 xi . uitti
cu . vii . bord . hnt . v . car . Ibi . vi . serui . 7 i . molin
de . xxxii . den . Ptu . viii . car . Silua . cc . porc . Valet
c . solid . Qdo recep . iiii . lib . T.R.E . tntd . Hoc m
tenuit Wilaf ho Leuuini comit . 7 uende potuit.

145 a

Rob de Tham ten de epo *CETEODE* . p . x . hid
se defd . Tra . e . v . car . In dnio sunt . ii . 7 vii . uitti
cu . ii . bord hnt . ii . car 7 dim . 7 dim pot fieri.
Ibi . vi . serui . 7 i . molin de . xxx . den . ptu . v . car.
Silua . c . porc . Val lx . sol . Qdo recep . xl . sol.
T.R.E . lx . sol . Hoc m tenuit Alnod chentiscus.
teign regis . E . 7 uende potuit.

32 Thurstan holds FOXCOTE from the Bishop. It answers for 6 hides. Land for 4 ploughs; in lordship 2.
1 villager with 2 smallholders have 2 ploughs.
1 slave; meadow for 4 ploughs; woodland, 30 pigs.
The value is and always was £3.
Leith, a thane of King Edward's, held this manor; he could sell.

33 Gilbert Maminot holds LECKHAMPSTEAD from the Bishop. It answers for 18 [hides]. Land for 12 ploughs; in lordship 3; a fourth possible.
18 villagers with 6 smallholders have 4 ploughs; another 4 possible.
2 slaves; meadow for 12 ploughs; woodland, 400 pigs.
The total value is and was £6; before 1066 £8.
Earl Leofwin held this manor.

In ROWLEY Hundred

34 Arnulf of Hesdin holds 7 hides in LENBOROUGH from the Bishop as one manor. Land for 5 ploughs; in lordship 2.
1 villager with 6 smallholders have 1 plough; a further 2 possible.
3 slaves; meadow for 5 ploughs; from the woodland 4s a year.
The value is and was 60s; before 1066 £4.
Wiglaf, Earl Leofwin's man, held this manor; he could sell.

35 Ansgot of Rots holds PRESTON (Bissett) from the Bishop. It answers for 15 hides. Land for 8 ploughs; in lordship 3.
11 villagers with 7 smallholders have 5 ploughs,
6 slaves; 1 mill at 32d; meadow for 8 ploughs; woodland, 200 pigs.
Value 100s; when acquired £4; before 1066 as much.
Wiglaf, Earl Leofwin's man, held this manor; he could sell.

36 Robert of Thaon holds CHETWODE from the Bishop. It answers for 10 hides. Land for 5 ploughs; in lordship 2. 145 a
7 villagers with 2 smallholders have 2½ ploughs; [another] ½ possible.
6 slaves; 1 mill at 30d; meadow for 5 ploughs; woodland, 100 pigs.
Value 60s; when acquired 40s; before 1066, 60s.
Alnoth the Kentishman, a thane of King Edward's, held this manor; he could sell.

ERnulf9 de Hesding ten de epo Bertone. p.x.hid se defd. Tra.e.v.car. In dnio.II.car. Ibi.III.bord hnt.I.car.7 II.car possunt fieri. Ibi.IIII.serui.ptu III.car. De pastura.xxx.sol. Silua.c.porc. IN totis ualent ual xIIII.lib. Qdo recep: xL.sol. T.R.E: LX.sol. Hoc M tenuit Wilaf teign comit' Leuuini.7 uende pot.

Ilbtus de Lacei ten de epo *TEDINWICHE*.p.x. hid se defd. Tra.e.VIII.car. In dnio sunt.III.7 III. uilli cu.II.bord hnt.IIII.car.7 V.pot fieri. Ibi.x. serui.7 I.molin de.IIII.sol.7 de alijs redditis uillæ. .xx.sol.ptu.VIII.car. Silua.octing porc. Inter totu ual.x.lib. Qdo recep: VI.lib. T.R.E: x.lib. Hoc M tenuit Alnod teign.R.E.7 uende potuit.

Ipse eps baiocsis ten.III.hid 7 III.uirg *IN LAMVA HD*. Tra.e.III.car. In dnio.II.hidæ.7 ibi est dim car. 7 I.car 7 dim pot fieri. Ibi.II.uilli cu.I.bord hnt dim car. Ibi.II.serui. Ptu.II.car. Val.xx.sol. Qdo recep: XIII.sol.7 IIII.den. T.R.E: XL.solid.

Robtus de Romenel ten de epo in Edintone.VI.hid. Tra.e.VI.car. In dnio sunt.II.7 VIII.uilli cu.II. bord hnt.III.car.7 IIII.pot fieri. Ibi.IIII.serui. ptu.VI.car. Val 7 ualuit.LX.sol. T.R.E: c.sol. Hoc M tenuit Goduin ho com Leuuini.7 uende potuit.

In Latesberie ten eps Lisiacsis *IN BONESTOV HD*. de epo Baiocsi.I.hid.v.pedes min. Tra.e.I.car. 7 ibi est cu.III.uillis.ptu.I.car. Val 7 ualuit.x.sol. T.R.E: xx.sol. Hanc tra tenuit Siric ho Leuuini comitis 7 uende potuit.

GATEHERST ten eps Lisiacsis de epo Baiocensi.7 Robt9 de nouuers de eo.p.v.hid se defd. Tra.e.IIII.car.

37 Arnulf of Hesdin holds BARTON (Hartshorn) from the Bishop.
It answers for 10 hides. Land for 5 ploughs; in lordship 2 ploughs.
3 smallholders have 1 plough; [another] 2 ploughs possible.
4 slaves; meadow for 3 ploughs; from the pasture, 30s; woodland, 100 pigs.
Total value £14; when acquired 40s; before 1066, 60s.
Wiglaf, a thane of Earl Leofwin's, held this manor; he could sell.

38 Ilbert of Lacy holds TINGEWICK from the Bishop. It answers for 10 hides. Land for 8 ploughs; in lordship 3.
3 villagers with 2 smallholders have 4 ploughs; a fifth possible.
10 slaves; 1 mill at 4s; from the other payments of the village, 20s; meadow for 8 ploughs; woodland, 800 pigs.
In total, value £10; when acquired £6; before 1066 £10.
Alnoth, a thane of King Edward's, held this manor; he could sell.

In LAMUA Hundred

39 The Bishop of Bayeux holds 3 hides and 3 virgates himself.
Land for 3 ploughs; in lordship 2 hides; ½ plough there; [another] 1½ ploughs possible.
2 villagers with 1 smallholder have ½ plough.
2 slaves; meadow for 2 ploughs.
Value 20s; when acquired 13s 4d; before 1066, 40s.

40 Robert of Romney holds 6 hides in ADDINGTON from the Bishop.
Land for 6 ploughs; in lordship 2.
8 villagers with 2 smallholders have 3 ploughs; a fourth possible.
4 slaves; meadow for 6 ploughs.
The value is and was 60s; before 1066, 100s.
Godwin, Earl Leofwin's man, held this manor; he could sell.

In BUNSTY Hundred

41 In LATHBURY the Bishop of Lisieux holds 1 hide less 5 feet from the Bishop of Bayeux. Land for 1 plough; it is there, with 3 villagers.
Meadow for 1 plough.
The value is and was 10s; before 1066, 20s.
Seric, Earl Leofwin's man, held this land; he could sell.

42 The Bishop of Lisieux holds GAYHURST from the Bishop of Bayeux, and Robert of Noyers from him. It answers for 5 hides.
Land for 4 ploughs; in lordship 2 ploughs.

In dn̄io sunt .IIæ. car. 7 x. uitti hn̄t. II. car. Ibi. II. serui.
7 I. molin̄ de. XIII. sol. 7 IIII. den. p̄tu̅. IIII. car. Silua
q̄ter xxti. porc. Int totu̅ ual 7 ualuit. c. sol. T.R.E.
VIII. lib. Hoc m̄ tenuit Siric hō Leuuini com. 7 uende pot.

In Brichella ten Turstin de epo. I. hid. Tra. ē
.I. car. s; n̄ est ibi car. nisi. III. uitti cu̅. II. bord.
Val 7 ualuit. XIIII. sol. T.R.E. xx. sol. Hoc m̄
tenuit Aluuin hō Estan. n̄ potuit dare nec uende
ext Brichelle m̄ Estani.

145 b

.V. TERRA EPI CONSTANT. *IN TICHESSELE HVND*

Eps Constantiensis ten *WERMELLE*. 7 Robt
ten de eo. p v. hid se defd sēp. Tra. ē. v. car. In dn̄io
sunt. II. 7 XVI. uitti cu̅. VI. bord hn̄t. III. car. Ibi. IIII.
serui. p̄tu̅. II. car. Silua. cc. porc. Val 7 ualuit. VI. lib.
T.R.E. VII. lib. Hoc m̄ tenuit Eddeua uxor Wluuardi.
sub regina Eddid. 7 uende potuit. *IN ESSEDENE HVND.*

Ipse eps ten *LOTEGARSER*. p IX. hid se defd. Tra. ē
VIII. car. In dn̄io. IIII. hide 7 ibi sunt. IIæ. car. 7 IIIcia. pot
fieri. Ibi. XIII. uitti cu̅. IIII. bord hn̄t. v. car. Ibi. v. serui.
P̄tu̅. VIII. car. Silua. XL. porc. In totis ualent ual 7 ua
luit. c. sol. T.R.E. VI. lib. Hoc m̄ tenuit Eddeua de
regina Eddid. 7 uende potuit.

Duo milites ten de epo *OLVONGE*. p x. hid se defd.
Tra. ē. IX. car. In dn̄io sunt. IIII. 7 quinta pot fieri.
Ibi XVIIIto. uitti hn̄t. III. car. 7 quarta pot fieri. Ibi. VIIIto.
bord. p̄tu̅. IIII. car. Silua. cc. porc. In totis ualent.
ual. x. lib. Qdo recep. c. sol. T.R.E. VII. lib. Hoc m̄
tenuit Eduuin teign. R.E. 7 uende potuit. *IN VOTESDON HD.*

In Merstone ten Rannulf sub epo. I. uirg. Tra. ē dim
car. 7 II. boues ibi sunt. Val 7 ualuit sēp. XL. den.
Hanc tra̅ tenuit Leuric hō Edduini 7 uende potuit.

10 villagers have 2 ploughs.
2 slaves; 1 mill at 13s 4d; meadow for 4 ploughs; woodland, 80 pigs.
In total, the value is and was 100s; before 1066 £8.
Seric, Earl Leofwin's man, held this manor; he could sell.

[In MOULSOE Hundred]

43 In (Little) BRICKHILL Thurstan holds 1 hide from the Bishop.
Land for 1 plough, but there is no plough there, only 3 villagers with 2 smallholders.
The value is and was 14s; before 1066, 20s.
Alwin, Estan's man, held this manor; he could not grant or sell outside Brickhill, Estan's manor.

5 LAND OF THE BISHOP OF COUTANCES

145 b

In IXHILL Hundred

1 The Bishop of Coutances holds WORMINGHALL; Robert holds from him.
It always answered for 5 hides. Land for 5 ploughs; in lordship 2.
16 villagers with 6 smallholders have 3 ploughs.
4 slaves; meadow for 2 ploughs; woodland, 200 pigs.
The value is and was £6; before 1066 £7.
Edeva, Wulfward's wife, held this manor under Queen Edith; she could sell.

In ASHENDON Hundred

2 The Bishop holds LUDGERSHALL himself. It answers for 9 hides.
Land for 8 ploughs; in lordship 4 hides; 2 ploughs there; a third possible.
13 villagers with 4 smallholders have 5 ploughs.
5 slaves; meadow for 8 ploughs; woodland, 40 pigs.
The total value is and was 100s; before 1066 £6.
Edeva held this manor from Queen Edith; she could sell.

3 Two men-at-arms hold OVING from the Bishop. It answers for 10 hides.
Land for 9 ploughs; in lordship 4; a fifth possible.
18 villagers have 3 ploughs; a fourth possible. 8 smallholders.
Meadow for 4 ploughs; woodland, 200 pigs.
Total value £10; when acquired 100s; before 1066 £7.
Edwin, a thane of King Edward's, held this manor; he could sell.

In WADDESDON Hundred

4 In (? North) MARSTON Ranulf holds 1 virgate under the Bishop.
Land for ½ plough; 2 oxen there.
The value is and always was 40d.
Leofric, Edwin's man, held this land; he could sell.

In Stiuelai ten Witts.III.hid 7 dim *In MVSELAI HVND*.
p uno M.Tra.ē.IX.car.In dn̄io sunt.II.car.Ibi.x.uitti
cū.x.bord hn̄t.VI.car 7 dim.7 adhuc dim pot fieri.
Ibi.v.serui.ptū.VIII.car.Val 7 ualuit sep.IIII.lib.
Hoc M tenuit Wluuard cild teign regis.E.
Ipse eps ten *SEVINESTONE*. *IN SIGELAI HVND*.
p VIII.hid 7 III.uirg.p uno M de Witto bonuaslet
in uadimonio.Tra.ē.VIII.car.In dn̄io sunt.III.hidæ.
7 ibi sunt.III.car.Ibi.XIII.uitti cū.II.bord hn̄t
v.car.Ibi.VI.serui.7 un molin de.x.sol.ptū.VIII.
car.In totis ualent ual.VI.lib.Qdo recep: xx.sol.
T.R.E: VIII.lib.Hoc M tenuit Edid regina.7 uende pot.
Ipse eps ten *ETONE*.p x.hid se defd.Tra.ē.XVIII.
car.In dn̄io.IIII.car.Ibi XXXV.uitti cū.VI.bord.
hn̄t XIIII.car.Ibi.XII.serui.7 I.molin de XX.sol.
ptū.XII.car.In totis ualent ual XII.lib.Qdo
recep: VIII.lib.T.R.E: X.lib.Hoc M tenuit Eddeua.
7 cui uoluit uende potuit. *IN BONESTOV HVND*.
LINFORDE ten Eddeua de epo.p.IIII.hid se defd.
Tra.ē.IIII.car.In dn̄io sunt.II.7 VI.uitti hn̄t
II.car.7 un molin de.VIII.sol.7 VIII.den.ptū
IIII.car.Silua.XL.porc.Val 7 ualuit.XL.sol.
T.R.E: LX.sol.Hoc M tenuit eadē Eddeua.T.R.E.
In Lateberie ten Witts de epo.v.hid p uno M.
Tra.ē.IIII.car.In dn̄io sunt.II.7 VI.uitti cū.VI.bord
hn̄t.II.car.Ibi.III.serui.7 ptū.IIII.car.Silua.c.porc.
Val.IIII.lib.Qdo recep: XL.sol.T.R.E: LX.sol.Hoc M
tenuit Edduin borgreti fili.teign.R.E.
In Telinghā ten Anschitill de epo.II.hid 7 dim.
7 III.part uni uirg.p uno M.Tra.ē.IIII.car.In dn̄io
sunt.III.7 III.uitti cū.VI.bord hn̄t.I.car.Ibi.IIII.serui.

In MURSLEY Hundred

5 In STEWKLEY William holds 3½ hides as one manor.
Land for 9 ploughs; in lordship 2 ploughs.
10 villagers with 10 smallholders have 6½ ploughs;
a further ½ possible.
5 slaves; meadow for 8 ploughs.
The value is and always was £4.
Young Wulfward, a thane of King Edward's, held this manor.

In SECKLOE Hundred

6 The Bishop holds SIMPSON himself for 8 hides and 3 virgates
as one manor in pledge from William Bonvallet. Land for 8 ploughs;
in lordship 3 hides; 3 ploughs there.
13 villagers with 2 smallholders have 5 ploughs.
6 slaves; 1 mill at 10s; meadow for 8 ploughs.
Total value £6; when acquired 20s; before 1066 £8.
Queen Edith held this manor; she could sell.

7 The Bishop holds (Water) EATON himself. It answers for 10 hides.
Land for 18 ploughs; in lordship 4 ploughs.
35 villagers with 6 smallholders have 14 ploughs.
12 slaves; 1 mill at 20s; meadow for 12 ploughs.
Total value £12; when acquired £8; before 1066 £10.
Edeva held this manor; she could sell to whom she would.

In BUNSTY Hundred

8 Edeva holds (Little) LINFORD from the Bishop. It answers for 4 hides.
Land for 4 ploughs; in lordship 2.
6 villagers have 2 ploughs.
1 mill at 8s 8d; meadow for 4 ploughs; woodland, 40 pigs.
The value is and was 40s; before 1066, 60s.
Edeva also held this manor before 1066.

9 In LATHBURY William holds 5 hides from the Bishop as one manor.
Land for 4 ploughs; in lordship 2.
6 villagers with 6 smallholders have 2 ploughs.
3 slaves; meadow for 4 ploughs; woodland, 100 pigs.
Value £4; when acquired 40s; before 1066, 60s.
Edwin son of Burgred, a thane of King Edward's, held this manor.

10 In TYRINGHAM Ansketel holds 2½ hides and 3 parts of 1 virgate from
the Bishop as one manor. Land for 4 ploughs; in lordship 3.
3 villagers with 6 smallholders have 1 plough. 4 slaves.

Int' totū ual . L. sol . Qdo recep: xx . sol. T.R.E: LX . sol.
H tra . ē de Excābio ꝑ bledone. Hoc m̄ tenuer̄ . II . teigni.
Vn⁹ hō Wallef comit . II . hid 7 dim uirg ꝑ uno m̄ hab.
7 alt . III . part uni⁹ uirg . tenuit . 7 uende potuer̄.
In Stoches ten qdā Anglic⁹ de epo . I . hid 7 I . uirg.
Tra . ē . I . car . 7 ibi est . cū . IIII . bord . ptū . I . car . Silua
L . porc . Val . xx . sol . Qdo recep: x . sol . T.R.E: xx . sol.
Hanc trā tenuer̄ . II . teigni ꝑ duob⁹ m̄ . Vnqsq; tenuit
II . uirg 7 dim . 7 uende potuer̄.

m̄ In *WESTONE* . ten eps VII . hid 7 dim . Tra . ē . VII . car
In dnio . ē . I . hida . 7 I . car . 7 IIII . uitti cū . III . bord hnt
VI . car . 7 cū eis sunt . VII . sochi 7 qdā francig . Ibi . III . serui.
ptū . VII . car . Silua . CC . porc . Val 7 ualuit . C . sol.
T.R.E: VI . lib . Hoc m̄ tenuer̄ . X . teigni hoes burgret
7 uende potuer̄ . 7 ibid fuit un⁹ hō Alrici . III . uirg
habuit . 7 uende potuit.

m̄ Ipse eps ten *OLNEI* . ꝑ x . hid se defd . Tra . ē . x . car.
In dnio . III . hidæ . 7 ibi sunt . III . car . Ibi XXIIII . uitti
cū . V . bord . hnt VII . car . Ibi . V . serui . 7 I . mol de XL
sol 7 CC . anguill . ptū . x . car . Silua . CCCC . porc.
Int' tot ual XII . lib . Qdo recep: VII . lib . T.R.E: XII . lib.
Hoc m̄ tenuit Borret . 7 ibi . I . sochs hō ej⁹ . I . uirg 7 dim
habuit . 7 uende potuit.

m̄ In Lauuendene ten eps . II . hid ꝑ uno m̄ . Tra . ē . IIII.
car . In dnio . I . hida 7 ibi . II . car . 7 IIII . uitti cū . III.
bord hnt . II . car . Ibi . III . serui . Ptū . I . car . Silua
C . porc . Val . XL . sol . Qdo recep: xx . sol . T . R . E: LX . sol.
Hoc m̄ tenuit un⁹ hō Borret . 7 uende potuit.
In ead uilla ten Witts de epo . IIII . hid 7 II . partes
uni⁹ uirg ꝑ uno m̄ . Tra . ē . IIII . car . In dnio . II . car.
7 VII . uitti cū . VI . bord hnt . II . car . Ibi . III . serui . 7 I . mol

145 c

In total, value 50s; when acquired 20s; before 1066, 60s.
This land is in exchange for Bleadon.
Two thanes held this manor; one, Earl Waltheof's man, had 2 hides and ½ virgate as one manor; the other held 3 parts of 1 virgate; they could sell.

1 In STOKE (Goldington) an Englishman holds 1 hide and 1 virgate from the Bishop. Land for 1 plough; it is there with
4 smallholders.
Meadow for 1 plough; woodland, 50 pigs.
Value 20s; when acquired 10s; before 1066, 20s.
Two thanes held this land as two manors; each held 2½ virgates; they could sell.

2 M. In WESTON (Underwood) the Bishop holds 7½ hides.
Land for 7 ploughs; in lordship 1 hide; 1 plough.
4 villagers with 3 smallholders have 6 ploughs;
with them are 7 Freemen and a Frenchman.
3 slaves; meadow for 7 ploughs; woodland, 200 pigs.
The value is and was 100s; before 1066 £6.
Ten thanes, Burgred's men, held this manor; they could sell.
A man of Alric's was also there; he had 3 virgates; he could sell.

3 M. The Bishop holds OLNEY himself. It answers for 10 hides.
Land for 10 ploughs; in lordship 3 hides; 3 ploughs there.
24 villagers with 5 smallholders have 7 ploughs.
5 slaves; 1 mill at 40s and 200 eels; meadow for 10 ploughs;
woodland, 400 pigs.
In total, value £12; when acquired £7; before 1066 £12.
Burgred held this manor; 1 Freeman, his man, had 1½ virgates; he could sell.

4 M. In LAVENDON the Bishop holds 2 hides as one manor.
Land for 4 ploughs; in lordship 1 hide; 2 ploughs there.
4 villagers with 3 smallholders have 2 ploughs.
3 slaves; meadow for 1 plough; woodland, 100 pigs.
Value 40s; when acquired 20s; before 1066, 60s.
A man of Burgred's held this manor; he could sell.

5 In the same village William holds 4 hides and 2 parts of 1 virgate from the Bishop as one manor. Land for 4 ploughs;
in lordship 2 ploughs.
7 villagers with 6 smallholders have 2 ploughs.

7 dim de xx.vii.sol 7 ccl. anguill. pastu. iiii. car. Silua lx. porc. Val. lx. sol. Qdo recep: xx. sol. T.R.E: iiii. lib. Hoc M tenuer. viii. teigni. 7 un eo Alli ho regis. E. senior alio fuit. Qms tra sua uende potuer.

In ead uilla ten Anschitill. i. hid 7 dim. 7 ii. part uni uirg de epo. Tra. e. i. car 7 dim. 7 ibi sunt. pstu similit. Silua xii. porc. Val xx. sol. Qdo recep: v. sol. T.R.E: xx. sol. Hanc tra tenuit Borgeret 7 Vluric ho ej. 7 uendere potuer.

In ead uilla ten. iii. sochi. i. hid de epo. 7 i. uirg. Tra e. i. car. Ibi. e dim. 7 dim pot fieri. Ibi un uills cu. ii. bord. pstu. iiii. bou. Silua. viii. porc. Val 7 ualuit x sol. T.R.E: xx. sol. Hanc tra tenuer. ii. teigni. Borret 7 Vluric ho di 7 uende potuer.

IN MOLESOVESLAV HVND.

In Clystone ten Morcar. i. hid 7 dim. de epo. Tra. e. ii. car. 7 ibi sunt. cu. vi. uillis 7 iiii. bord. Ibi un seruus. pstu. ii. car. 7 i. molin. Int tot ual 7 ualuit. xx. sol. T.R.E: xl. sol. Hoc M tenuit Alli teign. R.E. 7 uende potuit. H tra. e de Excabio p bledone. ut dnt hoes epi.

In ead uilla ten Turbt de epo. i. hid. Tra. e. i. car. 7 ibi est cu uno uillo. 7 iii. bord. Ibi un seruus. Pstu. i. car. Silua. xx. porc. Val 7 ualuit. x. sol. T.R.E: xx. sol. Hanc tra tenuit Wluuin ho di. 7 uende potuit.

145 d

M Ipse eps ten *SERINTONE*. p x. hid se defd. Tra. e. xi. car. In dnio. iii. hidae. 7 ibi sunt. iiii. car. Ibi. xx. ii. uilli cu. vi. bord hnt. vi. car. 7 vii. pot fieri. Ibi. viii. serui. 7 un molin de. xxvi. sol. pstu. iiii. car. Silua

3 slaves; 1½ mills at 27s and 250 eels; meadow for 4 ploughs; woodland, 60 pigs.
Value 60s; when acquired 20s; before 1066 £4.
Eight thanes held this manor; one of them, Aellic, King Edward's man, was senior to the others. All could sell their own land.

16 In the same village Ansketel holds 1½ hides and 2 parts of 1 virgate from the Bishop. Land for 1½ ploughs; they are there.
Meadow likewise; woodland, 12 pigs.
Value 20s; when acquired 5s; before 1066, 20s.
Burgred and Wulfric, his man, held this land; they could sell.

17 In the same village 3 Freemen hold 1 hide and 1 virgate from the Bishop. Land for 1 plough; ½ there; [another] ½ possible.
1 villager with 2 smallholders.
Meadow for 4 oxen; woodland, 8 pigs.
The value is and was 10s; before 1066, 20s.
Two thanes, Burgred and Wulfric, a man of God (?), held this land; they could sell.

In MOULSOE Hundred

18 In CLIFTON (Reynes) Morcar holds 1½ hides from the Bishop. Land for 2 ploughs; they are there, with
6 villagers and 4 smallholders.
1 slave; meadow for 2 ploughs; 1 mill.
In total, the value is and was 20s; before 1066, 40s.
Aellic, a thane of King Edward's, held this manor; he could sell. This land is in exchange for Bleadon, as the Bishop's men state.

19 In the same village Thorbert holds 1 hide from the Bishop. Land for 1 plough; it is there, with
1 villager and 3 smallholders.
1 slave; meadow for 1 plough; woodland, 20 pigs.
The value is and was 10s; before 1066, 20s.
Wulfwin, a man of God (?), held this land; he could sell.

20 M. The Bishop holds SHERINGTON himself. It answers for 10 hides. 145 d
Land for 11 ploughs; in lordship 3 hides; 4 ploughs there.
22 villagers with 6 smallholders have 6 ploughs; a seventh possible.
8 slaves; 1 mill at 26s; meadow for 4 ploughs; woodland, 100 pigs.

c.porc. Int totū uał.x.lib. Qdo recep: vii.lib. T.R.E: x.lib. De hoc ϖ tenuit Eduuin fili borret vi.hid p uno ϖ.7 Aluuin hō ej.i.hid p uno ϖ. 7 Osulf hō regis.E.habuit.iii.hid p uno ϖ.Isti duo potuer dare 7 uendere terrā suā.

In Ambretone ten duo teigni de epo.iii.hid.Tra.ē ii.car.7 ibi sunt.Ptū.ii.car.Silua.l.porc.Ibi sunt ii.uilli.7 ii.bord.Vał 7 ualuit xl.sol.T.R.E: iiii.lib. Istimet tenuer qui nc tenent.Vn eoꝝ Godric habuit .i.hid.7 alt Vluric.ii.hid p uno ϖ: 7 uende potuer.

.VI. TERRA EPI LISIACENSIS. *IN COTESLAV HVND.*

Eps Lisiacensis ten in *Croustone*.ii.hid 7 dim.Robert de Nouuers ten de eo p uno ϖ.Tra.ē.v.car. In dnio sunt.ii.7 iii.pot fieri.7 iiii.uilli cū.iiii.bord hnt.ii.car.Vał 7 ualuit.lx.sol.T.R.E: iiii.lib.Hoc ϖ tenuit Blacheman hō Tosti comit n potuit uende absq ejus licentia. *IN MOSLEI HVND.*

In *Brichellæ* ten Robt de epo.v.hid. Tra.ē.iiii.car.In dnio.ē una.7 vii.uilli cū.iii.bord hnt iii.car.Ibi un seruus.ptū.iiii.car.Silua.cl.porc. Vał 7 ualuit sep.iiii.lib.Hoc ϖ tenuit Blacheman hō Tosti comitis.7 uendere potuit.

.VII. TERRA SCI PETRI WESTMON. *IN STOCHES HVND.*

ϖ Abbas Sci Petri Westmonast ten *Daneham*.p.x.hid se defd.Tra.ē.xii.car.In dnio.iii.hidæ.7 ibi sunt.ii.car. Ibi xv.uilli cū.iii.bord.hnt.vii.car.7 adhuc.iii.poss fieri.Ptū.xii.car.7 ii.molini de.vii.sol.7 iii.piscar reddt.iii.sol.p annū.Silua.ccc.porc.In totis ualent uał.vii.lib.7 ualuit.T.R.E: x.lib.Hoc ϖ dedit Vlstan

In total, value £10; when acquired £7; before 1066 £10.

Of this manor, Edwin son of Burgred held 6 hides as one manor; Alwin, a man of his, 1 hide as one manor; and Oswulf, King Edward's man, had 3 hides as one manor. Those two could grant and sell their land.

21 In EMBERTON two thanes hold 3 hides from the Bishop.
Land for 2 ploughs; they are there.
Meadow for 2 ploughs; woodland, 50 pigs.
2 villagers; 2 smallholders.
The value is and was 40s; before 1066 £4.

The same men held as hold now. One of them, Godric, had 1 hide; the other, Wulfric, 2 hides as one manor; they could sell.

6 LAND OF THE BISHOP OF LISIEUX

In COTTESLOE Hundred

1 The Bishop of Lisieux holds 2½ hides in CRAFTON. Robert of Noyers holds from him, as one manor. Land for 5 ploughs; in lordship 2; a third possible.
4 villagers with 4 smallholders have 2 ploughs.
The value is and was 60s; before 1066 £4.

Blackman, Earl Tosti's man, held this manor; he could not sell without his permission.

In MOULSOE Hundred

2 In BRICKHILL Robert holds 5 hides from the Bishop.
Land for 4 ploughs; in lordship 1.
7 villagers with 3 smallholders have 3 ploughs.
1 slave; meadow for 4 ploughs; woodland, 150 pigs.
The value is and always was £4.

Blackman, Earl Tosti's man, held this manor; he could sell.

7 LAND OF ST. PETER'S OF WESTMINSTER

In STOKE Hundred

1 M. The Abbot of St. Peter's of Westminster holds DENHAM.
It answers for 10 hides. Land for 12 ploughs; in lordship 3 hides; 2 ploughs there.
15 villagers with 3 smallholders have 7 ploughs; a further 3 possible.
Meadow for 12 ploughs; 2 mills at 7s; 3 fisheries yield 3s a year; woodland, 300 pigs.
The total value is and was £7; before 1066 £10.

★ teign͡ S PEKO de Westmonast.7 ibi jacuit in dn̄io die qua Rex.E.fuit uiuus 7 mortuus. *IN BVRNEHĀ HVND.*

M Ipse abb̄ ten in *ESBVRNEHĀ*. VIII. hid. Tra. ē. VI. car. In dn̄io. IIII. hidæ. 7 ibi. ē una car. 7 VI. uitti cū. I. bord hn̄t. V. car̄. P̄tū. VI. car̄. Silua. C. porc. In totis ualent uat. C. sot 7 XXVIII. den. Q̄do recep̄: simil. T.R.E: VI. lib. Hoc M tenuer̄. III. teigni T.R.E. 7 uende potuer̄. 7 tam̄ ipsi. III. reddider̄ p annū. V. ores de c̄suetudine ad monasterium de Stanes. Hoz un Vluric. III. hid 7 III. uirg habuit. 7 alt III. hid 7. I. uirg. hō Edrici hab. 7 III. merlaue cius. una hid habuit. hō Seulfi fuit.

.VIII TERRA SC̄I ALBANI. *IN VOTESDON HVND.*

ABBAS DE SC̄O ALBANO ten *GRENESBERGA*. p V. hid se defd. Tra. ē. IX. car. In dn̄io. II. hide. 7 ibi sunt. II. car 7 VII. uitti cū. IIII. bord hn̄t. VII. car̄. Ibi un seruus. p̄tū. II. car. Int tot uat uat. C. sot. Q̄do recep̄: IIII. lib. T.R.E: C. sot. Hoc M jacuit 7 jacet in dn̄io æcctæ S Albani.

M Ipse abb̄ ten *ESTONE*. p X. hid *IN COTESLAI HVND.* se defd. Tra. ē. XII. car̄. In dn̄io. VI. hidæ. 7 ibi sunt. III. car. 7 adhuc duæ poss fieri. Ibi. VII. uitti cū. XII. bord hn̄t. VI. car. Ibi un seruus. P̄tū. III. car̄. Vat. X. lib. Q̄do recep̄: VI. lib. T.R.E: X. lib. Hoc M jacuit 7 jacet in dn̄io æcctæ S Albani.

146 a

M Ipse abb̄ ten *WENESLAI*. p XV. hid *IN MVSELAI HD.* se defd. Tra. ē XIX. car̄. In dn̄io. V. hidæ. 7 ibi sunt. III. car̄. 7 IIII. pot fieri. Ibi XVII. uitti cū. V. bord hn̄t XV. car. Ibi. III. serui. p̄tū. XIX. car̄. De silua. X. sot p annū. In totis ualent uat 7 ualuit sēp. XI. lib. 7 XIII. sot 7 IIII. den. Hoc M jacuit 7 jacet in dn̄io æcctæ S Albani.

The thane Wulfstan gave this manor to St. Peter's of Westminster; it lay there in lordship in 1066.

In BURNHAM Hundred

2 M. The Abbot holds 8 hides in EAST BURNHAM himself. Land for 6 ploughs; in lordship 4 hides; 1 plough there.
6 villagers with 1 smallholder have 5 ploughs.
Meadow for 6 ploughs; woodland, 100 pigs.
Total value 100s 28d; when acquired, the same; before 1066 £6.
Three thanes held this manor before 1066; they could sell. However these three paid 5 *ora* a year as a customary due to the monastery of Staines. One of them, Wulfric, had 3 hides and 3 virgates; the second, Edric of Marlow's man, had 3 hides and 1 virgate; the third had 1 hide; he was Saewulf's man.

8 LAND OF ST. ALBANS

In WADDESDON Hundred

1 The Abbot of St. Albans holds GRANBOROUGH. It answers for 5 hides. Land for 9 ploughs; in lordship 2 hides; 2 ploughs there.
7 villagers with 4 smallholders have 7 ploughs.
1 slave; meadow for 2 ploughs.
In total, value 100s; when acquired, £4; before 1066, 100s.
This manor lay and lies in the lordship of St. Albans Church.

In COTTESLOE Hundred

2 M. The Abbot holds ASTON (Abbots) himself. It answers for 10 hides. Land for 12 ploughs; in lordship 6 hides; 3 ploughs there; a further 2 possible.
7 villagers with 12 smallholders have 6 ploughs.
1 slave; meadow for 3 ploughs.
Value £10; when acquired £6; before 1066 £10.
This manor lay and lies in the lordship of St. Albans Church.

146 a

In MURSLEY Hundred

3 M. The Abbot holds WINSLOW himself. It answers for 15 hides. Land for 19 ploughs; in lordship 5 hides; 3 ploughs there; a fourth possible.
17 villagers with 5 smallholders have 15 ploughs. 3 slaves.
Meadow for 19 ploughs. From the woodland, 10s a year.
The total value is and always was £11 13s 4d.
This manor lay and lies in the lordship of St. Albans Church.

IX TERRA ECCLÆ DE BERCHINGES. *IN ERLAI HVND.*

ABBATISSA de Berchinges ten SLAPETONE. p vi. hid se defd. Tra. ē. vi. car. In dnio una hida. 7 ibi sunt. ii. car. 7 xviii. uitti cū. iiii. bord. hnt iiii. car. Ibi. iiii. serui. ptū. vi. car. In totis ualent uat 7 ualuit sep. vi. lib. Hoc m jacuit 7 jacet in æccla de Berchinges.

X TERRA CANONICOZ OXENEFORD *IN ESSEDEN HVND.*

CANONICI de Oxeneford ten de rege WITCHENDE. p x. hid se defd. Tra. ē. ix. car. In dnio una hida 7 dim. 7 ibi sunt. ii. car. 7 xviii. uitti cū uno bord. hnt. vii. car. Ibi. i. seruus. ptū. ii. car. In totis ualent uat 7 ualuit. vi. lib. T.R.E. viii. lib. Hoc m jacuit 7 jacet in dnio æcclæ canonicoz de Oxeneford.

.XI. TERRA REINBALDI PRBI *IN BVRNEHĀ HVND.*

RAINBALD pbr ten de rege. i. hidā in Boueniæ quæ jacet in æccla de Cochehā. Tra. ē. i. car. 7 ibi est. cū uno uitto. ptū. i. car. Vat 7 ualuit sep. x. sol. Istemet tenuit in elemosina de. E. rege.

XII. TERRA COMITIS MORITONIENS *IN STANES HVND.*

COMES MORITON ten jn Missedene. i. hid 7 Wigot ten de eo. Tra. ē. i. car 7 dim. Ibi. ē. i. car. 7 dimid pot fieri. Ibi. iiii. bord. ptū. i. car. Silua. c. porc. Vat 7 ualuit. c. sol. T.R.E. xl. sol. Hanc trā tenuit

9 LAND OF BARKING CHURCH

In YARDLEY Hundred

1 The Abbess of Barking holds SLAPTON. It answers for 6 hides. Land for 6 ploughs; in lordship 1 hide; 2 ploughs there.
18 villagers with 4 smallholders have 4 ploughs.
4 slaves; meadow for 6 ploughs.
The total value is and always was £6.
This manor lay and lies in (the lands of) Barking Church.

10 LAND OF THE CANONS OF OXFORD

In ASHENDON Hundred

1 The Canons of Oxford hold (Upper) WINCHENDON from the King. It answers for 10 hides. Land for 9 ploughs; in lordship 1½ hides; 2 ploughs there.
18 villagers with 1 smallholder have 7 ploughs.
1 slave; meadow for 2 ploughs.
The total value is and was £6; before 1066 £8.
This manor lay and lies in the lordship of the Church of the Canons of Oxford.

11 LAND OF REINBALD THE PRIEST

In BURNHAM Hundred

1 Reinbald the Priest holds 1 hide from the King in BOVENEY, which lies in (the lands of) the Church of Cookham. Land for 1 plough; it is there, with
1 villager.
Meadow for 1 plough.
The value is and always was 10s.
He held it himself in alms from King Edward.

12 LAND OF THE COUNT OF MORTAIN

In STONE Hundred

1 The Count of Mortain holds 1 hide in (Little) MISSENDEN; Wigot holds from him. Land for 1½ ploughs; 1 plough there; [another] ½ possible.
4 smallholders.
Meadow for 1 plough; woodland, 100 pigs.
The value is and was 100s; before 1066, 40s.

Aluuin' hō Syredi . f . Sybi . 7 uende potuit. *IN RISBERG*
In Horsedene ten Radulf' de com . vi . hid. *HVND*
7 III . uirg . Tra . ē . IIII . car . In dnio . ē una . 7 VII . uilli
cū uno bord hnt . III . car . Ibi . II . serui . 7 . I . molin nil
redd . pt̄ū . I . car . Val 7 ualuit . L . sol . T.R.E. c . sol.
Hoc m̄ tenuer . III . sochi . Hoꝝ . II . hoēs Heraldi comit
II . hid habuer . 7 III . hō Ingoldi . IIII . hid 7 III . uirg
habuit . Oms tam̄ uendere potuer.

m̄ IPSE comes ten *BLEDELAI* . p xxx . hid se defd.
Tra . ē . XVIII . car . In dnio . XVI . hidæ . 7 ibi sunt . IIII.
car . 7 XXXII . uilli cū . III . bord hnt . XIIII . car . Ibi
VIII . serui . 7 I . mol redd XXIIII . sūmas brasij.
Silua mille porc . 7 de reddit siluæ ferra car suffici
enter . pt̄ū . XVIII . car . In totis ualent ual XXII . lib.
Qdo recep: XII . lib . T.R.E: XX . lib . Hoc m̄ tenuit
Edmer Atule . teign' R.E. 7 uende potuit.

In Elmodeshā ten Almar de com *IN BVRNEHĀ HD.*
dim hid . Tra . ē . II . car . 7 ibi sunt cū . I . uillo 7 I . bord.
pt̄ū . II . car . Silua . XX . porc . Val 7 ualuit sēp XX . sol.
Hanc trā tenuit Siuuard hō Aldeue . 7 potuit uende.

In Wicūbe ten . Wills de com *IN DVSTENBERG HD.*
dim hid . Tra . ē dim car . 7 ibi . ē cū uno bord . Valet
7 ualuit sēp . x . sol . Hanc trā tenuit . I . sochs hō . S.
archiepi . n̄ potuit dare uel uende ext maneriū
de Wicūbe . die qua rex . E . fuit uiuus 7 mortuus . ut
Hund testat.

146 b

In Iforde ten monachi de Greisten VI . hid *IN TICHESSELE HD.*
de comite . Tra . ē . VI . car . In dnio . III . hidæ . 7 ibi sunt . II . car.
7 aliæ . II . possunt . ee . Ibi . III . uilli cū . X . bord hnt . II . car.

Alwin, Sired son of Sibbi's man, held this land;
he could sell.

In RISBOROUGH Hundred

2 In HORSENDEN Ralph holds 6 hides and 3 virgates from the Count.
Land for 4 ploughs; in lordship 1.
7 villagers with 1 smallholder have 3 ploughs.
2 slaves; 1 mill yields nothing; meadow for 1 plough.
The value is and was 50s; before 1066, 100s.
3 Freemen held this manor; two of these, Earl Harold's men, had 2 hides; the third, Ingold's man, had 4 hides and 3 virgates. However all could sell.

3 M. The Count holds BLEDLOW himself. It answers for 30 hides.
Land for 18 ploughs; in lordship 16 hides; 4 ploughs there.
32 villagers with 3 smallholders have 14 ploughs.
8 slaves; 1 mill pays 24 loads of malt; woodland, 1,000 pigs; from the returns of the woodland, enough ploughshares; meadow for 18 ploughs.
Total value £22; when acquired £12; before 1066 £20.
Edmer Ator, a thane of King Edward's, held this manor; he could sell.

In BURNHAM Hundred

4 In AMERSHAM Aelmer holds ½ hide from the Count. Land for 2 ploughs; they are there, with
1 villager and 1 smallholder.
Meadow for 2 ploughs; woodland, 20 pigs.
The value is and always was 20s.
Siward, Aldeva's man, held this land; he could sell.

In DESBOROUGH Hundred

5 In (West) WYCOMBE William holds ½ hide from the Count.
Land for ½ plough; it is there, with
1 smallholder.
The value is and always was 10s.
1 Freeman, a man of Archbishop Stigand's, held this land.
He could not grant or sell outside the manor of Wycombe, in 1066, as the Hundred testifies.

In IXHILL Hundred 146 b

6 In ICKFORD the Monks of Grestain hold 6 hides from the Count.
Land for 6 ploughs; in lordship 3 hides; 2 ploughs there; another 2 possible.
3 villagers with 10 smallholders have 2 ploughs.

Ptũ . VI . car. Vał 7 ualuit . VI . lib . T.R.E.' VII . lib . Hoc Ⓜ
tenuit Vlf hõ Heraldi comitis . 7 uende potuit.

Ⓜ Ipse comes ten *WITEHUNGE* . p v . hid *IN COTESLAI HD.*
se defd . Tra . ẽ XL . car . In dnio est . I . hida . 7 ibi sunt . IIII . car.
Ibi . LI . uitts cũ XX^{ti} . bord hnt . XXI . car . 7 adhuc . XV.
car poss fieri . Ptũ . XXV . car . De pastura ferr ad . V . car.
In totis ualent uał XXXI . lib . Qdo recep̃' similit . T.R.E.'
XXXII . lib . Hoc Ⓜ tenuit Eduuard cilt hõ com Heraldi . 7 uende pot.

In Crouſtone ten monachi de S Nicolao . II . hid 7 dim
de comite . Tra . ẽ . V . car . In dnio sunt . III . 7 VIII . uitti hnt
II . car . ptũ . V . car . Vał 7 ualuit . IIII . lib . T.R.E.' VI . lib.
Hoc Ⓜ tenuit Eduuard cilt . 7 uende potuit.

In Withungraue . ten Alan . I . hid 7 dim de comite.
Tra . ẽ . I . car . Ibi . ẽ una . 7 dim pot fieri . Ibi . I . uitts 7 I . bord.
ptũ . I . car . Vał 7 ualuit sep . XX^{ti} . sol . Hanc trã tenuit
Ordmær hõ Brictric . 7 uende potuit.

In Helpestorp . ten Rannulf de comite . III . uirg.
Tra . ẽ . I . car . 7 ibi est cũ . II . bord . Ibi . I . seruus . 7 ptũ
. I . car . Vał 7 ualuit sep . XX . sol . Hanc trã tenuit
Leuuin hõ Godrici . 7 uende potuit.

In Harduich ten Almar de com . II . hid . Tra . ẽ . II . car
7 ibi sunt cũ . II . uittis 7 I . bord . Ibi . I . seruus . Ptũ . II . car.
Vał 7 ualuit sep . XL . sol . Hanc trã tenuit Sauuard
hõ comitis Heraldi . 7 uende potuit.

In Bricstoch . ten Alan de comite . II . hid . Tra . ẽ . II . car.
In dnio est una . 7 III . uitti cũ . I . bord hnt . I . car . ptũ . II . car.
Vał . XXX . sol . Qdo recep̃' X . sol . T.R.E.' XL . sol . Hanc
trã tenuer . III . teigni . Vnoꝝ un hõ Leuuini com . Alt hõ
Goduini cilt abbis Westmon . tcius hõ Alueradi de Withũga.
7 oms trã suã uende potuer.

Meadow for 6 ploughs.
The value is and was £6; before 1066 £7.
Ulf, Earl Harold's man, held this manor; he could sell.

In COTTESLOE Hundred

7 M. The Count holds WING himself. It answers for 5 hides.
Land for 40 ploughs; in lordship 1 hide; 4 ploughs there.
51 villagers with 20 smallholders have 21 ploughs;
a further 15 ploughs possible.
Meadow for 25 ploughs. From the pasture, shares for 5 ploughs.
Total value £31; when acquired the same; before 1066 £32.
Young Edward, Earl Harold's man, held this manor; he could sell.

8 In CRAFTON the monks of St. Nicholas' hold 2½ hides from the Count. Land for 5 ploughs; in lordship 3.
8 villagers have 2 ploughs.
Meadow for 5 ploughs.
The value is and was £4; before 1066 £6.
Young Edward held this manor; he could sell.

9 In WINGRAVE Alan holds 1½ hides from the Count. Land for 1 plough; 1 there; [another] ½ possible.
1 villager and 1 smallholder.
Meadow for 1 plough.
The value is and always was 20s.
Ordmer, Brictric's man, held this land; he could sell.

10 In HELSTHORPE Ranulf holds 3 virgates from the Count.
Land for 1 plough; it is there, with
2 smallholders.
1 slave; meadow for 1 plough.
The value is and always was 20s.
Leofwin, Godric's man, held this land; he could sell.

1 In HARDWICK Aelmer holds 2 hides from the Count.
Land for 2 ploughs; they are there, with
2 villagers and 1 smallholder.
1 slave; meadow for 2 ploughs.
The value is and always was 40s.
Saeward, Earl Harold's man, held this land; he could sell.

2 In BURSTON Alan holds 2 hides from the Count. Land for 2 ploughs; in lordship 1.
3 villagers with 1 smallholder have 1 plough.
Meadow for 2 ploughs.
Value 30s; when acquired 10s; before 1066, 40s.
Three thanes held this land, of whom one was Earl Leofwin's man; the second a man of Young Godwin, Abbot of Westminster; the third Alfred of Wing's man; all could sell their land.

In eađ uilla ten Almær. I. uirg de comite. 7 ibi sunt. II. uitti. Vał 7 ualuit. v. sot. Hanc trā tenuit Siuuard hō com Heraldi. 7 uendere potuit.

IN ERLAI HVND.

In Draitone ten Witts fili Nigelli. I. hiđ 7 dim. Tra. ē. I. car. ptū. I. car. Silua. xxv. porc. Vał 7 ualuit sēp xx. sot. Hanc trā tenuit una uidua de Brictric. 7 uende pot.

In eađ uilla ten Lepsi de comite. I. hiđ 7 dim. 7 II. part uni uirg. Tra. ē. I. car. Ibi. II. uitti 7 II. serui. ptū. I. car. Silua. xxv. porc. Vał 7 ualuit sēp. xx. sot. Hanc trā tenuit Wiga hō. R.E. 7 uendere potuit.

In Pincelestorne ten Radulf de com. III. hiđ 7. I. uirg p uno M. Tra. ē. I. car. 7 ibi est cū uno borđ. Silua. xxx. porc. Vał. xx. sot. Qdo recep: v. sot. T.R.E: xxv. sot. Hanc trā tenuit Aluied de Elesberie. 7 uende pot.

In eađ uilla ten Bernard de com. III. hiđ 7 I. uirg p uno M. Tra. ē. I. car. Ibi. ē dim. 7 dimiđ pot fieri. Ibi. II. borđ. Silua. xxx. porc. Vał 7 ualuit sēp. xx. sot. Hanc trā tenuer. II. hōēs abbis de S Albano. 7 uende pot.

In eađ uilla ten Fulcold de com. I. hiđ 7 I. uirg. Tra. ē. IIII. bobz. 7 ibi sunt. Silua. x. porc. Vał 7 ualuit sēp. x. sot. Hanc trā tenuit Gladuin hō abbis S Albani. 7 uende pot.

146 c

De Manerio Pincelestorne sūpsit Turgisus hō comitis VI. hiđ. quas ipse com injuste ten in dnio suo.

In Estone ten Radulf de comite. III. uirg. Tra. ē dim car. 7 ibi est cū uno uitto. Vał 7 ualuit. v. sot. T.R.E: x. sot. Hanc trā tenuit Goduin pbr. S. Arch. 7 uende pot.

13 In the same village Aelmer holds 1 virgate from the Count.
2 villagers.
The value is and was 5s.
Siward, Earl Harold's man, held this land; he could sell.

In YARDLEY Hundred

14 In DRAYTON (Beauchamp) William son of Nigel holds 1½ hides.
Land for 1 plough.
Meadow for 1 plough; woodland, 25 pigs.
The value is and always was 20s.
A widow of Brictric's held this land; she could sell.

15 In the same village Leofsi holds 1½ hides and 2 parts of 1 virgate from the Count. Land for 1 plough.
2 villagers and 2 slaves.
Meadow for 1 plough; woodland, 25 pigs.
The value is and always was 20s.
Wicga, King Edward's man, held this land; he could sell.

16 In PITSTONE Ralph holds 3 hides and 1 virgate from the Count as one manor. Land for 1 plough; it is there, with
1 smallholder.
Woodland, 30 pigs.
Value 20s; when acquired 5s; before 1066, 25s.
Alfgeat of Aylesbury held this land; he could sell.

17 In the same village Bernard holds 3 hides and 1 virgate from the Count as one manor. Land for 1 plough; ½ there; [another] ½ possible.
2 smallholders.
Woodland, 30 pigs.
The value is and always was 20s.
Two of the Abbot of St. Albans' men, held this land; they could sell.

18 In the same village Fulkhold holds 1 hide and 1 virgate from the Count.
Land for 4 oxen; they are there.
Woodland, 10 pigs.
The value is and always was 10s.
Gladwin, the Abbot of St. Albans' man held this land; he could sell.

19 From the manor of PITSTONE Thorgils, the Count's man, took 6 hides which the Count himself wrongfully holds, in his lordship. 146 c

20 In (Ivinghoe) ASTON Ralph holds 3 virgates from the Count.
Land for ½ plough; it is there, with
1 villager.
The value is and was 5s; before 1066, 10s.
Godwin, a priest of Archbishop Stigand's, held this land; he could sell.

In Cetedone teñ Radulf de comite.I.hid 7 I.uirg.
Tra.ē.I.car.7 ibi.ē cū.I.bord.Val 7 ualuit sēp.x.sol.
Hanc trā tenuer.III.hões.S Archiepi.7 uende potuer.
In ead uilla teñ Rannulf de com dim hid.Tra est
dim car.7 ibi.ē cū uno uitto.Val 7 ualuit sēp.x.sol.
Hanc trā tenuit Leuing hō abbis S Albani.7 uende pot.
In Hortone teñ Alestan de com.I.uirg.Tra.ē.II.bob.
Val 7 ualuit.II.sol.T.R.E.III.sol.Hanc trā tenuit
Bruman hō.S.archiepi.7 uende potuit. *IN MVSELAI HD.*
In Sueneberne teñ Radulf 7 Almarus.v.hid.
Tra.ē.v.car.Ibi una.ē.7 IIII.poss fieri.Ibi.II.uitti.
ptū.v.car.H tra ual.XL.sol.Qdo recep.VI.lib.
T.R.E.C.sol.De hoc m tenuit Brixtuin teign.R.E.
IIII.hid 7 dim.7 Almar hō com Heraldi.I.hid 7 dim.
In Sceldene teñ Radulf de com 7 uende pot.
III.hid 7 dim uirg p uno m.Tra.ē.III.car.7 ibi sunt
cū.III.uittis 7 II.bord.ptū.III.car.Val 7 ualuit XXX.
sol.T.R.E.XL.sol.Hoc m tenuer.IIII.teigni.Hoz
un hō Aluuini.7 alt hō Aluuini de Neuhā.7 tcius hō
Aluuardi.7 IIII tus.hō Azori.Oms hi uende potuer.
In Muselai teñ Aluerad de com.I.hid.Tra.ē dim
car.Val 7 ualuit.VII.sol.T.R.E.x.sol.Hanc
trā tenuit Eduin hō Azorii.7 uende potuit.
In Betesdene teñ isd com.III.uirg. *IN STOFALD HD.*
Tra.ē.I.car.sz uastata.ē.Hanc trā tenuit Alric
hō Aluuini.f.Goding.7 uende potuit. *IN ROVELAI HD.*
In Ilesdone.teñ Rannulf de com.I.hid.Tra.ē.I.car.
7 ibi.ē cū.III.bord.ptū.I.car.Silua.x.porc.Val
XXX.sol.Qdo recep.XII.sol.T.R.E.XXX.sol.Hanc
trā tenuit Leuuin hō Alric.f.Goding.7 uende pot.

21 In CHEDDINGTON Ralph holds 1 hide and 1 virgate from the Count.
Land for 1 plough; it is there, with
1 smallholder.
The value is and always was 10s.
Three of Archbishop Stigand's men held this land; they could sell.

22 In the same village Ranulf holds ½ hide from the Count.
Land for ½ plough; it is there, with
1 villager.
The value is and always was 10s.
Leofing, the Abbot of St. Albans' man, held this land; he could sell.

23 In HORTON Alstan holds 1 virgate from the Count. Land for 2 oxen.
The value is and was 2s; before 1066, 3s.
Bruman, Archbishop Stigand's man, held this land; he could sell.

In MURSLEY Hundred

24 In SWANBOURNE Ralph and Aelmer hold 5 hides. Land for 5 ploughs.
1 there; [another] 4 possible.
2 villagers.
Meadow for 5 ploughs.
Value of this land, 40s; when acquired £6; before 1066, 100s.
Brictwin, a thane of King Edward's, held 4½ hides of this manor, and Aelmer, Earl Harold's man, 1½ hides; they could sell.

25 In SALDEN Ralph holds 3 hides and ½ virgate from the Count as one manor. Land for 3 ploughs; they are there, with
3 villagers and 2 smallholders.
Meadow for 3 ploughs.
The value is and was 30s; before 1066, 40s.
Four thanes held this manor; one of these [was] a man of Alwin's, the second a man of Alwin of Nuneham's, the third a man of Alfward's, the fourth a man of Azor's; all of them could sell.

26 In MURSLEY Alfred holds 1 hide from the Count. Land for ½ plough.
The value is and was 7s; before 1066, 10s.
Edwin, Azor's man, held this land; he could sell.

In STOTFOLD Hundred

27 In BIDDLESDEN the Count also holds 3 virgates. Land for 1 plough; but it has been laid waste.
Alric, Alwin son of Goding's man, held this land; he could sell.

In ROWLEY Hundred

28 In HILLESDEN Ranulf holds 1 hide from the Count. Land for 1 plough; it is there, with
3 smallholders.
Meadow for 1 plough; woodland, 10 pigs.
Value 30s; when acquired 12s; before 1066, 30s.
Leofwin, Alric son of Goding's man, held this land; he could sell.

In *MERSA* ten monachi de Grestein *IN LAMVE HD*.
xi. hid de com. Tra. e. xiii. car. In dnio. iiii. hidæ.
7 ibi sunt. iii. car. Ibi. xvii. uilli cu. iii. bord. hnt. x.
car. Ibi. viii. serui. Int totu uat 7 ualuit sep. viii. lib.
Hoc M tenuit Vlf. f. Borgerete. 7 uende potuit.
7 un ho Bondi stalre habuit ibi dim hid. 7 uende pot.
In Caldecote ten Aluered. iiii. hid 7 i. uirg *IN SIGELAI HD*.
de com p uno M. Tra. e. iiii. car. In dnio est una 7 dim.
7 adhuc dim pot fieri. Ibi sunt. ii. uauassores redd
xxx. ii. sol 7 vi. den. 7 un uills 7 v. bord cu. ii. car. Ibi
un seruus. 7 i. molin de. v. ores 7 iiii. den. ptu. ii. car.
Silua. xxiiii. porc. 7 xxviii. den de csuetud. In totis
ualent uat 7 ualuit sep. iiii. lib. Hoc M tenuer. iiii.
teigni. T.R.E. 7 uende potuer. 7 dare cui uoluer.
In Vlchetone ten Radulf de com. iiii. hid p. i. M.
Tra. e. iiii. car. In dnio. e una 7 alia pot fieri. Ibi. iii. uilli
cu. vi. bord hnt. i. car. 7 alia pot fieri. Ibi. ii. serui.
ptu. iiii. car. Int tot uat. iii. lib. Qdo recep: iiii. lib.
T.R.E: iii. lib. Hoc M tenuer. viii. teigni. Hoz. iiii.

146 d

uaru choes Alurici dim hid habuer. 7 un ho Alrici. f. Godin.
. i. hid 7 dim uirg. 7 un ho Vluuardi. f. Eddeue
una hid 7 i. uirg. 7 un ho Leuuini. f. Estan. dim hid.
7 un ho Balduini dim hid. 7 un ho Morcar dim hid.
7 un ho Seuuolt. i. uirg habuit. Oms hi uende pot.
In Lochintone ten Walter de com dim hid.
Tra. e dim car. 7 ibi. e cu uno uillo. H tra uat. xx. sol.
Qdo recep: v. sol. T.R.E: xx. sol. Hanc tra tenuit
Elmær ho Aluric. f. Goding. 7 uende potuit.
In Linforde ten Rannulf de com. ii. hid. Tra. e
ii. car. 7 ibi sunt cu. iiii. uillis 7 iii. bord 7 i. seruo.

In LAMUA Hundred

9 In MARSH (Gibbon) the monks of Grestain hold 11 hides from the Count. Land for 13 ploughs; in lordship 4 hides; 3 ploughs there.
17 villagers with 3 smallholders have 10 ploughs. 8 slaves.
In total, the value is and always was £8.
Ulf son of Borgred held this manor; he could sell. A man of Bondi the Constable's had ½ hide there; he could sell.

In SECKLOE Hundred

0 In CALDECOTE Alfred holds 4 hides and 1 virgate from the Count as one manor. Land for 4 ploughs; in lordship 1½; a further ½ possible.
2 vavassors pay 32s 6d; 1 villager and 5 smallholders with 2 ploughs.
1 slave; 1 mill at 5 *ora* and 4d; meadow for 2 ploughs; woodland, 24 pigs, and 28d as a customary due.
The total value is and always was £4.
Four thanes held this manor before 1066; they could sell and grant to whom they would.

1 In WOUGHTON Ralph holds 4 hides from the Count as one manor. Land for 4 ploughs; in lordship 1; another possible.
3 villagers with 6 smallholders have 1 plough; another possible.
2 slaves; meadow for 4 ploughs.
In total, value £3; when acquired £4; before 1066 £3.
Eight thanes held this manor; four of these, men of Alfric Varus', had ½ hide; one, a man of Alric son of Goding's, 1 hide and ½ virgate; one, a man of Wulfward son of Edeva's, 1 hide and 1 virgate; one, a man of Leofwin son of Estan's, ½ hide; one, a man of Baldwin's, ½ hide; one, a man of Morcar's, ½ hide; and one, a man of Saeward's, had 1 virgate; all these could sell. 146 d

2 In LOUGHTON Walter holds ½ hide from the Count. Land for ½ plough; it is there, with
1 villager.
Value of this land, 20s; when acquired 5s; before 1066, 20s.
Aelmer, Aelfric son of Goding's man, held this land; he could sell.

3 In (Great) LINFORD Ranulf holds 2 hides from the Count. Land for 2 ploughs; they are there, with
4 villagers, 3 smallholders and 1 slave.

pt͡u .II. car̄. Vał 7 ualuit sēp.XL.ſoł. Hanc t͛ram tenuer̄.II. hoēs Alric.f. Godingi.7 uend͛e potuer̄.

In Weſtone ten̄ Iuo de comite *IN BONESTOV HD̄.*
.I.hid 7 II.part͛ uni͛ uirg.T͛ra.ē.I.car͛.Ibi ſunt.II.
boues cū.II.bord.pt͡u.I.car̄.Silua.XX.porc͛.Vał
7 ualuit sēp.XX.ſoł.Hanc t͛rā tenuer̄.III.teigni.
Hoꝝ.II.hoēs Burgeret.III.uirg͛ 7 II.part͛.I.uirg͛ ha
buer̄.III.hō Alrici.f.Goding.I.uirg͛.7 uend͛e potuer̄.

In Lauuendene ten͛ Hunfrid͛ de com̄.II.hid 7 dim͛
p uno M.T͛ra.ē.II.car͛.7 dim͛.In dn̄io.I.hid 7 dim̄.
7 ibi.ē una.car̄.7 III.uilli cū.v.bord.hn̄t.I.car̄ 7 dim͛.
Ibi.II.ſerui.7 I.moł de.X.ſoł 7 L.anguilł.pt͡u
II.car̄.Silua.XL.porc̄.Vał.XL.ſoł.Q͞do recep̄:
XX.ſoł.T.R.E:IIII.lib.Hoc M tenuit un͛ hō Alrici
filij Goding.7 uend͛e potuit. *IN MOLESLOV HVND.*

In Wauendone ten͛ Radulf͛ de com͛.II.hid p uno
M.T͛ra.ē.II.car͛ 7 dim͛.In dn̄io.ē una.7 II.uilli
cū.III.bord hn̄t.I.car̄.7 dim͛ pot͛ fieri.Ibi.I.ſeru͛.
7 pt͡u.II.car̄.Silua.XV.porc͛.Vał.XX.ſoł.Q͞do re
cep:X.ſoł.T.R.E:XL.ſoł.Hoc M tenuit Golnil
huſcarle regis.E.7 uend͛e potuit.

In ead ten͛ Walteri͛ de com͛.II.hid p uno M.T͛ra.ē.
II.car͛ 7 dim͛.In dn̄io.ē una.7 II.uilli cū.III.bord hn̄t
.I.car͛.7 adhuc poſs fac͛e dimid.Ibi.II.ſerui.Pt͡u.II.
car̄.Silua.XV.porc͛.Vał.XX.ſoł.Q͞do recep:X.ſoł.
T.R.E:XL.ſoł.Hoc M tenuit Brictuin͛ hō Heraldi com̄

In ead uilla ten͛ Hunfrid͛ de comite 7 uend͛e pot͛.
III.uirg͛.T͛ra.ē.I.car̄.Ibi.I.bord.pt͡um.I.car̄.
Vał 7 ualuit.V.ſoł.T.R.E:X.ſoł.Hanc t͛rā tenuit
Chentis hō Leuenot.f.Oſmundi.7 uend͛e potuit.

Meadow for 2 ploughs.
The value is and always was 40s.
Two of Alric son of Goding's men held this land: they could sell.

In BUNSTY Hundred

34 In WESTON (Underwood) Ivo holds 1 hide and 2 parts of 1 virgate from the Count. Land for 1 plough; 2 oxen there, with
2 smallholders.
Meadow for 1 plough; woodland, 20 pigs.
The value is and always was 20s.
Three thanes held this land; two of these, Burgred's men, had 3 virgates and 2 parts of 1 virgate; the third, Alric son of Goding's man, 1 virgate; they could sell.

35 In LAVENDON Humphrey holds 2½ hides from the Count as one manor. Land for 2½ ploughs; in lordship 1½ hides; 1 plough there.
3 villagers with 5 smallholders have 1½ ploughs.
2 slaves; 1 mill at 10s and 50 eels; meadow for 2 ploughs; woodland, 40 pigs.
Value 40s; when acquired 20s; before 1066 £4.
A man of Alric son of Goding's held this manor; he could sell.

In MOULSOE Hundred

36 In WAVENDON Ralph holds 2 hides from the Count as one manor. Land for 2½ ploughs; in lordship 1.
2 villagers with 3 smallholders have 1 plough; [another] ½ possible.
1 slave; meadow for 2 ploughs; woodland, 15 pigs.
Value 20s; when acquired 10s; before 1066, 40s.
Godnir, King Edward's Guard, held this manor; he could sell.

37 In the same [village] Walter holds 2 hides from the Count as one manor. Land for 2½ ploughs; in lordship 1.
2 villagers with 3 smallholders have 1 plough; a further ½ possible.
2 slaves; meadow for 2 ploughs; woodland, 15 pigs.
Value 20s; when acquired 10s; before 1066, 40s.
Brictwin, Earl Harold's man, held this manor; he could sell.

38 In the same village Humphrey holds 3 virgates from the Count. Land for 1 plough.
1 smallholder.
Meadow for 1 plough.
The value is and was 5s; before 1066, 10s.
Kentish, Leofnoth son of Osmund's man, held this land; he could sell.

.XIII. TERRA HVGONIS COMITIS. *IN COTESLAI HVND.*

M HVGO Comes ten *MENTEMORE*. Robt ten de eo. p xviii. hid se desd. Tra. e. x. car. In dnio. iiii. car. 7 xviii. uitti hnt. vi. car. Ibi. iii. serui. ptu iiii. car. In totis ualent uat. xii. lib. Qdo recep: x. lib. T.R.E: xiiii. lib. Hoc M tenuit Eddeua pulchra.

Hugo ten de comite *SENELAI* *IN SIGELAI HVND.* p ii. hid se desd. Tra. e. x. car. In dnio sunt. iii. car. 7 v. uitti cu. vi. seruis hnt. v. car. 7 adhuc. ii. poss fieri. ptu. v. car. Silua. l. porc. Vat 7 ualuit. c. sol. T.R.E: vi. lib. Hoc M tenuit Burcard Huscarle regis. E. 7 uende potuit.

147 a

In Senelai. ten Hugo de comite Hugone. v. hid. p uno M. Tra. e. v. car. 7 ibi sunt. iiii. car. 7 v. ta pot fieri. Ibi. viii. uitti. ptu. v. car. Silua. l. porc. In toto ualent uat 7 ualuit. iii. lib. T.R.E: iiii. lib. Hoc M tenuit Burchard teignus regis. E. *IN MOISSELAI HD.*

Wills ten Brichella p. ix. hid se desd. Tra. e. ix. car. In dnio. iiii. car. 7 xvi. uitti cu. vi. bord hnt. vi. car. Ibi. vi. serui. 7 ii. molini de. xxx. sol. ptu. x. car. Silua. c. porc. Int tot uat. ix. lib. Qdo recep: vii. lib. T.R.E: x. lib. Hoc M tenuit Tosti comes.

.XII. TERRA WALTERIJ GIFARD *IN STANES HVND.*

WALTERIVS Gifard 7 Hugo de Molebec de eo ten in Herdeuuelle. ii. hid. Tra. e. ii. car. 7 ibi sunt cu iiii. uiltis 7 iii. bord. Ibi. iiii. serui. Vat 7 ualuit semp xxx. sol. Hanc tra tenuer. ii. hoes Sired. 7 uende potuer. 7 m tenent.

M Ipse Hugo ten de Walterio *CHENEBELLA*. p. xx. ti hid se desd. Tra. e. xi. car. 7 dim. In dnio sunt. ii. 7 tcia æ pot fieri. Ibi. xxii. uitti cu. viii. bord hnt. viii. to car

13 LAND OF EARL HUGH

In COTTESLOE Hundred

1 M. Earl Hugh holds MENTMORE; Robert holds from him. It answers for 18 hides. Land for 10 ploughs; in lordship 4 ploughs.
18 villagers have 6 ploughs.
3 slaves; meadow for 4 ploughs.
Total value £12; when acquired £10; before 1066 £14.
Edeva the Fair held this manor.

In SECKLOE Hundred

2 Hugh holds SHENLEY (Church End) from the Earl. It answers for 2 hides. Land for 10 ploughs; in lordship 3 ploughs.
5 villagers with 6 slaves have 5 ploughs; a further 2 possible.
Meadow for 5 ploughs; woodland, 50 pigs.
The value is and was 100s; before 1066 £6.
Burghard, one of King Edward's Guards, held this manor; he could sell.

3 In SHENLEY (Church End) Hugh holds 5 hides from Earl Hugh as one manor. Land for 5 ploughs; 4 ploughs there; a fifth possible. 147 a
8 villagers.
Meadow for 5 ploughs; woodland, 50 pigs.
The total value is and was £3; before 1066 £4.
Burghard, a thane of King Edward's, held this manor.

In MOULSOE Hundred

4 William holds (Great) BRICKHILL. It answers for 9 hides. Land for 9 ploughs; in lordship 4 ploughs.
16 villagers with 6 smallholders have 6 ploughs.
6 slaves; 2 mills at 30s; meadow for 10 ploughs; woodland, 100 pigs.
In total, value £9; when acquired £7; before 1066 £10.
Earl Tosti held this manor.

14 LAND OF WALTER GIFFARD

In STONE Hundred

1 Walter Giffard, and Hugh of Bolbec from him, holds 2 hides in HARTWELL. Land for 2 ploughs; they are there, with
4 villagers and 3 smallholders. 4 slaves.
The value is and always was 30s.
Two of Sired's men held this land; they could sell; they hold now.

2 M. Hugh holds (Great) KIMBLE himself from Walter. It answers for 20 hides. Land for 11½ ploughs; in lordship 2, a third possible.
22 villagers with 8 smallholders have 8½ ploughs.

7 dimid . Ibi . vi . serui . p̄tū . xi . car . Nem ad sepes.
In totis ualent uat 7 ualuit sēp . x . lib . Hoc m̄ tenuit
Sired teign regis . E . 7 uende potuit.

m̄ Turstin filius Rolf ten de Walterio *MISSEDENE*.
p x . hid se defd . Tra . ē . viii . car . In dn̄io sun̄ . ii . 7 ix.
uilli cū uno bord hn̄t . vi . car . Ibi . ii . serui . p̄tū . ii . car.
Silua qngent porc . 7 de reddita siluæ . iiii . ores p ann.
In totis ualent uat 7 ualuit . iiii . lib . T.R.E. vii . lib . Hoc m̄
tenuit Sired . f. Alueue . teign . R.E . 7 uende potuit.

m̄ Herbrand ten de Waltio *FALELIE*. *IN DVSTENBERG HD.*
p x . hid se defd . Tra . ē . xiiii . car . In dn̄io sunt . ii . car.
7 xiii . uilli cū . i . bord . hn̄t . xii . car . Ibi . v . serui . p̄tū
ii . car . Silua . c . porc . Int totū uat . vi . lib . Qdo recep.
c . sol . T.R.E. vi . lib . Hoc m̄ tenuit comes Tosti.

m̄ Ipse Walteri ten *CREDENDONE*. *IN TICHESHELE HD.*
p xx . hid se defd . Tra . ē . xxv . car . In dn̄io . x . hidæ.
7 ibi sunt . v . car . 7 lii . uilli cū . x . bord hn̄t . xx . car.
Ibi . x . serui . 7 i . molin de . xviii . sol . p̄tū . x . car . Silua
c . porc . 7 parc ibi bestiarū siluaticarū . In totis ualent
uat xx . lib . Qdo recep 7 T.R.E. xv . lib . Hoc m̄ tenuit
Seric Alueue filius.

m̄ Hugo ten de Walterio *EDDINGRAVE* . p . iii . hid 7 dim
se defd . Tra . ē . iiii . car . In dn̄io sunt . ii . 7 ii . uilli cū . vii.
bord hn̄t . iii . car . Ibi un seruus . p̄tū . i . car . Int totū
uat . lx . sol . Qdo recep . xl . sol . T.R.E. iiii . lib . Hoc m̄
tenuit Vluuard hō Eddid reginæ . 7 uende potuit.

m̄ Ipse Walteri ten *CILTONE* . p x . hid se defd . Tra . ē
x . car . In dn̄io . iiii . hidæ . 7 ibi sunt . iiii . car . 7 x . uilli
cū . iiii . bord hn̄t . vi . car . Ibi . iii . serui . p̄tū . iii . car.
Silua . c . porc . Int totū uat . vii . lib . Qdo recep . viii . lib.
7 tntd . T.R.E. Hoc m̄ tenuit Alric fili Goding . teign . R.E.

6 slaves; meadow for 11 ploughs; wood for fences.
The total value is and always was £10.
Sired, a thane of King Edward's, held this manor; he could sell.

3 M. Thurstan son of Rolf holds (Great) MISSENDEN from Walter. It answers for 10 hides. Land for 8 ploughs; in lordship 2.
9 villagers with 1 smallholder have 6 ploughs.
2 slaves; meadow for 2 ploughs; woodland, 500 pigs; and from the returns of the woodland, 4 ora a year.
The total value is and was £4; before 1066 £7.
Sired son of Aelfeva, a thane of King Edward's, held this manor; he could sell.

In DESBOROUGH Hundred
4 M. Herbrand holds FAWLEY from Walter. It answers for 10 hides. Land for 14 ploughs; in lordship 2 ploughs.
13 villagers with 1 smallholder have 12 ploughs.
5 slaves; meadow for 2 ploughs; woodland, 100 pigs.
In total, value £6; when acquired 100s; before 1066 £6.
Earl Tosti held this manor.

In IXHILL Hundred
5 M. Walter holds (Long) CRENDON himself. It answers for 20 hides. Land for 25 ploughs; in lordship 10 hides; 5 ploughs there.
52 villagers with 10 smallholders have 20 ploughs.
10 slaves; 1 mill at 18s; meadow for 10 ploughs; woodland, 100 pigs, and a park there for woodland beasts.
Total value £20; when acquired and before 1066 £15.
Seric son of Aelfeva held this manor.

6 M. Hugh holds ADDINGROVE from Walter. It answers for 3½ hides. Land for 4 ploughs; in lordship 2.
2 villagers with 7 smallholders have 3 ploughs.
1 slave; meadow for 1 plough.
In total, value 60s; when acquired 40s; before 1066 £4.
Wulfward, Queen Edith's man, held this manor; he could sell.

7 M. Walter holds CHILTON himself. It answers for 10 hides. Land for 10 ploughs; in lordship 4 hides; 4 ploughs there.
10 villagers with 4 smallholders have 6 ploughs.
3 slaves; meadow for 3 ploughs; woodland, 100 pigs.
In total, value £7; when acquired £8; before 1066 as much.
Alric son of Goding, a thane of King Edward's, held this manor.

M Rogerius ten de Walterio HESINTONE . p . v . hid se
defd . Tra . e . IIII . car . In dnio sunt . II . 7 . v . uitti hnt . II .
Ibi . II . serui . 7 ptu . II . car . Val 7 ualuit sep . LX . sol .
Hoc M tenuit Alric fili Goding . 7 uende potuit .
M Ipse Walteri ten DORTONE . p . v . hid se defd . Tra
. e . VII . car . In dnio . II . hidæ 7 dim . 7 ibi sunt . III . car .

147 b
Ibi . XII . uitti cu . VI . bord hnt . IIII . car . Ibi . III . serui .
ptu . III . car . Silua . C . porc . In totis ualent ual 7 ualuit sep
. C . sol . Hoc M tenuit Alricus teign regis . E . 7 uende pot .
M Ipse Walterius ten POLICOTE . p . x . hid IN ESSEDEN HD .
se defd . Tra . e . VIII . car . Duo milit ten de Walterio . In dnio
. IIII . car . 7 XIII . uitti cu . I . bord hnt . IIII . car . Ibi . IIII . serui .
Ptu . VIII . car . In totis ualent ual 7 ualuit . VI . lib . T.R.E .
VII . lib . De hoc M tenuit Alric filius Goding . v . hid . 7 III[es] .
frs tenuer . v . hid . 7 cui uoluer uende potuer .
M In ASSEDONE ten Ricard de Walterio . VIII . hid . Tra . e
VI . car . In dnio sunt . II . 7 IIII . uitti cu . IIII . bord hnt . IIII[or] . car .
Ibi . II . serui . 7 ptu . VI . car . In totis ualent ual . III . lib . Qdo
recep . IIII . lib . T.R.E . C . sol . Hoc M tenuer . III . frs . 7 cui
uoluer uende potuer .
M In CERLESLAI ten Ernulf 7 Goisfrid de Walterio
VIII . hid 7 dim . Tra . e . VI . car . In dnio . IIII . car . 7 VI .
uitti cu . II . bord hnt . II . car . Ibi . IIII . serui . ptu . VI . car .
Val 7 ualuit . VI . lib . T.R.E . VII . lib . Hoc M tenuer . VI .
teigni . 7 uende potuer cui uoluer .
M Ipse Walteri ten WICHENDONE . p x . hid se defd . Tra
e . XI . car . In dnio . III . hidæ 7 ibi sunt . III . car . 7 XXIII .
uitti cu . VIII . bord hnt . VIII . car . Ibi un seruus . 7 ptu . VII .
car . 7 I . molin de XX[ti] . sol 7 qt XX[ti] . anguitt . in totis ualent
ual 7 ualuit sep . XII . lib . Hoc M tenuit Eddeda regina Eddeua[de] .

8 M. Roger holds EASINGTON from Walter. It answers for 5 hides.
Land for 4 ploughs; in lordship 2.
5 villagers have 2 [ploughs].
2 slaves; meadow for 2 ploughs.
The value is and always was 60s.
Alric son of Goding held this manor; he could sell.

9 M. Walter holds DORTON himself. It answers for 5 hides. Land for 7 ploughs; in lordship 2½ hides; 3 ploughs there.
12 villagers with 6 smallholders have 4 ploughs. 147 b
3 slaves; meadow for 3 ploughs; woodland, 100 pigs.
The total value is and always was 100s.
Alric, a thane of King Edward's, held this manor; he could sell.

In ASHENDON Hundred

10 M. Walter holds POLLICOT himself. It answers for 10 hides.
Land for 8 ploughs. Two men-at-arms hold from Walter.
In lordship 4 ploughs.
13 villagers with 1 smallholder have 4 ploughs.
4 slaves; meadow for 8 ploughs.
The total value is and was £6; before 1066 £7.
Alric son of Goding held 5 hides of this manor, and three brothers held 5 hides; they could sell to whom they would.

11 M. In ASHENDON Richard holds 8 hides from Walter.
Land for 6 ploughs; in lordship 2.
4 villagers with 4 smallholders have 4 ploughs.
2 slaves; meadow for 6 ploughs.
Total value £3; when acquired £4; before 1066, 100s.
Three brothers held this manor; they could sell to whom they would.

12 M. In CHEARLSEY Arnulf and Geoffrey hold 8½ hides from Walter.
Land for 6 ploughs; in lordship 4 ploughs.
6 villagers with 2 smallholders have 2 ploughs.
4 slaves; meadow for 6 ploughs.
The value is and was £6; before 1066 £7.
Six thanes held this manor; they could sell to whom they would.

13 M. Walter holds (Lower) WINCHENDON himself. It answers for 10 hides.
Land for 11 ploughs; in lordship 3 hides; 3 ploughs there.
23 villagers with 8 smallholders have 8 ploughs. 1 slave.
Meadow for 7 ploughs; 1 mill at 20s and 80 eels.
The total value is and always was £12.
Edith held this manor from Queen Edith.

M Radulf⁹ ten de Walterio *OLTONE*. p. x. hid se defd.
Tra. e. x. car. In dnio sunt. III. 7 x. uitti cu XIII. bord
hnt. VII. car. Ibi. v. serui. 7 ptu. v. car. Silua. cc. porc. Int
totu uat 7 ualuit. VII. lib. T.R.E. VIII. lib. Hoc M tenuit
Eddeua uxor Vluuardi. 7 uende potuit. *IN COTESLAI HD*
Duo Angli ten de Walterio in hoc hund una uirg. Tra. e
dim car. ptu dim car. Vat 7 ualuit sep. III. sol 7 dim.
Istimet q ten tenuer. T.R.E. 7 uende potuer.
M Hugo de Bolebec ten de Walterio *WICHERCE*. p. VIII.
hid se defd. Tra. e XII. car. In dnio. III. car. 7 II. poss fieri.
Ibi. XIIII. uitti cu. II. bord hnt. VII. car. Ibi. VIII. serui.
ptu. VI. car. Int totu uat 7 ualuit. VIII. lib. T.R.E. x. lib.
Hoc M tenuer. II. frs teigni regis. E. p. II. M. 7 uende potuer.
In Litecota ten Robt de Walterio. II. hid 7 dim p uno M.
Tra. e. III. car. In dnio. II. car. 7 II. uitti cu. III. bord
hnt. I. car. Ibi. III. serui. 7 ptu. I. car. H tra uat 7 ualuit
XL. sol. T.R.E. LX. sol. Hoc M tenuit Wiga teign regis. E.
7 uende potuit.
In Bricstoch ten Turstin de Walterio. I. hid. Tra. e. I. car.
7 ibi. e cu. II. bord. 7 I. seruo. ptu. I. car. Vat. xx. sol.
Qdo recep. x. sol. T.R.E. xx. sol. Hanc tra tenuit Aluuen
quæda femina sub Siuuardo. 7 uende potuit. *IN ERLAI HD*.
Radulf⁹ ten de Walter in Pincenestorne. v. hid 7 dim p uno
Maner. Tra. e. II. car. 7 ibi sunt cu. III. uittis 7 III. bord.
7 I. seruo. Silua. XL. porc. Vat. XL. sol. Qdo recep. xx. sol.
T.R.E. XL. sol. Hoc M tenuit Toroi ho com Leuuini. 7 uende pot.
Witts ten de Walter In *SOENEBERNO* *IN MUSELAI HD*
VII. hid 7 III. uirg p uno M. Tra. e. VII. car. In dnio

14 M. Ralph holds WOTTON (Underwood) from Walter. It answers for 10 hides. Land for 10 ploughs; in lordship 3.
10 villagers with 13 smallholders have 7 ploughs.
5 slaves; meadow for 5 ploughs; woodland, 200 pigs.
In total, the value is and was £7; before 1066 £8.
Edeva, Wulfward's wife, held this manor; she could sell.

In COTTESLOE Hundred

15 Two Englishmen hold 1 virgate from Walter in this Hundred. Land for ½ plough.
Meadow for ½ plough.
The value is and always was 3½s.
The present holders held before 1066; they could sell.

16 M. Hugh of Bolbec holds WHITCHURCH from Walter. It answers for 8 hides. Land for 12 ploughs; in lordship 3 ploughs; [another] 2 possible.
14 villagers with 2 smallholders have 7 ploughs.
8 slaves; meadow for 6 ploughs.
In total, the value is and was £8; before 1066 £10.
Two brothers, thanes of King Edward's, held this manor as two manors; they could sell.

17 In LITTLECOTE Robert holds 2½ hides from Walter as one manor. Land for 3 ploughs; in lordship 2 ploughs.
2 villagers with 3 smallholders have 1 plough.
3 slaves; meadow for 1 plough.
The value of this land is and was 40s; before 1066, 60s.
Wicga, a thane of King Edward's, held this manor; he could sell.

18 In BURSTON Thurstan holds 1 hide from Walter. Land for 1 plough; it is there, with
2 smallholders and 1 slave.
Meadow for 1 plough.
Value 20s; when acquired 10s; before 1066, 20s.
Aelfwen, a woman, held this land under Siward; she could sell.

In YARDLEY Hundred

19 Ralph holds 5½ hides in PITSTONE from Walter as one manor. Land for 2 ploughs; they are there, with
3 villagers, 3 smallholders and 1 slave.
Woodland, 40 pigs.
Value 40s; when acquired 20s; before 1066, 40s.
Thorulf, Earl Leofwin's man, held this manor; he could sell.

In MURSLEY Hundred

20 William holds 7 hides and 3 virgates in SWANBOURNE from Walter as one manor. Land for 7 ploughs; in lordship 2.

sunt . II . 7 VII . uitti cũ . v . bord hnt . IIII . car . Ibi . II . serui.
ptũ . VI . car . Int totũ uat 7 ualuit . IIII . lib . T.R.E. c . sol.

147 c

Hoc M̃ tenuer . II . teigni . Aluuard 7 Aluui hõ ej . p duob
v. hid . I . v' man'. II . hid 7 III . uirg'
Man habuer . 7 uendere potuer.

M̃ Ipse Walteri ten *HEREWORDE* . p x . hid se defd . Tra . ẽ
.IX . car . In dnio . v . hide . 7 ibi sunt . IIII . car . 7 VIII . uitti cũ
.x . bord hnt . v . car . Ibi . II . serui . 7 ptũ . IX . car . Silua
c . porc . In totis ualentijs uat 7 ualuit sep . VII . lib . Hoc M̃
tenuit Aluuard cilt . teign regis . E.

Walter de Bec ten de Waltio Sincleberia . p . VI . hid
se defd . Tra . ẽ . VI . car . In dnio sunt . III . car . 7 IIII . uitti
cũ . IIII . bord hnt . III . car . Ibi . IIII . serui . 7 ptũ . III . car.
Silua . XL . porc . In totis ualentijs uat 7 ualuit sep
IIII . lib . Hoc M̃ tenuit Eduuard cilt teign regis . E.

M̃ Ipse Walt ten *WADONE* . p x . hid se defd . Tra . ẽ
x . car . In dnio . v . hidæ . 7 ibi sunt . v . car . 7 XIIII . uitti
cũ . IX . bord hnt . v . car . Ibi . x . serui . ptũ . x . car . Silua
.c . porc . In totis ualent uat 7 ualuit semp . VIII . lib.
Hoc M̃ tenuit Eduuard cilt teign regis . E.

M̃ In *MUSELAI* . ten Witts de Waltio : v . hid p uno M̃.
Tra . ẽ . IIII . car . In dnio sunt . II . 7 II . uitti cũ . v . bord hnt
II . car . Ibi . II . serui . Ptũ . II . car . Vat 7 ualuit sep . III . lib.

In *LANPORT* . ten Berner de Waltio . III . hid 7 dimid
p uno M̃ . Tra . ẽ . IIII . car . In dnio est una . 7 alia pot
fieri . Ibi . II . uitti cũ . II . bord hnt . II . car . Ibi . II . serui.
ptũ . II . car . Silua . L . porc . Vat 7 ualuit sep . XL . sol.
Hoc M̃ tenuit Suen Suert hõ Eduini . 7 uende pot.
comit'.

Robt ten de Waltio *ACHELEI* . p . III . hid se defd.
Tra . ẽ . IIII . car . In dnio sunt . IIII . boues . 7 II . car poss
or
fieri . Ibi . II . uitti . cũ . IIII . bord . hnt . II . car 7 dimid.

7 villagers with 5 smallholders have 4 ploughs.
2 slaves; meadow for 6 ploughs.
In total, the value is and was £4; before 1066, 100s.
Two thanes held this manor; Alfward, 5 hides less 1 virgate, and Alwin, his man, 2 hides and 3 virgates; they had it as two manors; they could sell. 147 c

21 M. Walter holds (Great) HORWOOD himself. It answers for 10 hides.
Land for 9 ploughs; in lordship 5 hides; 4 ploughs.
8 villagers with 10 smallholders have 5 ploughs.
2 slaves; meadow for 9 ploughs; woodland, 100 pigs.
The total value is and always was £7.
Young Alfward, a thane of King Edward's, held this manor.

22 Walter of Bec holds SINGLEBOROUGH from Walter. It answers for 6 hides. Land for 6 ploughs; in lordship 3 ploughs.
4 villagers with 4 smallholders have 3 ploughs.
4 slaves; meadow for 3 ploughs; woodland, 40 pigs.
The total value is and always was £4.
Young Edward, a thane of King Edward's, held this manor.

23 M. Walter holds WHADDON himself. It answers for 10 hides.
Land for 10 ploughs; in lordship 5 hides; 5 ploughs there.
14 villagers with 9 smallholders have 5 ploughs.
10 slaves; meadow for 10 ploughs; woodland, 100 pigs.
The total value is and always was £8.
Young Edward, a thane of King Edward's, held this manor.

24 M. In MURSLEY William holds 5 hides from Walter as one manor.
Land for 4 ploughs; in lordship 2.
2 villagers with 5 smallholders have 2 ploughs.
2 slaves; meadow for 2 ploughs.
The value is and always was £3.

[In STOTFOLD Hundred]

25 In LAMPORT Berner holds 3½ hides from Walter as one manor.
Land for 4 ploughs; in lordship 1; another possible.
2 villagers with 2 smallholders have 2 ploughs.
2 slaves; meadow for 2 ploughs; woodland, 50 pigs.
The value is and always was 40s.
Swein Swarthy, Earl Edwin's man, held this manor; he could sell.

26 Robert holds AKELEY from Walter. It answers for 3 hides.
Land for 4 ploughs; in lordship 4 oxen; 2 ploughs possible.
2 villagers with 4 smallholders have 2½ ploughs.

Ibi . II . serui . pt̃u . I . car . Silua octingent porc . 7 VI.
In totis ualent uat 7 ualuit XL . sot . T.R.E.: LX . sot.
Hoc M tenuit Alricus fili Goding . 7 uende potuit.
M Hugo ten de Waltio *LELINCHESTANE* . p . V . hid
se defd . Tra . e . V . car . In dnio . e una 7 dim . 7 dimid
pot fieri . Ibi . VI . uitti cu . V . bord hnt . II . car . 7 III . pot
fieri . pt̃u . V . car . Silua . mille 7 CC . porc . Vat . XL . sot.
Qdo recep: XL . sot . T.R.E.: L . sot . Hoc M tenuit
Syric ho Eddid regine . 7 uende potuit.
In *MORTONE* ten Turstin de Waltio . II . hid . Tra . e . II.
car . 7 ibi . e una 7 dim . 7 dim pot fieri . Ibi . II . uitti
7 IIII . bord . pt̃u . II . car . Vat . XXX . sot . Qdo recep: X . sot.
T.R.E.: XX . sot . Hoc M tenuit Vluric ho Alrici filij
Goding . 7 uende potuit.
In ead uilla ten isd Torstin de Waltio . IIII . hid p uno
Man . Tra . e . IIII . car . In dnio sunt . II . 7 aliæ . II . poss . ee.
Ibi un uitts cu . III . bord . Pt̃u . IIII . car . Vat . IIII . lib
Qdo recep: XX . sot . T.R.E.: LX . sot . De hoc M tenuit
Alric . f . Goding . II . hid p uno M . 7 Ederic ho Asgari
. I . hid 7 dim p uno M . 7 Sauuard ho Azor filij Toti
dimid hid tenuit . 7 dare 7 uende potuer.
In Lechamestede ten Hugo de Walterio . II . hid.
Tra . e . I . car . 7 ibi est . cu uno uitto 7 II . bord . 7 I . seruo.
Ibi unu molin de XX . den . Ptu . I . car . Silua . L . porc.
147 d
In totis ualent uat XXX . sot . Qdo recep: XX . sot . T.R.E.:
XXX . sot . Hoc M tenuit ho Asgari stalre Suartinus.
nec uende neq dare potuit præter ej licentia.
In Bccentone ten Hugo de Waltio *IN ROVELAI HD.*
V . hid p uno M . Tra . e . V . car . In dnio sunt . II . 7 V . uitti
cu . IX . bord hnt . III . car . Ibi un seruus 7 I . molin de

2 slaves; meadow for 1 plough; woodland, 800 pigs
and 6 [s. too?].
The total value is and was 40s; before 1066, 60s.
Alric son of Goding held this manor; he could sell.

27 M. Hugh holds LILLINGSTONE (Dayrell) from Walter. It answers for 5 hides. Land for 5 ploughs; in lordship 1½; [another] ½ possible.
6 villagers with 5 smallholders have 2 ploughs;
a third possible.
Meadow for 5 ploughs; woodland, 1,200 pigs.
Value 60s; when acquired 40s; before 1066, 50s.
Seric, Queen Edith's man, held this manor; he could sell.

28 In (Maids) MORETON Thurstan holds 2 hides from Walter.
Land for 2 ploughs; 1½ there; [another] ½ possible.
2 villagers and 4 smallholders.
Meadow for 2 ploughs.
Value 30s; when acquired 10s; before 1066, 20s.
Wulfric, Alric son of Goding's man, held this manor; he could sell.

29 In the same village Thurstan also holds 4 hides from Walter as one manor. Land for 4 ploughs; in lordship 2; another 2 possible.
1 villager with 3 smallholders.
Meadow for 4 ploughs.
Value £4, when acquired 20s; before 1066, 60s.
Alric son of Goding held 2 hides of this manor as one manor; Edric, Asgar the Constable's man, 1½ hides as one manor; and Saeward, Azor son of Toti's man, held ½ hide; they could grant and sell.

30 In LECKHAMPSTEAD Hugh holds 2 hides from Walter. Land for 1 plough; it is there, with
1 villager, 2 smallholders and 1 slave.
1 mill at 20d; meadow for 1 plough; woodland, 50 pigs.
Total value 30s; when acquired 20s; before 1066, 30s. 147 d
Swarting, Asgar the Constable's man, held this manor;
he could neither sell nor grant without his permission.

In ROWLEY Hundred

31 In BEACHAMPTON Hugh holds 5 hides from Walter as one manor.
Land for 5 ploughs; in lordship 2.
5 villagers with 9 smallholders have 3 ploughs;
1 slave; 1 mill at 10s; meadow for 2 ploughs.

x . sol . Ptu . II . car. In totis ualent uat . IIII . lib . Qdo
recep: xxx . sol . T.R.E: IIII . lib 7 x . sol . Hoc m tenuit
Alric ho 7 teign regis . E . 7 uende potuit.

Isde Hugo ten Burtone de Waltio . p una hida
se defd . Tra . e . II . car . In dnio . e una . 7 II . uitti cu . II .
bord hnt . I . car . Ptu . II . car . Vat 7 ualuit . xxx . sol .
T.R.E: xx . sol . Hoc m tenuit Alric teign regis . E.

In Edingeberge ten Radulf de Walterio . III . hid p uno m . Tra . e . II . car . Ibi est una .
7 alia pot fieri . Ibi . II . bord . 7 ptu . II . car . Vat . xxx . sol .
Qdo recep: LX . sol . T.R.E: XL . sol . Hoc m tenuit Touui .
Alrici ho filij Godingi . 7 uende potuit.

In Vlesdone ten Hugo de Waltio XVIII . hid p . I . m .
Tra . e . XIIII . car . In dnio sunt . IIII . 7 XVII . uitti cu . IX .
bord hnt . X . car . Ibi . VII . serui . 7 I . molin de . IIII . sol .
Ptu . XIIII . car . Silua . c . porc . In totis ualent uat
VI . lib . Qdo recep: VIII . lib . 7 tntd T.R.E. Hoc m
tenuit Alric teign . R.E . 7 uende potuit.

Radulf ten de Waltio *ACHECOTE* . p . v . hid se defd .
Tra . e . VIII . car . In dnio sunt . II . 7 x . uitti cu . IX . bord
hnt . VI . car . Ibi . II . serui . ptu . II . car . Silua . c . porc .
In totis ualent uat 7 ualuit sep . c . sol . Hoc m tenuer
IIII . teigni . Hoz un Aluuin hab . II . hid 7 dim p . I . m .
7 alt Eduuin . I . hid 7 . I . uirg p uno m . 7 Almar dim
hid . 7 Thori huscarle regis . E . III . uirg . Oms u uende potuer.

In Wlsiestone ten Radulf
de Waltio . III . hid 7 dim p uno m . Tra . e . III . car .
In dnio sunt . II . 7 IIII . uitti hnt . I . car . Ptu . II . car .
7 un molin de . x . sol . Vat . XL . sol . Qdo recep: xx . sol .
T.R.E: LX . sol . Hoc m tenuit Eduuard teign . R.E.

Total value £4; when acquired 30s; before 1066 £4 10s.
Alric, King Edward's man and thane, held this manor; he could sell.

32 Hugh also holds BOURTON from Walter. It answers for 1 hide. Land for 2 ploughs; in lordship 1.
2 villagers with 2 smallholders have 1 plough.
Meadow for 2 ploughs.
The value is and was 30s; before 1066, 20s.
Alric, a thane of King Edward's, held this manor; he could sell.

33 In LENBOROUGH Ralph holds 3 hides from Walter as one manor. Land for 2 ploughs; 1 there; another possible.
2 smallholders.
Meadow for 2 ploughs.
Value 30s; when acquired 60s; before 1066, 40s.
Tovi, Alric son of Goding's man, held this manor; he could sell.

34 In HILLESDEN Hugh holds 18 hides from Walter as one manor. Land for 14 ploughs; in lordship 4.
17 villagers with 9 smallholders have 10 ploughs.
7 slaves; 1 mill at 4s; meadow for 14 ploughs; woodland, 100 pigs.
Total value £6; when acquired £8; before 1066 as much.
Alric, a thane of King Edward's, held this manor; he could sell.

[In LAMUA Hundred]

35 Ralph holds EDGCOTT from Walter. It answers for 5 hides. Land for 8 ploughs; in lordship 2.
10 villagers with 9 smallholders have 6 ploughs.
2 slaves; meadow for 2 ploughs; woodland, 100 pigs.
The total value is and always was 100s.
Four thanes held this manor; one of these, Alwin, had 2½ hides as one manor; the second, Edwin, 1 hide and 1 virgate as one manor; Aelmer, ½ hide; and Thori, one of King Edward's Guards, 3 virgates; all could sell.

[In SECKLOE Hundred]

36 In (Little) WOOLSTONE Ralph holds 3½ hides from Walter as one manor. Land for 3 ploughs; in lordship 2.
4 villagers have 1 plough.
Meadow for 2 ploughs; 1 mill at 10s.
Value 40s; when acquired 20s; before 1066, 60s.
Edward, a thane of King Edward's, held this manor; he could sell.

In Vlsiestone ten monachi S Petri culturæ 7 uende pot. de Waltio. v. hid p uno m. Tra. e. v. car. In dnio sunt. II. 7 VIII. uitti cu uno bord hnt. III. car. Ibi un molin de. VI. sot 7 IIII. den. Ptu. IIII. car. Silua. c. porc. Vat 7 ualuit. III. lib. T.R.E. IIII. lib. Hoc m tenuit Alric filius Goding. 7 uende potuit.

m Ipse Walteri ten NEVTONE. p x. hid se defd. Tra. e. XII. car. In dnio. IIII. hidæ. 7 ibi sunt. IIII. car. 7 XX. uitti cu. VIII. bord hnt. VIII. car. Ibi. XI. serui. 7 ptu. VI. car. In totis ualent uat XII. lib. Qdo recep. X. lib. 7 tntd. T.R.E. Hoc m tenuit Eduuard cilt.

In Lochintone. ten Iuo de Waltio. IIII. hid 7 dim. Tra. e. IIII. car 7 dim. In dnio sunt. II. 7 v. uitti cu. II. bord hnt. I. car. 7 alia 7 dim pot fieri. Ptu IIII. car. Vat LX. sot. Qdo recep. XXX. sot. T.R.E. IIII. lib. Hoc m tenuer. v. teigni. 7 uende potuer.

148 a

In Bradeuuelle ten Walter Achet de Waltio Gifard. I. hid 7 dim. Tra. e. II. car. In dnio. e una. 7 alia pot fieri. Ibi. I. bord 7 I. seruus. Ptu. I. car. Vat XX. solid. Qdo recep. X. sot. T.R.E. XXX. sot. Hanc tra tenuit Aluiet ho Eddid reginæ. 7 uende potuit.

m In Linforde ten Hugo de Waltio. II. hid 7 I. uirg 7 dim. p uno m. Tra. e. v. car. In dnio. e una. 7 XVI. uitti cu II. bord hnt. IIII. car. Ibi. IIII. serui. 7 ptu. IIII. car. Vat. III. lib. Qdo recep. XL. sot. T.R.E. IIII. lib. Hoc m tenuit Alric Goding fili. 7 uende potuit. IN BONESTOV HD

m Isd Hugo ten de Waltio RAVENESTON. p. v. hid se defd. Tra. e. VI. car. In dnio sunt. II. 7 X. uitti cu. VI. bord hnt. IIII. car. Ibi. IIII. serui. 7 I. molin de. XXV. sot. Ptu. VI. car. Silua. CCC. porc. Vat 7 ualuit. C. sot. T.R.E. VI. lib. Hoc m tenuit Leuuin teign. R.E. 7 uende pot.

37 In (Great) WOOLSTONE the monks of St. Peter's of La Couture hold 5 hides from Walter as one manor. Land for 5 ploughs; in lordship 2.
8 villagers with 1 smallholder have 3 ploughs.
1 mill at 6s 4d; meadow for 4 ploughs; woodland, 100 pigs.
The value is and was £3; before 1066 £4.
Alric son of Goding held this manor; he could sell.

38 M. Walter holds NEWTON (Longville) himself. It answers for 10 hides. Land for 12 ploughs; in lordship 4 hides; 4 ploughs there.
20 villagers with 8 smallholders have 8 ploughs.
11 slaves; meadow for 6 ploughs.
Total value £12; when acquired £10; before 1066 as much.
Young Edward held this manor.

39 In LOUGHTON Ivo holds 4½ hides from Walter. Land for 4½ ploughs; in lordship 2.
5 villagers with 2 smallholders have 1 plough; another 1½ possible.
Meadow for 4 ploughs.
Value 60s; when acquired 30s; before 1066 £4.
Five thanes held this manor; they could sell.

40 In BRADWELL Walter Hackett holds 1½ hides from Walter Giffard. 148 a
Land for 2 ploughs; in lordship 1; another possible.
1 smallholder and 1 slave.
Meadow for 1 plough.
Value 20s; when acquired 10s; before 1066, 30s.
Alfgeat, Queen Edith's man, held this land; he could sell.

41 M. In (Great) LINFORD Hugh holds 2 hides and 1½ virgates from Walter as one manor. Land for 5 ploughs; in lordship 1.
16 villagers with 2 smallholders have 4 ploughs.
4 slaves; meadow for 4 ploughs.
Value £3; when acquired 40s; before 1066 £4.
Alric son of Goding held this manor; he could sell.

In BUNSTY Hundred

42 M. Hugh also holds RAVENSTONE from Walter. It answers for 5 hides. Land for 6 ploughs; in lordship 2.
10 villagers with 6 smallholders have 4 ploughs.
4 slaves. 1 mill at 25s; meadow for 6 ploughs; woodland, 300 pigs.
The value is and was 100s; before 1066, £6.
Leofwin, a thane of King Edward's, held this manor; he could sell.

In Lauuedene ten Radulf de Waltio . II . hid . 7 unā uirg 7 IIII . part uni uirgæ . Tra . ē . II . car. In dn̄io . ē una. 7 v . uilli cū . VIII . bord hn̄t . I . car . p̄tū . I . car . Silua xxx . porc . Val . xxv . sol . Qdo recep: x . sol . T.R.E: XL . sol . Hanc trā tenuit un hō Wluui epi . 7 uende pot.

M In Horelmede ten Hugo de Waltio *IN MOSLAI HD*.
II . hid 7 dim p uno M . Tra . ē . II . car 7 dim . 7 ibi sunt cū . IIII . uill 7 II . bord . p̄tū . I . car . Silua . L . porc . Val 7 ualuit sēp . XL . sol . Hoc M tenuit un hō Alrici . f. Godin 7 uende potuit.

M Ricard ten de Waltio *MOLESHOV* . p . x . hid se defd . Tra . ē . VII . car . In dn̄io . ē una . 7 VII . uilli cū IX . bord hn̄t . VI . car . Ibi . I . seruus . 7 p̄tū . v . car . Silua . c . porc . Int tot ual . VI . lib . Qdo recep: c . sol . T.R.E: VIII . lib . Hoc M tenuer . VIII . teigni 7 uende potuer. Vn hoz Aluuin . II . hid tenuit p uno M . 7 alt Vlf hō Asgari stalre . II . hid p uno M . 7 Algar hō Eduuardi cilt . I . hid 7 dim p uno M . Elsi . I . hid . Turchil . I . hid . Lodi . I . hid . Osulf . I . hid . Elricus dim hid.

M In Brotone ten Hugo de Waltio . IIII . hid p uno M . Tra . ē . v . car . In dn̄io . I . car . 7 VIII . uilli cū . v . bord hn̄t IIII . car . Ibi . II . serui . 7 I . molin in dn̄io . P̄tū . III . car . Val 7 ualuit . LX . sol . T.R.E: IIII . lib . Hoc M tenuit Osuui hō Alrici . f. Goding . 7 uende potuit.

In Mideltone ten Hugo de Waltio dim hid . Tra . ē una car . s; n̄ est ibi . P̄tū . I . car . Val . IIII . sol . T.R.E: x . sol . Hanc trā tenuit hō Alrici Osuui . 7 uende potuit.

M In Brichelle ten Radulf de Waltio . v . hid p uno M . Tra . ē . v . car . In dn̄io sunt . II . 7 VIII . uilli cū . II . bord hn̄t III . car . Ibi . II . serui . p̄tū . v . car . Val . LX . sol . Qdo recep:

3 In LAVENDON Ralph holds 2 hides, 1 virgate, and the fourth part of 1 virgate from Walter. Land for 2 ploughs; in lordship 1.
5 villagers with 8 smallholders have 1 plough.
Meadow for 1 plough; woodland, 30 pigs.
Value 25s; when acquired 10s; before 1066, 40s.
A man of Bishop Wulfwy's held this land; he could sell.

In MOULSOE Hundred

4 M. In HARDMEAD Hugh holds 2½ hides from Walter as one manor.
Land for 2½ ploughs; they are there, with
4 villagers and 2 smallholders.
Meadow for 1 plough; woodland, 50 pigs.
The value is and always was 40s.
A man of Alric son of Goding's held this manor; he could sell.

5 M. Richard holds MOULSOE from Walter. It answers for 10 hides.
Land for 7 ploughs; in lordship 1.
7 villagers with 9 smallholders have 6 ploughs.
1 slave; meadow for 5 ploughs; woodland, 100 pigs.
In total, value £6; when acquired 100s; before 1066 £8.
Eight thanes held this manor; they could sell. One of them, Alwin, held 2 hides as one manor; the second, Ulf, Asgar the Constable's man, 2 hides as one manor; Algar, Young Edward's man, 1½ hides as one manor; Alfsi, 1 hide; Thorkell, 1 hide; Lodi, 1 hide; Oswulf 1 hide, and Alric, ½ hide.

6 M. In BROUGHTON Hugh holds 4 hides from Walter as one manor.
Land for 5 ploughs; in lordship 1 plough.
8 villagers with 5 smallholders have 4 ploughs.
2 slaves; 1 mill, in lordship; meadow for 3 ploughs.
The value is and was 60s; before 1066 £4.
Oswy, Alric son of Goding's man, held this manor; he could sell.

7 In MILTON (Keynes) Hugh holds ½ hide from Walter. Land for 1 plough, but it is not there.
Meadow for 1 plough.
Value 4s; before 1066, 10s.
Oswy, Alric's man, held this land; he could sell.

48 M. In BRICKHILL Ralph holds 5 hides from Walter as one manor.
Land for 5 ploughs; in lordship 2.
8 villagers with 2 smallholders have 3 ploughs.
2 slaves; meadow for 5 ploughs.
Value 60s; when acquired 40s; before 1066, 100s.

XL . sol . T.R.E.' c . sol . De hac tra tenuit Goduin hō Wluui
epi . II . hid p uno m . Godbold . I . hid . Alric . I . hid . Ordric
. I . hid . 7 oms trā suā uende potuer.

m In ead uilla ten Robt de Waltio . IIII . hid p uno m.
Tra . ē . v . car . In dnio . sunt . III . 7 IX . uitti cū . v . bord hnt
II . car . Ibi . III . serui . 7 I . molin de . x . sol . ptū . v . car.
Silua . c . porc . Val 7 ualuit sep . c . sol . de hac tra
ten Goduin hō epi Wluui . II . hid p uno m . 7 alij . v.
teigni aliā trā idest . II . hid tenuer . 7 uende potuer.

148 b

.XV. TERRA WILLI DE WARENE. *IN ELESBERIE HVND.*

WILLELM de Warenna ten *BROTONE* . p . x . hid
se defd . Tra . ē . VIII . car . In dnio . II . hidæ 7 ibi sunt . II . car.
7 XIII . uitti cū . v . bord . hnt . VI . car . Ibi . IIII . serui . 7 I . molin
de . x . sol . ptū . v . car . Silua . c . porc . In totis ualent ualet
7 ualuit . VIII . lib . T.R.E.' x . lib . Hoc m tenuit Eduuard
teign . R.E. 7 uende potuit. *IN ROVELAI HVND.*

m Brienz ten de Witto *CAVREFELLE* . p . v . hid se defd.
Tra . ē . VIII . car . In dnio sunt . III . 7 XII . uitti cū . IX . bord hnt
v . car . Ibi . ē uiuariū pisciū . In totis ualent ual 7 ualuit sep
c . sol . Hoc m tenuit Eduuard hō Tosti com . 7 uende potuit.

.XVI. TERRA WILLI PEVREL. *IN STANES HVND.*

m WILLELM peurel ten *HERDEWELLE* . VI . hid 7 III . uirg.
Tehel ten de eo . Tra . ē . VIII . car . In dnio sunt . III . 7 XVI.
uitti cū . IIII . bord . hnt . v . car . Ibi . IIII . serui . 7 ptū . VIII.
car . In totis ualent 7 ual 7 ualuit . c . sol . T.R.E.' VII . lib.
Hoc m tenuit Aluuin teign . R.E. 7 uende potuit.
In Vpetone ten Robt de Witto . III . hid 7 dim . Tra . ē . v . car.
In dnio sunt . II . 7 VIII . uitti cū . III . bord hnt . III . car . Ibi . III.

Godwin, Bishop Wulfwy's man, held 2 hides of this land as one manor; Godbold, 1 hide; Alric, 1 hide, and Ordric, 1 hide; all could sell their land.

49 M. In the same village Robert holds 4 hides from Walter as one manor. Land for 5 ploughs; in lordship 3.
9 villagers with 5 smallholders have 2 ploughs.
3 slaves; 1 mill at 10s; meadow for 5 ploughs; woodland, 100 pigs.
The value is and always was 100s.
Godwin, Bishop Wulfwy's man, held 2 hides of this land as one manor; five other thanes held the other land, that is 2 hides; they could sell.

15 LAND OF WILLIAM OF WARENNE

148 b

In AYLESBURY Hundred

1 William of Warenne holds BROUGHTON. It answers for 10 hides. Land for 8 ploughs; in lordship 2 hides; 2 ploughs there.
13 villagers with 5 smallholders have 6 ploughs.
4 slaves; 1 mill at 10s; meadow for 5 ploughs; woodland, 100 pigs.
The total value is and was £8; before 1066 £10.
Edward, a thane of King Edward's, held this manor; he could sell.

In ROWLEY Hundred

2 M. Bryant holds CAVERSFIELD from William. It answers for 5 hides. Land for 8 ploughs; in lordship 3.
12 villagers with 9 smallholders have 5 ploughs.
A fishpond.
The total value is and always was 100s.
Edward, Earl Tosti's man, held this manor; he could sell.

16 LAND OF WILLIAM PEVEREL

In STONE Hundred

1 M. William Peverel holds HARTWELL; 6 hides and 3 virgates. Teuthael holds from him. Land for 8 ploughs; in lordship 3.
16 villagers with 4 smallholders have 5 ploughs.
4 slaves; meadow for 8 ploughs.
The total value is and was 100s; before 1066 £7.
Alwin, a thane of King Edward's, held this manor; he could sell.

2 In UPTON Robert holds 3½ hides from William. Land for 5 ploughs; in lordship 2.
8 villagers with 3 smallholders have 3 ploughs.

serui.7 p̃tũ.v.car̃.Val̃ 7 ualuit sẽp.LX.sol̃.Hoc M̃ tenuit Aluuin̄ hõ Eddid regine.7 uendẽ pot̃. *IN ESSEDENE HVND.*

M̃ Pagan̄ ten̄ de Witto Tochingeuuiche p̃.II.hid.Tra.ẽ.II.car̃. In dn̄io.ẽ.I.7 III.uitti hñt.II.car̃.Ibi.I.seru̅.p̃tũ.II.car̃. Silua.L.porc̃.H̃ tra ual̃.XXX.sol̃.Q̃do recep̃:XX.sol̃.T.R.E.: XXX.sol̃.Hoc M̃ tenuit Aluuin̄ teign̄.R.E.7 uendẽ potuit.

In Sibdone ten̄ Witts.I.hid.Tra.ẽ dim̄ car̃.7 ibi.ẽ cũ uno uitto.Val̃ 7 ualuit.V.sol̃.Hanc trã tenuit Aluuin̄ teign̄.R.E.

M̃ Ipse Witts ten̄ *GLAINDONE*.p̃ X.hid se defd̃. *IN VOTESDONE HD.* Tra.ẽ.X.car̃.In dn̄io.III.hidæ.7 ibi sunt.III.car̃.7 XVI. uitti cũ.II.bord.hñt.V.car̃.7 adhuc.II^æ.poss̃ fieri.Ibi .III.serui.p̃tũ.IIII.car̃.Silua.CL.porc̃.In totis ualent̃ ual̃.X.lib̃.Q̃do recep̃:XII.lib̃.T.R.E.:X.lib̃.Hoc M̃ tenuit Aluuin̄ teign̄.R.E.

M̃ Ipse Witts ten̄ *HOCSAGA*.p̃.V.hid se defd̃.Tra.ẽ.III. car̃ 7 dim̄.In dn̄io.III.hidæ.7 ibi sunt.II.car̃.7 VI.uitti cũ.II.bord hñt.I.car̃ 7 dim̄.p̃tũ.III.car̃.Silua.XL.porc̃. Val̃ 7 ualuit sẽp.LX.sol̃.Hoc M̃ tenuit Aluuin̄ teign̄.R.E.

M̃ Radulf̄ ten̄ in Claindone de Witto.III.hid 7 I.uirg̃ p̃ uno M̃.Tra.ẽ.III.car̃.In dn̄io.ẽ una.7 IIII.uitti hñt aliã.7 III.pot̃ fieri.p̃tũ.I.car̃.Nem̄ ad sepes.Val̃ 7 ua luit sẽp.XL.sol̃.Hoc M̃ tenuit Aluuin̄ teign̄.R.E.7 uendẽ pot̃. De hac tra tenuit q̄da hõ ej̄.I.uirg.7 potuit uendẽ p̃t ej̄ lictiã.

M̃ Ambrosius ten̄ de Witto *EDESTOCHA*.p̃ X.hid se defd̃. Tra.ẽ.VII.car̃.In dn̄io sunt.III.7 V.uitti cũ.II.bord hñt III.car̃.7 IIII.pot̃ fieri.p̃tũ.VII.car̃.In totis ualent̃ ual̃ 7 ualuit C.sol̃.T.R.E.:VIII.lib̃.Hoc M̃ tenuit Gethe uxor comitis Radulfi.

3 slaves; meadow for 5 ploughs.
The value is and always was 60s.
Alwin, Queen Edith's man, held this manor; he could sell.

In ASHENDON Hundred

3 M. Payne holds TETCHWICK from William, for 2 hides. Land for 2 ploughs; in lordship 1.
3 villagers have 2 ploughs.
1 slave; meadow for 2 ploughs; woodland, 50 pigs.
Value of this land, 30s; when acquired 20s; before 1066, 30s.
Alwin, a thane of King Edward's, held this manor; he could sell.

4 In SHIPTON (Lee) William holds 1 hide. Land for ½ plough; it is there, with
1 villager.
The value is and was 5s.
Alwin, a thane of King Edward's, held this land.

In WADDESDON Hundred

5 M. William holds (Middle) CLAYDON himself. It answers for 10 hides. Land for 10 ploughs; in lordship 3 hides; 3 ploughs there.
16 villagers with 2 smallholders have 5 ploughs; a further 2 possible.
3 slaves; meadow for 4 ploughs; woodland, 150 pigs.
Total value £10; when acquired £12; before 1066 £10.
Alwin, a thane of King Edward's, held this manor.

6 M. William holds HOGSHAW himself. It answers for 5 hides. Land for 3½ ploughs; in lordship 3 hides; 2 ploughs there.
6 villagers with 2 smallholders have 1½ ploughs.
Meadow for 3 ploughs; woodland, 40 pigs.
The value is and always was 60s.
Alwin, a thane of King Edward's, held this manor.

7 M. Ralph holds 3 hides and 1 virgate in (East) CLAYDON from William as one manor. Land for 3 ploughs; in lordship 1.
4 villagers have another; a third possible.
Meadow for 1 plough; wood for fences.
The value is and always was 40s.
Alwin, a thane of King Edward's, held this manor; he could sell. A man of his held 1 virgate of this land; he could sell without his permission.

[In LAMUA Hundred]

8 M. Ambrose holds ADSTOCK from William. It answers for 10 hides. Land for 7 ploughs; in lordship 3.
5 villagers with 2 smallholders have 3 ploughs; a fourth possible.
Meadow for 7 ploughs.
The total value is and was 100s; before 1066 £8.
Gytha, Earl Ralph's wife, held this manor; she could sell.

M̄ Ipse Wills ten HAVRESHA̅. p x. hid se defd. 7 uende pot. IN BONESTOV HVND.

Tra. ē. x. car. In dnio sunt hidæ. 7 ibi. I. car 7 dim. 7 altera 7 dim pot fieri. Ibi. XVI. uitti cū. VIII. bord. hnt. VII. car. Ibi. v. serui. 7 I. molin de. VIII. sol. 7 LXXV. anguill. ptū IX. car. Silua. CCC. porc. Val 7 ualuit. VI. lib. T.R.E. VII. lib. Hoc M̄ tenuit Gueth comitissa.

M̄ Drogo ten de Witto Stoches. III. hid 7 III. uirg p uno M̄. Tra. ē. IIII. car. In dnio sunt. II. 7 v. uitti cū. IIII. bord hnt. II. car. Ibi. II. serui. ptū. IIII. car. Silua. CC. porc. Val 7 ualuit sēp. IIII. lib. Hoc M̄ tenuit Gueth comitissa.

148 c

XVII. TERRA WILLI FILIJ ANSCVLFI. IN STANES HVND.

WILLELM filius Ansculfi ten in hoc hund dim hid. 7 qdā Anglic de eo. Tra. ē dim car. 7 ibi ē cū uno bord. Val 7 ualuit sēp. x. sol. Hanc tram tenuit Leuuin fr Alsi. 7 uende potuit. IN ELESBERIE HD.

M̄ Radulf ten de Witto in ESENBERGE. XIII. hid 7 dim. Tra. ē. XI. car. In dnio sunt. II. 7 XVII. uitti cū. III. bord hnt. IX. car. Ibi. II. serui. 7 ptū. II. car. Silua. C. 7 v. porc. In totis ual 7 ualuit. VIII. lib. T.R.E. IX. lib. Hoc M̄ tenuit Herald com. 7 ipsū M̄ excābiauit Ansculf de pinchengi p dim Risenbga. ctra Radulfū talge bosch jussu regis Witti.

In ead uilla ten Otbtus de Witto. I. hid 7 dim. Tra ē. II. car. 7 ibi sunt. II. boues cū uno uitto. Val 7 ualuit. v. sol. T.R.E. XX. sol. Hanc trā tenuit Balduin hō Stig Arciepi. 7 uende potuit.

M̄ Isd Otbt ten de Witto HĀDENĀ. p. III. hid se defd. Tra. ē. v. car. In dnio sunt. II. 7 IIII. uitti hnt. III. car. Ibi. II. serui. Silua. qngent porc. 7 de reddita silue

In BUNSTY Hundred

9 M. William holds HAVERSHAM himself. It answers for 10 hides. Land for 10 ploughs; in lordship ... hides; 1½ ploughs there; another 1½ possible.

16 villagers with 8 smallholders have 7 ploughs.

5 slaves; 1 mill at 8s, and 75 eels; meadow for 9 ploughs; woodland, 300 pigs.

The value is and was £6; before 1066 £7.

Countess Gytha held this manor.

10 M. Drogo holds STOKE (Goldington) from William; 3 hides and 3 virgates as one manor. Land for 4 ploughs; in lordship 2.

5 villagers with 4 smallholders have 2 ploughs.

2 slaves; meadow for 4 ploughs; woodland, 200 pigs.

The value is and always was £4.

Countess Gytha held this manor.

17 LAND OF WILLIAM SON OF ANSCULF

148 c

In STONE Hundred

1 William son of Ansculf holds ½ hide in this Hundred, and an Englishman from him. Land for ½ plough; it is there, with

1 smallholder.

The value is and always was 10s.

Leofwin, Alfsi's brother, held this land; he could sell.

In AYLESBURY Hundred

2 M. Ralph holds 13½ hides from William in ELLESBOROUGH. Land for 11 ploughs; in lordship 2.

17 villagers with 3 smallholders have 9 ploughs.

2 slaves; meadow for 2 ploughs; woodland, 105 pigs.

The total value is and was £8; before 1066 £9.

Earl Harold held this manor; Ansculf of Picquigny exchanged this manor with Ralph Tallboys for half of (Princes) Risborough by order of King William.

3 In the same village Odbert holds 1½ hides from William. Land for 2 ploughs; 2 oxen there, with

1 villager.

The value is and was 5s; before 1066, 20s.

Baldwin, Archbishop Stigand's man, held this land; he could sell.

4 M. Odbert also holds HAMPDEN from William. It answers for 3 hides. Land for 5 ploughs; in lordship 2.

4 villagers have 3 ploughs.

2 slaves; woodland, 500 pigs, and from the returns of woodland, shares for 2 ploughs.

ferra.II.car.Val 7 ualuit.IIII.lib.T.R.E: c.sol.Hoc
M tenuit Balduin ho Stig Arch.7 uende potuit.

Walteri ten de Witto *DITONE*. *IN STOCHES HVND*
p.v.hid se desd.Tra.e.III.car.In dnio.e.I.7 IIII.uitti
hnt.II.car.Ibi.I.seruus.7 ptu.III.car.Silua.XVI.porc.
Val 7 ualuit XXX.sol.T.R.E: XL.sol.Hoc M tenuit
Sired ho com Heraldi.7 uende potuit.

M Isd Walteri ten de Witto *STOCHES*.p x.hid se desd.
Tra.e.x.car.In dnio sunt.II.7 x.uitti cu.III.bord
hnt.VI.car.7 adhuc possunt fieri.II.Ibi.IIII.serui.
7 I.molin de.IIII.sol.Silua qngent porc.In totis ua
lentijs ual.v.lib.Qdo recep: III.lib.T.R.E: VI.lib.
Hoc M tenuit Siret ho com Heraldi.7 uende pot.7 de hac tra
tenuit.I.hida qda sochs ho Tubi.7 uende potuit.

M In *MERSTONE* ten Rannulf *IN VOTESDONE HD*.
de Witto.VI.hid 7 dim p uno M.Tra.e.VI.car.In dnio
sunt.II.7 VIII.uitti cu.III.bord hnt.III.car.7 IIII.pot fieri.
ptu.II.car.Int totu ual.c.sol.Qdo recep: LX.sol.T.R.E:
IIII.lib.De hoc M tenuit Leuric ho com Eduini.v.hid p.I.M.
7 Alt ho habuit.I.hid 7 I.uirg de soca regis.E.7 Brictuin
ho Tosti comitis.I.uirg habuit.Oms hi uende potuer.

In ead uilla ten Bernard de Witto.I.hida.Tra.e
.I.car.7 ibi.e cu.I.bord.Val 7 ualuit.x.sol.T.R.E.
.XX.sol.Hanc tra tenuit Aluui ho Brictric.7 de soca
regis fuit.7 uendere potuit.

In Hochestone ten Pagan de Witto.VIII.hid 7 II.uirg
7 dim.Tra.e.x.car.In dnio sunt.II.7 XII.uitti cu.VII.
bord.hnt.VIII.car.Ibi.v.serui.Ptu.x.car.Int totu
ual 7 ualuit.VII.lib.T.R.E: c.sol.De hoc M tenuit

The value is and was £4; before 1066, 100s.
Baldwin, Archbishop Stigand's man, held this manor; he could sell.

In STOKE Hundred

5 Walter holds DITTON from William. It answers for 5 hides.
Land for 3 ploughs; in lordship 1.
4 villagers have 2 ploughs.
1 slave; meadow for 3 ploughs; woodland, 16 pigs.
The value is and was 30s; before 1066, 40s.
Sired, Earl Harold's man, held this manor; he could sell.

6 M. Walter also holds STOKE (Poges) from William. It answers for 10 hides.
Land for 10 ploughs; in lordship 2.
10 villagers with 3 smallholders have 6 ploughs; a further 2 possible.
4 slaves; 1 mill at 4s; woodland, 500 pigs.
Total value £5; when acquired £3; before 1066 £6.
Sired, Earl Harold's man, held this manor; he could sell. A Freeman, Tubbi's man, held 1 hide of this land; he could sell.

In WADDESDON Hundred

7 M. In (North) MARSTON Ranulf holds 6½ hides from William as one manor.
Land for 6 ploughs; in lordship 2.
8 villagers with 3 smallholders have 3 ploughs; a fourth possible.
Meadow for 2 ploughs.
In total, value 100s; when acquired 60s; before 1066 £4.
Leofric, Earl Edwin's man, held 5 hides of this manor as one manor; a second man had 1 hide and 1 virgate, of King Edward's jurisdiction; and Brictwin, Earl Tosti's man, had 1 virgate; all of them could sell.

8 In the same village Bernard holds 1 hide from William.
Land for 1 plough; it is there, with
1 smallholder.
The value is and was 10s; before 1066, 20s.
Alwin, Brictric's man, held this land; it was of the King's jurisdiction; he could sell.

[In MURSLEY Hundred]

9 In HOGGESTON Payne holds 8 hides and 2½ virgates from William.
Land for 10 ploughs; in lordship 2.
12 villagers with 7 smallholders have 8 ploughs.
5 slaves; meadow for 10 ploughs.
In total, the value is and was £7; before 1066, 100s.

148 c

Almer̃.vii.hid̃ ꝑ uno ᗰ.hō Bundi stalri.7 unꝰ hō abbatisse de Berchinges.i.hid̃.7 unꝰ hō Eddeuæ pulchræ .ii.uirḡ 7 dim̃ ten̄.7 hi om̄s uendē potuer̃. *IN COTESLAI*
In Soleberie ten̄ Pagan̄ de Willo.v.hid̃. *HUND*.
7 dim̃.7 iii.part̃.i.uirḡ.Tra.ē.xvii.car̃.In dn̄io sunt.iii.7 xiiii.uilli cū.v.bord̃ hn̄t.ix.car̃.7 adhuc .v.car̃ poss fieri.Ibi.iii.serui.7 i.molin̄ de.xvi.sol̃. p̃tū.iii.car̃.Int̃ totū ual̃ 7 ualuit.vii.lib̃.T.R.E.' viii.lib̃.Hoc ᗰ tenuer̃.xi.sochi.7 uendē potuer̃.

148 d

In Holendone ten̄ Pagan̄ de Willo.iii.uirḡ 7 dim̃. Tra.ē.i.car̃.7 ibi.ē.cū.iii.uillis.Val̃ 7 ualuit sep̄.x. sol̃.Hanc trā tenuer̃.iiii.sochi.Hoꝝ.iii.hōes Bric trici.ii.uirḡ 7 dim̃ habuer̃.7 iiii.hō Wige.i.uirḡ habuit.7 hi om̄s trā suā uendē potuer̃.

In Litecote ten̄ Pagan̄ de Willo.i.hid̃ 7 dim̃.Tra.ē .i.car̃ 7 dim̃.Ibi.ē una cū.i.bord̃.7 dim̃ pot̃ fieri. p̃tū.i.car̃.Val̃.xx.sol̃.Q̃do recep̄.' xl.sol̃.T.R.E.' xxx.sol̃.Hanc trā tenuer̃.ii.hōes Brictric.7 uendē pot̃.

In *CETEDENE* ten̄ Suertin de Willo *IN ERLAI HUND*.
dim̃ hid̃.Tra.ē.ii.bob̃.Val̃ 7 ualuit.v.sol̃.T.R.E.' x.sol̃. Hanc trā tenuit Leuing hō.R.E.7 uendē pot̃. *IN MUSELAI*

In Sueneberie ten̄ Pagan̄ de Villo.i.uirḡ. *HUND*.
Tra.ē.ii.bou̅.Val̃ 7 ualuit sep̄.ii.sol̃.Hanc terrā tenuit Osuui.hō Brictrici.7 uendē potuit. *IN LAMUA*

Balduinꝰ ten̄ de Willo ad firmā.ii.hid̃ *HUND*.
Tra.ē.i.car̃ 7 dim̃.7 ibi sunt.cū.i.uillo.7 i.bord̃. p̃tū.i.car̃.Int̃ totū ual̃ 7 ualuit.xxvi.sol̃.Istemet tenuit.T.R.E.7 uendē potuit.

Aelmer, Bondi the Constable's man, held 7 hides of this manor as one manor; a man of the Abbess of Barking's, 1 hide; and a man of Edeva the Fair's held 2½ virgates; all of them could sell.

In COTTESLOE Hundred

10 In SOULBURY Payne holds 5½ hides and the third part of 1 virgate from William. Land for 17 ploughs; in lordship 3.

14 villagers with 5 smallholders have 9 ploughs; a further 5 ploughs possible.

3 slaves; 1 mill at 16s; meadow for 3 ploughs.

In total the value is and was £7; before 1066 £8.

11 Freemen held this manor; they could sell.

11 In HOLLINGDON Payne holds 3½ hides from William. 148 d

Land for 1 plough; it is there, with

3 villagers.

The value is and always was 10s.

Four Freemen held this land; three of these, men of Brictric's, had 2½ virgates; the fourth, a man of Wicga's, had 1 virgate; all of them could sell their land.

12 In LITTLECOTE Payne holds 1½ hides from William.

Land for 1½ ploughs; 1 there, with

1 smallholder; [another] ½ possible.

Meadow for 1 plough.

Value 20s; when acquired 40s; before 1066, 30s.

Two of Brictric's men held this land; they could sell.

In YARDLEY Hundred

13 In CHEDDINGTON Swarting holds ½ hide from William. Land for 2 oxen.

The value is and was 5s; before 1066, 10s.

Leofing, King Edward's man, held this land; he could sell.

In MURSLEY Hundred

14 In SWANBOURNE Payne holds 1 virgate from William. Land for 2 oxen.

The value is and always was 2s.

Oswy, Brictric's man, held this land; he could sell.

In LAMUA Hundred

15 Baldwin holds 2 hides from William at a revenue.

Land for 1½ ploughs; they are there, with

1 villager and 1 smallholder.

Meadow for 1 plough.

In total, the value is and was 26s.

He held it himself before 1066; he could sell.

In *Merse* ten Ailric de Witto.IIII.hid p uno ω
Tra.e.v.car.In dnio.II.7 v.uitti cu.III.bord hnt
III.car.Ibi.III.serui.Ptu.v.car.Silua.XXX.porc.
Val 7 ualuit sep.LXX.sol.Istemet tenuit T.R.E.sed m
tenet ad firma de Witto grauit 7 miserabiliter.

ω Ipse Witts ten *Nevport*. *In Sigelai hvnd.*
p.v.hid se defd.Tra.e.IX.car.In dnio.IIII.carucatæ
terræ.7 ibi sunt.IIII.car.7 v.uitti hnt.v.car.Bur
genses hnt.VI.car 7 dim.aliorq houm ext.v.hid
laborantes.Ibi.IX.serui.7 II.mol de XL.sol.ptu
omib car.7 x.sol.Silua.CCC.porc 7 II.sol.7 adhuc
IIII.sol de hoib q manent in silua.7 in omib alijs red
ditis p annu reddit.c.sol.7 XVI.sol 7 IIII.denar.
In totis ualent ual.XX.lib.7 ualuit.T.R.E.XXIIII.lib.
Hoc ω tenuit Vlf teign.R.E.

In Caldecote.ten Witts.III.hid 7 I.uirg.Tra.e.II.car.
In dnio.e una.7 alia pot fieri.Ibi.I.uitts 7 I.molin
de.VIII.sol.7 qda miles ibi ht dim hid.cu dim car.
ptu.I.car.Silua.c.porc.Val 7 ualuit sep XL.sol.
Hoc ω tenuer.II.hoes Vlf.7 uende potuer.

In Vlsiestone.ten Witts.I.hid 7 dim.Tra.e.I.car
7 dim.In dnio.e una.7 un uitts ht dim car.Ibi.II.serui.
Val 7 ualuit XX.sol.T.R.E.XXX.sol.Hanc tra tenuit
Vlf teign.R.E.7 uende potuit.

In Bradeuuelle.ten Witts.III.uirg.Tra.e.I.car.7 ibi
est cu.I.uitto 7 II.bord.7 I.seruo.ptu.I.car.Val 7 ua
luit sep.x.sol.Hanc tra tenuit Aluuard.ho Goding.
7 uende potuit.De hac tra desaisiuit Ansculf Wittum
de Celsi.qdo uicecomes erat.injuste ut dnt hoes de
Hund.7 sine libatore regis uel alicujus.

16 In MARSH (Gibbon) Alric holds 4 hides from William as one manor. Land for 5 ploughs; in lordship 2.
5 villagers with 3 smallholders have 3 ploughs.
3 slaves; meadow for 5 ploughs; woodland, 30 pigs.
The value is and always was 70s.
He held it himself before 1066, but now he holds it from William at a revenue, harshly and wretchedly.

In SECKLOE Hundred

17 M. William holds NEWPORT (Pagnell) himself. It answers for 5 hides. Land for 9 ploughs; in lordship 4 carucates of land; 4 ploughs there.
5 villagers have 5 ploughs; the Burgesses have 6½ ploughs of the other men who work outside the 5 hides.
9 slaves; 2 mills at 40s; meadow for all the ploughs and 10s too; woodland, 300 pigs and 2s too; a further 4s from the men who live in the woodland; in all other payments it pays 116s 4d a year.
The total value is and was £20; before 1066 £24.
Ulf, a thane of King Edward's, held this manor.

18 In CALDECOTE William holds 3 hides and 1 virgate. Land for 2 ploughs; in lordship 1; another possible.
1 villager.
1 mill at 8s; a man-at-arms has ½ hide, with ½ plough; meadow for 1 plough; woodland, 100 pigs.
The value is and always was 40s.
Two of Ulf's men held this manor; they could sell.

19 In (Little) WOOLSTONE William holds 1½ hides. Land for 1½ ploughs; in lordship 1.
1 villager has ½ ploughs. 2 slaves.
The value is and was 20s; before 1066, 30s.
Ulf, a thane of King Edward's, held this land; he could sell.

20 In BRADWELL William holds 3 virgates. Land for 1 plough; it is there, with
1 villager, 2 smallholders and 1 slave.
Meadow for 1 plough.
The value is and always was 10s.
Alfward, Goding's man, held this land; he could sell.
When he was Sheriff, Ansculf dispossessed William of Cholsey of this land, wrongfully, as the men of the Hundred state, and without the King's or anyone's deliverer.

In Linforde ten Robtus de Witto . I . uirg . Tra . ē . II . bob; . 7 ibi . un uitts . Val 7 ualuit sep . II . sol . Hanc trā tenuit Grimbald hō Bisi . 7 uende potuit.

In *TEDLINGHĀ* ten Acardus de Witto . VII . hid . 7 unā uirg 7 IIII . part tam uni uirg p uno m . Tra . ē . VIII . car . In dnio sunt . III . 7 IX . uitti cū . VI . bord hnt . V . car . Ibi . VI . serui . ptū . VIII . car . Silua . CC . porc . 7 XXVI . denar de minutis csuetudinib; . Int totū ual . VI . lib.

149 a

Qdo recep : VIII . lib . 7 tntd T . R . E . Hoc m tenuer V . teigni . Herold un eo; habuit . III . hid p uno m . 7 Goduin pbr dim hid . Estan . II . hid p uno m . Godric hō Heraldi . I . uirg . 7 Alueua uxor Heroldi . I . hid 7 dim p uno m . Hi oms potuer uende cui uoluer.

Wibtus ten de Witto . IIII . hid *IN MOSLEIE HD* p uno m . Tra . ē . IIII . car . In dnio . ē una . 7 VII . uitti cū . VI . bord hnt . III . car . Ibi un seruus . 7 I . mold de XX . sol . ptū . III . car . Silua . CL . porc . 7 XVI . den . Val 7 ualuit . XL . sol . T . R . E : IIII . lib . Hoc m tenuer duo teigni Herald 7 Aluui . 7 uende potuer.

IN CICELAI . ten Balduin de Witto . III . hid p uno m . Tra . ē . III . car . In dnio . ē una . 7 V . uitti cū . IIII . bord hnt . II . car . ptū . I . car . Silua . C . porc . Val 7 ualuit sep . XL . sol . Istemet tenuit . T . R . E . 7 uende potuit.

In ead ten Andreas de Witto . III . hid p uno m . Tra . ē . III . car . In dnio . ē una . 7 VII . uitti cū . IIII . bord hnt . II . car . Ibi . II . serui . ptū . II . car . Silua C . porc . Val 7 ualuit sep . XL . sol . Hoc m tenuit Edestan hō Alnodi chentis . 7 uende potuit.

21 In (Great) LINFORD Robert holds 1 virgate from William.
Land for 2 oxen.
1 villager.
The value is and always was 2s.
Grimbald, Bisi's man, held this land; he could sell.

[In BUNSTY Hundred]

22 In TYRINGHAM Acard holds 7 hides, 1 virgate, and the fourth part of 1 virgate from William as one manor. Land for 8 ploughs; in lordship 3.
9 villagers with 6 smallholders have 5 ploughs.
6 slaves; meadow for 8 ploughs; woodland, 200 pigs, and 26d from minor customary dues.
In total, value £6; when acquired £8; before 1066 as much. 149 a
Five thanes held this manor; one of them, Harold, had 3 hides as one manor; Godwin the priest, ½ hide; Estan, 2 hides as one manor; Godric, Harold's man, 1 virgate; and Aelfeva, Harold's wife, 1½ hides as one manor; all of them could sell to whom they would.

In MOULSOE Hundred

23 Wibert holds 4 hides from William as one manor. Land for 4 ploughs; in lordship 1.
7 villagers with 6 smallholders have 3 ploughs.
1 slave; 1 mill at 20s; meadow for 3 ploughs; woodland, 150 pigs and 16d too.
The value is and was 40s; before 1066 £4.
Two thanes, Harold and Alwin, held this manor; they could sell.

24 In CHICHELEY Baldwin holds 3 hides from William as one manor.
Land for 3 ploughs; in lordship 1.
5 villagers with 4 smallholders have 2 ploughs.
Meadow for 1 plough; woodland, 100 pigs.
The value is and always was 40s.
He also held before 1066; he could sell.

25 In the same [village] Andrew holds 3 hides from William as one manor. Land for 3 ploughs; in lordship 1.
7 villagers with 4 smallholders have 2 ploughs.
2 slaves; meadow for 2 ploughs; woodland, 100 pigs.
The value is and always was 40s.
Athelstan, Alnoth the Kentishman's man, held this manor; he could sell.

In eađ ten̄ Pagan̄ de Wiłło.iii.hiđ 7 iii.uirḡ
p̱ uno M̄.Tra.ē.iiii.car̄.In dn̄io.ē una.7 v.uiłłi
cū.vi.borđ hn̄t.iii.car̄.P̄tū car̄.Vał.lx.soł.
Q̄do recep̄:c.soł.T.R.E:iiii.lib̄.Hoc M̄ tenuer̄
nouē teigni.7 uendē potuer̄ sine licentia Dn̄oꝝ suoꝝ.
M̄ Ipse Wiłłs ten̄ *TICHEFORDE*.p̱ v.hiđ se desđ.
Tra.ē.viii.car̄.In dn̄io.ii.carucatæ træ.7 ibi.ii.
carucæ.P̄ter.v.hiđ.Ibi.vi.uiłłi cū.iiii.seruis
hn̄t.vi.car̄.p̄tū.v.car̄.Silua.l.porc̄.Ibi.v.sochi
reddunt.xxvii.soł.Vał.c.soł.Q̄do recep̄:vi.
lib̄.7 tn̄tđ T.R.E.Hoc M̄ tenuit Vlf teign̄.R.E.
7 ibi fuer̄.v.teigni qui.iii.uirḡ 7 dim̄ de hac tra
tenuer̄.7 cui uoluer̄ uendere potuer̄.
In Herouldmede ten̄ Herueus.i.hiđ dim̄ uirḡ min̄
p̱ uno M̄.de Wiłło.Tra.ē.i.car̄.7 ibi.ē.cū.ii.uiłłis
7 ii.borđ 7 i.seruo.Silua.xx.iiii.porc̄.Vał 7 ualuit
xii.soł.T.R.E:xx.soł.Hanc trā tenuit Goduin̄
hō Vlf.7 uendē potuit.
In eađ ten̄ Pagan̄ de Wiłło dim̄ uirḡ.Tra.ē.ii.
boꝫ.7 ibi sunt.p̄tū.ii.bob̄.Silua.v.porc̄.Valet
7 ualuit.ii.soł.T.R.E:ii.ł. Hanc trā tenuit
Godric hō Osuui.7 uendē potuit.
In eađ ten̄ Balduin̄.i.hiđ de Wiłło p̱ uno M̄.
Tra.ē.i.car̄.7 ibi.ē cū.iii.uiłłis.Vał 7 ualuit
sēp̱ unā mark̄ Argenti.Hoc M̄ tenuer̄.iii.frs
Vn̄ eoꝝ hō Tochi.7 ii.hōēs Balduini fuer̄.7 uendē
potuer̄.De hac tra jacet dim̄ uirga in monastio
Sc̄i Firmini de Crauelai.7 jacuit.T.R.E.
In Midueltone ten̄ Otb̄tus de Wiłło.i.hiđ.Tra.ē
.i.car̄.Ibi.i.uiłłs 7.v.borđ.7 i.seruus.P̄tū.i.car̄.
Vał.v.soł.Q̄do recep̄:xx.soł.7 tn̄tđ.T.R.E.
Hanc trā tenuit Sauuold hō Wl[cilt]uuardi.7 uendē pot.

26 In the same [village] Payne holds 3 hides and 3 virgates from William as one manor. Land for 4 ploughs; in lordship 1.
5 villagers with 6 smallholders have 3 ploughs.
Meadow for ... ploughs.
Value 60s; when acquired 100s; before 1066 £4.
Nine thanes held this manor; they could sell without the permission of their lords.

27 M. William holds TICKFORD himself. It answers for 5 hides. Land for 8 ploughs; in lordship 2 carucates of land; 2 ploughs there, besides the 5 hides.
6 villagers with 4 slaves have 6 ploughs.
Meadow for 5 ploughs; woodland, 50 pigs. 5 Freemen pay 27s.
Value 100s; when acquired £6; before 1066 as much.
Ulf, a thane of King Edward's, held this manor; there were five thanes there who held 3½ virgates of this land; they could sell to whom they would.

28 In HARDMEAD Harvey holds 1 hide less ½ virgate from William as one manor. Land for 1 plough; it is there, with
2 villagers, 2 smallholders and 1 slave.
Woodland, 24 pigs.
The value is and was 12s; before 1066, 20s.
Godwin, Ulf's man, held this land; he could sell.

29 In the same [village] Payne holds ½ virgate from William. Land for 2 oxen; they are there.
Meadow for 2 oxen; woodland, 5 pigs.
The value is and was 2s; before 1066, 2 or ...
Godric, Oswy's man, held this land; he could sell.

30 In the same [village] Baldwin holds 1 hide from William as one manor. Land for 1 plough; it is there, with
3 villagers.
The value is and always was one silver mark.
Three brothers held this manor; one of them was Toki's man, two were Baldwin's men; they could sell. ½ virgate of this land lies in the (lands of the) monastery of St. Firmin's of Crawley, and lay (there) before 1066.

31 In MILTON (Keynes) Osbert holds 1 hide from William. Land for 1 plough.
1 villager, 5 smallholders and 1 slave.
Meadow for 1 plough.
Value 5s; when acquired 20s; before 1066 as much.
Saewold, Young Wulfward's man, held this land; he could sell.

.XVII. TERRA ROBERTI DE TODENI. *IN STANES HVND.*

ROTBERT' de Todeni.7 Gislebt' de eo ten VII.hid

In Stanes. Tra.ē.VI.car. In dnio sunt.II.7 VII.uilli

cū.XI.bord hnt.IIII.car.Ibi.IIII.serui.7 I.sochs reddit

XV.sol p annū.In totis ualent ual 7 ualuit semp.c.sol.

Hoc ϖ tenuit Vlf Huscarle.R.E. *IN ERLAI HVND.*

ϖ In Cetendone ten Gislebt' de Robto.v.hid 7 dim

p uno ϖ.Tra.ē.III.car 7 dim.In dnio.ē una.7 alia pot

fieri.Ibi.VI.uilli hnt.I.car 7 dim.Ibi.IIII.serui.ptū

II.car.Val 7 ualuit.LX.sol.T.R.E.c.sol.Hoc ϖ tenuit

Osulf Frani filius.teign'.R.E.7 uende potuit. *IN MOSLAI HD.*

ϖ In CLISTONE ten Wills de boscroard 7 fr ej' de Robto

.IIII.hid p uno ϖ.Tra.ē.IIII.car.In dnio sunt.II.7 VI.uilli

cū.VII.bord hnt.II.car.Ibi.III.serui.Ptū.IIII.car.Silua

CCCC.porc.Int tot ual 7 ualuit.c.sol.T.R.E.VI.lib.Hoc ϖ

tenuit Osulf teign'.R.E.7 uende potuit.In hac uilla

Clistone ten Siuert 7 Turbt'.III.uirg.quas Wills 7 Rogeri'

hnt occupatas 7 celatas sup regē ut hoēs de hund dnt.

De.IIII.hid supscriptis tenuit Alric hō Osulfi.I.uirg.

7 uende potuit cui uoluit.

.XIX. TERRA ROBERTI DE OILGI. *IN STOCHES HVND.*

ϖ ROTBERT' de Olgi ten *EVREHAM*.p XVII.hid se desd.

Tra.ē.XXX.car.In dnio.II.hidæ.7 ibi.IIII.car.7 XXXII.

uilli hnt.XXVI.car.De his uillis.v.hnt VI.hid.Ibi

VI.bord 7 IIII.serui.7 III.molend de XL.IIII.sol.ptū

XXX.car.De.IIII.piscar.mille 7 qngent anguill.7 pisces

p dies ueneris ad op' ppositi uillæ.Silua octingent porc.7 II.

arpendi uineæ.In totis ualent ual XXII.lib.Qdo recep.

c.sol.T.R.E.XII.lib.Hoc ϖ tenuit Tochi teign'.R.E.

7 ibi fuer.III.sochi.Hoz un' hō Tochi.III.uirg tenuit.

18 LAND OF ROBERT OF TOSNY 149 b

In STONE Hundred

1 Robert of Tosny, and Gilbert from him, holds 7 hides in STONE.
Land for 6 ploughs; in lordship 2.
7 villagers with 11 smallholders have 4 ploughs. 4 slaves.
1 Freeman pays 15s a year.
The total value is and always was 100s.
Ulf, one of King Edward's Guards, held this manor.

In YARDLEY Hundred

2 M. In CHEDDINGTON Gilbert holds 5½ hides from Robert as one manor.
Land for 3½ ploughs; in lordship 1; another possible.
6 villagers have 1½ ploughs.
4 slaves; meadow for 2 ploughs.
The value is and was 60s; before 1066, 100s.
Oswulf, son of Fran, a thane of King Edward's, held this manor; he could sell.

In MOULSOE Hundred

3 M. In CLIFTON (Reynes) William of Bosc-le-hard (?) and his brother hold 4 hides from Robert as one manor. Land for 4 ploughs; in lordship 2.
6 villagers with 7 smallholders have 2 ploughs;
3 slaves; meadow for 4 ploughs; woodland, 400 pigs.
In total, the value is and was 100s; before 1066 £6.
Oswulf, a thane of King Edward's, held this manor; he could sell.
In this village, Clifton, Siferth and Thorbert hold 3 virgates, which William and Roger have appropriated and concealed, against the King, as the men of the Hundred say. Of the 4 hides mentioned above, Alric, Oswulf's man, held 1 virgate; he could sell to whom he would.

19 LAND OF ROBERT D'OILLY

In STOKE Hundred

1 M. Robert d'Oilly holds IVER. It answers for 17 hides.
Land for 30 ploughs; in lordship 2 hides; 4 ploughs there.
32 villagers have 26 ploughs; 5 of these villagers have 6 hides.
6 smallholders and 4 slaves.
3 mills at 44s; meadow for 30 ploughs; from 4 fisheries 1,500 eels, and fish every Friday for the village reeve's work; woodland, 800 pigs; 2 *arpents* of vines.
Total value £22; when acquired 100s; before 1066 £12.
Toki, a thane of King Edward's, held this manor; there were three Freemen there. One of these, Toki's man, held 3 virgates,

sed uende n̄ potuit p̄ter ej licentiā.7 alt hō regine Eddid
II.hid 7 dim̄.7 tcius hō Seulf.II.hid 7 dim habuit.hi.II.
potuer̄ dare t uende cui uoluer̄.7 ad hoc m̄ n̄ ptinuer̄.
Hoc m̄ excābiauit Robt Clarenboldo de maresc pro
Pateberie.7 est de feudo suæ feminæ. *IN DUSTENBERG HD*

M̄ Ipse Robt ten *WICUBE* de feudo suæ feminæ.p x.hid
se desd.Tra.ē.xxx.car.In dn̄io.IIII.hidæ.7 ibi sunt.III.
car.Ibi.XL.uitti cū.VIII.bord hn̄t.XXVII.car̄.Ibi.VIII.
serui.7 IIII.buri.7 VI.molini de.LXXV.sol p annū.
p̄tū.III.car̄.7 ad eqs de curia.7 car uittis.Silua qngent
porc.In totis ualent uat.XXVI.lib.Qdo recep:x.lib.T.R.E:XII.lib.
Hoc m̄ tenuit Brictric de regina Eddid. *IN TICHESSELE*

Rotbt filius Walterij ten de Robto *ACHELEI*. *HUND*.
p.V.hid 7 III.uirg se desd.Tra.ē.VII.car.In dn̄io
sunt.III.7 IX.uitti cū.VII.bord hn̄t.IIII.car.Ibi.III.serui.
Silua.CC.porc.nisi.eet parcus regis in quó jacet.
In totis ualent uat 7 ualuit.VI.lib.T.R.E:VII.lib.
Hæ.V.hidæ 7 III.uirgæ sunt.VIII.hidæ.De his tenuit
Aluuid puella.II.hid.quas potuit dare t uende cui
uoluit.7 de dn̄ica firma regis.E.habuit ipsa dim hidā.
quā Godric uicecom ei cessit quādiu uicecom.eet.
ut illa doceret filiā ej Aurifrisiū opari.Hanc trā
ten m̄ Robt filius Walterij.testante hundret.

149 c

Radulf basset ten de Robto *MISSEVORDE*. *IN ERLAI*
p xx.hid se desd.Tra.ē.IX.car.In dn̄io sunt.IIII.
7 XXII.uitti hn̄t.V.car̄.Ibi.VIII.serui.7 III.molin
de.XV.sol.P̄tū.VI.car.Silua octingent porc.In
totis ualent uat 7 ualuit sep.XX.lib.Hoc m̄ tenuit
Brictric teign regis.E.7 uende potuit.

but he could not sell without his permission; the second, Queen Edith's man, 2½ hides; the third, Saewulf's man, had 2½ hides. These two could grant or sell to whom they would; they did not belong to this manor. Robert exchanged this manor with Clarenbold of Le Marais for Padbury. It is of his wife's Holding.

In DESBOROUGH Hundred

2 M. Robert holds (High) WYCOMBE himself from his wife's Holding. It answers for 10 hides. Land for 30 ploughs; in lordship 4 hides; 3 ploughs there.

40 villagers with 8 smallholders have 27 ploughs.

8 slaves and 4 boors; 6 mills at 75s a year; meadow for 3 ploughs, for the horses of the court, and for the villagers' ploughs; woodland, 500 pigs.

Total value £26; when acquired £10; before 1066 £12.

Brictric held this manor from Queen Edith.

In IXHILL Hundred

3 Robert son of Walter holds OAKLEY from Robert. It answers for 5 hides and 3 virgates. Land for 7 ploughs; in lordship 3.

9 villagers with 7 smallholders have 4 ploughs.

3 slaves; woodland, 200 pigs, if it were not for the King's park in which it lies.

The total value is and was £6; before 1066 £7.

These 5 hides and 3 virgates are 8 hides. Aelfgeth, a girl, held 2 of these hides, which she could grant or sell to whom she would; and from King Edward's household revenue she had ½ hide herself, which Godric the Sheriff assigned to her for as long as he should be Sheriff, so that she might teach his daughter gold embroidery. Robert son of Walter now holds this land, as the Hundred testifies.

In YARDLEY [Hundred] 149 c

4 Ralph Basset holds MARSWORTH from Robert. It answers for 20 hides. Land for 9 ploughs; in lordship 4.

22 villagers have 5 ploughs.

8 slaves; 3 mills at 15s; meadow for 6 ploughs; woodland, 800 pigs.

The total value is and always was £20.

Brictric, a thane of King Edward's, held this manor; he could sell.

In Cetendone ten Radulf de Robto.I.hid 7 dim.
Tra.e.I.car.7 ibi est cu.II.bord.Ptu.I.car.Vat
7 ualuit sep.xx.sol.Hanc tra tenuit Fin dan.7 uende pot.
In CELDESTONE ten Robt de Robto IN STOFALD HD.
IIII.hid p uno m.Tra.e.v.car.In dnio.II.car.
7 IIII.uitti cu.III.bord hnt.III.car.Ibi.IIII.serui.
Silua.L.porc.H tra uat XL.sol.Qdo recep:XXX.sol.
T.R.E:LX.sol.Hoc m tenuit Azor toti filius.7 uende pot.
m STRADFORD ten Turstin de Robto.p VIII.hid
se desd.Tra.e.VIII.car.In dnio sunt.III.7 x.uitti
cu.v.bord hnt.v.car.Ibi.III.serui.7 I.molin de
VIII.solid.ptu.VI.car.Vat.VII.lib.Qdo recep:
c.sol.T.R.E:VII.lib.Hoc m tenuit Azor filius
Toti.7 uende potuit.

.XX. TERRA ROBERTI GERNON. IN STOCHES HD.

m ROTBERTUS Gernon ten WIRECESBERIE.
p xx.hid se desd.Tra.e.XXV.car.In dnio.v.hidæ.
7 ibi sunt.II.car.7 XXXII.uitti cu.XVIII.bord hnt
XV.car.7 adhuc.VIII.car poss fieri.Ibi.VII.serui.
7 II.molini de.XL.p Annu.ptu.v.car.7 fenu ad
animalia curiæ.Silua qngent porc.7 IIII.piscar
in Tamesia.de.XXVII.sol.IIII.den min.In totis
ualent uat 7 ualuit.xx.lib.T.R.E:XXII.lib.Hoc m
tenuit Edmund teign.R.E.

.XXI. TERRA GOISFR DE MANNEVILE. IN BURNEHA HD.

m GOISFRID de Manneuille.ten ELNODESHAM
p VII.hid 7 dim se desd.Tra.e.XVI.car.In dnio
II.hide.7 ibi sunt.III.car.7 XIIII.uitti cu.IIII.bord.
hnt.IX.car.adhuc.IIII.poss fieri.Ibi.VII.serui.
ptu.XVI.car.Silua.CCCC.porc.In totis ualent

5 In CHEDDINGTON Ralph holds 1½ hides from Robert.
Land for 1 plough; it is there, with
2 smallholders.
Meadow for 1 plough.
The value is and always was 20s.
Fin the Dane held this land; he could sell.

In STOTFOLD Hundred
6 In SHALSTONE Robert holds 4 hides from Robert as one manor.
Land for 5 ploughs; in lordship 2 ploughs.
4 villagers with 3 smallholders have 3 ploughs.
4 slaves; woodland, 50 pigs.
Value of this land, 40s; when acquired 30s; before 1066, 60s.
Azor son of Toti held this manor; he could sell.

7 M. Thurstan holds (Water) STRATFORD from Robert. It answers for 8 hides. Land for 8 ploughs; in lordship 3.
10 villagers with 5 smallholders have 5 ploughs.
3 slaves; 1 mill at 8s; meadow for 6 ploughs.
Value £7; when acquired 100s; before 1066 £7.
Azor son of Toti held this manor; he could sell.

20 LAND OF ROBERT GERNON

In STOKE Hundred
1 M. Robert Gernon holds WRAYSBURY. It answers for 20 hides.
Land for 25 ploughs; in lordship 5 hides; 2 ploughs there.
32 villagers with 18 smallholders have 15 ploughs;
a further 8 ploughs possible.
7 slaves; 2 mills at 40[s] a year; meadow for 5 ploughs;
hay for the cattle of the court; woodland 500 pigs;
4 fisheries in the Thames at 27s less 4d.
The total value is and was £20; before 1066 £22.
Edmund, a thane of King Edward's, held this manor.

21 LAND OF GEOFFREY DE MANDEVILLE

In BURNHAM Hundred
1 M. Geoffrey de Mandeville holds AMERSHAM. It answers for 7½ hides.
Land for 16 ploughs; in lordship 2 hides; 3 ploughs there.
14 villagers with 4 smallholders have 9 ploughs;
a further 4 possible.
7 slaves; meadow for 16 ploughs; woodland 400 pigs.

uat 7 ualuit IX . lib . T . R . E : XVI . lib . Hoc m̄ Eddid regina

In Waldruge ten Suerting *IN TICHESELE HD.* tenuit.
de Goisfrido dim hid . Tra . ē . I . car . 7 ibi est . ptu
. I . car . Vat 7 ualuit . x . sol . T.R.E : xv . sol . Hanc
tra tenuit Dodinz ho Asgari Stalri . 7 uende pot.

m̄ In Claindone ten Goisfrid *IN VOTESDONE HD.*
VII . hid p uno m̄ . Tra . ē . v . car . In dnio . III . hidæ.
7 ibi sunt . II . car . 7 IIII . uitti cu . III . bord hnt . III . car.
ptu . II . car . Silua . XL . porc . Int totu uat . IIII . lib.
Qdo recep : III . lib . T.R.E : v . lib . Hoc m̄ tenuit
Suen ho Asgari stalre . n potuit dare t uende

m̄ Ipse Goisfrid ten *QVERENDONE.* pt ej licentia.
p x . hid se desd . Tra . ē . x . car . In dnio . IIII . hidæ.
7 ibi sunt . IIII . car . 7 XX . uitti cu . VIII . bord hnt
VIII . car.

149 d

ptu . x . car . Silua . CCC . porc . In totis ualent uat
VIII . lib . Qdo recep : c . sol . T.R.E : VI . lib . Hoc m̄
tenuit Suen ho Asgari stalre . n potuit uende
pt ej licentia. *IN ERLAI HVND.*

m̄ In *ESTONE* . ten Germund de Goisfrido . IIII . hid
7 I . uirg p uno m̄ . Tra . ē . III . car 7 dim . In dnio
sunt . II . car . 7 un uitts cu . IIII . seruis hnt . I . car
7 dim . ptu . III . car . Vat 7 ualuit . L . sol . T.R.E :
LX . sol . Hoc m̄ tenuit in dnio Asgar stalre.

Ipse Goisfrid ten in Sueneberie *IN MVSELAI HD.*
II . hid . Tra . ē . II . car . In dnio . I . hid 7 ibi . ē una car.
7 III . uitti cu . II . bord hnt . I . car . ptu . II . car . Vat
7 ualuit sep . XXX . sol . Hoc m̄ tenuit Suen ho
Asgari stalre . n potuit uende pter ej lictia. *IN STOFALD*

m̄ In Lechastede ten Osbt de Goisfr . III . hid. *HVND.*

The total value is and was £9; before 1066 £16.
Queen Edith held this manor.

In IXHILL Hundred

2 In WALDRIDGE Swarting holds ½ hide from Geoffrey. Land for 1 plough; it is there.
Meadow for 1 plough.
The value is and was 10s; before 1066, 15s.
Doding, Asgar the Constable's man, held this land; he could sell.

In WADDESDON Hundred

3 M. In (East) CLAYDON Geoffrey holds 7 hides as one manor. Land for 5 ploughs; in lordship 3 hides; 2 ploughs there.
4 villagers with 3 smallholders have 3 ploughs.
Meadow for 2 ploughs; woodland, 40 pigs.
In total, value £4; when acquired £3; before 1066 £5.
Swein, Asgar the Constable's man, held this manor; he could not grant or sell except with his permission.

4 M. Geoffrey holds QUARRENDON himself. It answers for 10 hides. Land for 10 ploughs; in lordship 4 hides; 4 ploughs there.
20 villagers with 8 smallholders have 8 ploughs.
Meadow for 10 ploughs; woodland, 300 pigs.
Total value £8; when acquired 100s; before 1066 £6. 149 d
Swein, Asgar the Constable's man, held this manor; he could not sell except with his permission.

In YARDLEY Hundred

5 M. In (Ivinghoe) ASTON Germund holds 4 hides and 1 virgate from Geoffrey as one manor. Land for 3½ ploughs; in lordship 2 ploughs.
1 villager with 4 slaves have 1½ ploughs.
Meadow for 3 ploughs.
The value is and was 50s; before 1066, 60s.
Asgar the Constable held this manor in lordship.

In MURSLEY Hundred

6 Geoffrey holds 2 hides in SWANBOURNE himself. Land for 2 ploughs; in lordship 1 hide; 1 plough there.
3 villagers with 2 smallholders have 1 plough.
Meadow for 2 ploughs.
The value is and always was 30s.
Swein, Asgar the Constable's man, held this manor; he could not sell except with his permission.

In STOTFOLD Hundred

7 M. In LECKHAMPSTEAD Osbert holds 3 hides from Geoffrey.

Tra.ē.III.car.In dn̄io.ē una.7 uitti hn̄t.I.car
7 dim.7 adhuc dim pot fieri. Silua.CL.porc.
Vat.xxx.sot. Q̃do recep: xx.sot. T.R.E: xxx.sot.
Hoc m̄ tenuit Suarting hō Asgari.n̄ potuit uende.
Witts de cahainges ten in *LAMVA HVND*.
de Goisfrido.III.hid 7 dim̄ p uno m̄.Tra.ē.III.
car 7 dim.In dn̄io.ē una.7 III.uitti cū uno bord
hn̄t.II.car 7 dim pot fieri.Ibi un9 seruus.p̃tū
III.car.In totis ualent uat 7 ualuit sēp.XL.sot.
Hoc m̄ tenuit Vlf hō Asgari stalre.7 uende pot.
7 De ead tra tenuit Aluui.dim hid.hō Aluuini fuit. [uari]
7 uende potuit.

.XXII TERRA GISLEB̄TI DE GAND. *IN ERLAI HVND*.

m̄ GISLEBERTVS de Gand ten *EDDINBERGE*.
p.xx.hid se defd.Tra.ē.XIIII.car.In dn̄io.x.
hidæ.7 ibi sunt.IIII.car.7 XXVI.uitti cū.IIII.bord
hn̄t.x.car.Ibi.x.serui.7 II.molini de.XV.sot
7 IIII.den.p̃tū.IIII.car.Silua.CCCC.porc.In totis
ualent uat XIII.lib.7 ualuit.T.R.E: XIIII.lib.
Hoc m̄ tenuit Vlf teign9 R.E.7 uende potuit.
In Hortone ten Suarting de Gisleb̄to.III.uirg.
ad dim car tra.ē.7 ibi.ē.car.H̄ tra uat 7 ualuit sēp
VI.sot 7 VIII.den.Hanc trā tenuit q̇dā hō Vlf.
n̄ potuit dare t uende p̃ter ej9 licentiā.

.XXIII. TERRA MILONIS CRISPIN. *IN STANES HVND*.

MILO Crispin9 ten in Opetone.I.hid 7 dim
7 Alric9 ten de eo.Tra.ē.I.car.7 ibi.ē.cū
uno uitto 7 II.bord.Ibi.II.serui.Vat 7 ualuit sēp.
xx.sot.Istemet tegn9 tenuit T.R.E. *IN BVRNEHĀ HD*.
m̄ Radulf9 ten de Milone *DORNEI*.p.III.hid se defd.
Tra.ē.III.car.In dn̄io.ē una.7 V.uitti cū.IIII.bord

Land for 3 ploughs; in lordship 1.
... villagers have 1½ ploughs; a further ½ possible.
Woodland, 150 pigs.
Value 30s; when acquired 20s; before 1066, 30s.
Swarting, Asgar's man, held this manor; he could not sell.

8 William of Keynes holds 3½ hides in Lamua Hundred as one manor from Geoffrey. Land for 3½ ploughs; in lordship 1.
3 villagers with 1 smallholder have 2 ploughs; [another] ½ possible.
1 slave; meadow for 3 ploughs.
The total value is and always was 40s.
Ulf, Asgar the Constable's man, held this manor; he could sell. Alwin held ½ hide of this land; he was Alwin Varus' man; he could sell.

22 LAND OF GILBERT OF GHENT

In YARDLEY Hundred

1 M. Gilbert of Ghent holds EDLESBOROUGH. It answers for 20 hides.
Land for 14 ploughs; in lordship 10 hides; 4 ploughs there.
26 villagers with 4 smallholders have 10 ploughs.
10 slaves; 2 mills at 15s 4d; meadow for 4 ploughs; woodland, 400 pigs.
Total value £13; value before 1066 £14.
Ulf, a thane of King Edward's, held this manor; he could sell.

2 In HORTON Swarting holds 3 virgates from Gilbert.
Land for ½ plough; a plough there.
The value of this land is and always was 6s 8d.
A man, Ulf, held this land; he could not grant or sell except with his permission.

23 LAND OF MILES CRISPIN

In STONE Hundred

1 Miles Crispin holds 1½ hides in UPTON. Alric holds from him.
Land for 1 plough; it is there, with
1 villager and 2 smallholders. 2 slaves.
The value is and always was 20s.
This thane also held before 1066.

In BURNHAM Hundred

2 M. Ralph holds DORNEY from Miles. It answers for 3 hides.
Land for 3 ploughs; in lordship 1.
5 villagers with 4 smallholders have 2 ploughs.

hn̄t . II . car' . Ibi . II . ſerui . p̄tū . III . car' 7 eq̄s . 7 I . piſcar'
de q̄ngent' Anguill' . Silua . c . L . porc' . Val' . xxx . ſol'.
Q̄do recep̄ : x . ſol' . T.R.E : LX . ſol' . Hoc m̄ tenuit
Aldred hō com Morcari . 7 uende' potuit.
Radulf' 7 Rogeri' ten' de Milone *HVCHEHĀ* . p̄ . VI.
hid' ſe defd' . Tra . ē . VI . car̄ . In dn̄io ſunt . II.æ 7 VIII.
uill'i hn̄t . IIII . car̄ . Ibi . III . ſerui . P̄tū car̄ . Silua . c . porc'.

150 a

De una piſcar' q̄ngent' anguill' . In totis ualent' ual'
IIII . lib' . Q̄do recep̄ : xx . ſol' . T.R.E : c . ſol' . Hoc m̄ tenuit
Haming' teign' . R . E . 7 uende' potuit. *IN DVSTENBERG HD̄.*
In Merlaue ten' Radulf' 7 Rogeri' de Milone . VIII.
hid' 7 dim' . 7 dim' uirg' . Tra . ē . VI . car̄ . In dn̄io ſunt
II.æ 7 XIIII . uill'i cū . VI . bord' hn̄t . IIII . car̄ . Ibi . II . ſerui.
p̄tū . VI . car̄ . Silua . cc . porc' . 7 XII . den' . Val' 7 ualuit
LX . ſol' . T.R.E : IIII . lib' . Hanc tra' tenuit haming
teign' . R . E . 7 uende' potuit.
In Santeſdune ten' Osb̄t' de Milone . v . hid' . Tra
ē . v . car̄ . In dn̄io ſunt . II . 7 XIII . uill'i cū . v . bord'
hn̄t . III . car' . Ibi . II . ſerui . 7 II . molend' de . VIII . ſol'.
p̄tū . I . car̄ . Silua . L . porc' . Val' 7 ualuit . c . ſolid'.
T.R.E : VI . lib' . Hoc m̄ tenuit Alric hō comitis Heraldi
In Eſtone ten' . II . hoēs de Milone 7 uende' pot'.
dim' hid' . Tra . ē dim' car' . 7 ibi eſt cū . II . uill'is . p̄tū
dim' car' . Val' 7 ualuit . x . ſol' . T.R.E : xv . ſol' . Hanc
tra' tenuer̄ Vluric 7 Coleman hoēs Brictric 7 uende' potuer̄.
m̄ Ipſe Milo ten' *SOBINTONE*. *IN TICHESELE HD̄.*
p̄ x . hid' ſe defd' . Tra . ē . x . car' . In dn̄io ſunt . III . hidæ.
7 ibi . III . car' . 7 XII . uill'i cū . VII . bord' hn̄t . VII . car̄.
Ibi . VI . ſerui . 7 I . molin̄ de x . ſol' . p̄tū . VI . car̄.
De piſcaria . c . anguil' . Silua . c . porc' . Hoc m̄ ual'

2 slaves; meadow for 3 ploughs and for horses; 1 fishery at 500 eels; woodland, 150 pigs.
Value 30s; when acquired 10s; before 1066, 60s.
Aldred, Earl Morcar's man, held this manor; he could sell.

3 Ralph and Roger hold HITCHAM from Miles. It answers for 6 hides.
Land for 6 ploughs; in lordship 2.
8 villagers have 4 ploughs.
3 slaves; meadow for a plough; woodland, 100 pigs; from 1 fishery 500 eels. **150 a**
Total value £4; when acquired 20s; before 1066, 100s.
Haming, a thane of King Edward's, held this manor; he could sell.

In DESBOROUGH Hundred

4 In MARLOW Ralph and Roger hold 8½ hides and ½ virgate from Miles.
Land for 6 ploughs; in lordship 2.
14 villagers with 6 smallholders have 4 ploughs.
2 slaves; meadow for 6 ploughs; woodland, 200 pigs and 12d too.
The value is and was 60s; before 1066 £4.
Haming, a thane of King Edward's, held this land; he could sell.

5 In SAUNDERTON Osbert holds 5 hides from Miles.
Land for 5 ploughs; in lordship 2.
13 villagers with 5 smallholders have 3 ploughs.
2 slaves; 2 mills at 8s; meadow for 1 plough; woodland, 50 pigs.
The value is and was 100s; before 1066 £6.
Alric, Earl Harold's man, held this manor; he could sell.

[In IXHILL Hundred]

6 In ? ASTON (Sandford) two men hold ½ hide from Miles.
Land for ½ plough; it is there, with
2 villagers.
Meadow for ½ plough.
The value is and was 10s; before 1066, 15s.
Wulfric and Colman, Brictric's men, held this land; they could sell.

In IXHILL Hundred

7 M. Miles holds SHABBINGTON himself. It answers for 10 hides.
Land for 10 ploughs; in lordship 3 hides; 3 ploughs there.
12 villagers with 7 smallholders have 7 ploughs.
6 slaves; 1 mill at 10s; meadow for 6 ploughs; from the fishery 100 eels; woodland, 100 pigs.

7 ualuit sēp . x . lib̄ . Wigot de Walingeford tenuit.
In Iforde ten Ricard de Milone . IIII . hid.
Tra . ē . IIII . car . In dn̄io . ē una . 7 VI . uitti hn̄t
III . car . Ibi . II . serui . Ptū . IIII . car . In totis ua
lentijs uat . III . lib̄ . Qdo recep: IIII . lib̄ . T.R.E: tntd
In Assedune ten Wichin *IN ESSEDEN HD.*
de Milone . II . hid . Tra . ē . II . car . 7 ibi sunt
cū . III . bord . ptū . II . car . Vat 7 ualuit sēp
xxx . sol . Istemet tenuit T.R.E. 7 uende potuit.
In Cerdeslai ten Ricard de milone . I . hid 7 dim.
Tra . ē . I . car . 7 ibi . ē . cū uno uitto 7 I . bord . Ibi . II . serui.
ptū . I . car . Vat 7 ualuit sēp XXII . sol . Hanc trā
tenuit Alden hō com Heraldi . 7 uende potuit.
In Sortelai . ten . II . hōes de Milone . I . hid . Tra . ē
. I . car . 7 ibi . ē cū uno uitto 7 I . bord . ptū . I . car.
Silua . xxx . porc . Vat 7 ualuit sēp x . sol . Hanc trā
tenuer . II . teigni hōes Brictric . 7 uende potuer.
M In *CHENTONE* . ten Milo . VII . hid 7 dim . Tra . ē
IX . car . In dn̄io . III . hidæ . 7 ibi sunt . III . car . 7 XXI.
uitts cū . VI . bord hn̄t . VI . car . Ibi . VI . serui . ptū
. II . car . Silua . c . porc . Ptū . II . car . Silua . c . porc.
In totis ualent uat 7 ualuit . VII . lib̄ . T.R.E: VIII . lib̄.
Hoc M tenuit Wigot de Walingeford.
Duo hōes ten de Milo..e Bichedone . p . II . hid.
Tra . ē . II . car . 7 ibi sunt cū . II . uittis 7 III . bord . Ptū
II . car . Vat 7 ualuit sēp xxv . sol . Istimet tenuer
T.R.E . un hō Brictric 7 alt hō Azoris . 7 uende potuer.
M Ipse Milo ten *VOTESDONE* . *IN VOTESDONE HD.*
p XXVII . hid se desd . Tra . ē XXVIII . car . In dn̄io

The value of this manor is and always was £10.
Wigot of Wallingford held it.

8 In ICKFORD Richard holds 4 hides from Miles. Land for 4 ploughs; in lordship 1.
6 villagers have 3 ploughs.
2 slaves; meadow for 4 ploughs.
Total value £3; when acquired £4; before 1066 as much.

In ASHENDON Hundred

9 In ASHENDON Vicking holds 2 hides from Miles. Land for 2 ploughs; they are there, with
3 smallholders.
Meadow for 2 ploughs.
The value is and always was 30s.
He held it himself before 1066; he could sell.

10 In CHEARSLEY Richard holds 1½ hides from Miles.
Land for 1 plough; it is there, with
1 villager and 1 smallholder.
2 slaves; meadow for 1 plough.
The value is and always was 22s.
Haldane, Earl Harold's man, held this land; he could sell.

11 In 'SHORTLEY' two men hold 1 hide from Miles. Land for 1 plough; it is there, with
1 villager and 1 smallholder.
Meadow for 1 plough; woodland, 30 pigs.
The value is and always was 10s.
Two thanes, Brictric's men, held this land; they could sell.

12 M. In QUAINTON Miles holds 7½ hides. Land for 9 ploughs; in lordship 3 hides; 3 ploughs there.
21 villagers with 6 smallholders have 6 ploughs.
6 slaves; meadow for 2 ploughs; woodland, 100 pigs.
The total value is and was £7; before 1066 £8.
Wigot of Wallingford held this manor.

13 Two men hold BEACHENDON from Miles for 2 hides. Land for 2 ploughs; they are there, with
2 villagers and 3 smallholders.
Meadow for 2 ploughs.
The value is and always was 25s.
They also held it before 1066, one Brictric's man, the other Azor's man; they could sell.

In WADDESDON Hundred

14 M. Miles holds WADDESDON himself. It answers for 27 hides.

x. hidæ. 7 ibi sunt. VIII. car. 7 L. uitti cū. x. bord hnt. xx. car.
Ibi XVII. serui. 7 I. molin de. XII. sol. ptū. XXVIII. car.
Silua. CL. porc. In totis ualent. uat. xxx. lib. Qdo recep:
XVI. lib. T.R.E: xxx. lib. Hoc m tenuit Brictric hō Eddid. reginæ.
In Claidone ten. II. Angli de Milone. II. hid. Tra. ē. I. car.
7 ibi. ē cū. III. bord. ptū. I. car. Vat 7 ualuit sēp. xx. sol.
Istimet tenuer. T.R.E. hōes haming fuer. 7 uende potuer.
In Claidone ten Gaufrid de Milone. VII. hid. 7 III. uirg
p uno m. Tra. ē. v. car. In dnio sunt. II. 7 IIII. uitti cū. III.
bord hnt. III. car. Ibi. III. serui. Ptū. II. car. Silua. c. porc.
Int totū uat. IIII. lib. Qdo recep: xx. sol. T.R.E: IIII. lib.
In Merstone ten Seric de Milone. I. hid. Tra. ē. I. car. 7 ibi
est cū. I. bord. ptū. I. car. Vat 7 ualuit sēp. xx. sol.
Istemet tenuit. T.R.E. hō Brictrici fuit. 7 uende potuit.
In Soleberie. Rogeri ten de Milone *IN COTESHALE HD.*
.I. hid 7 I. uirg 7 dim. Tra. ē. III. car. In dnio. ē una. 7 II.
uitti hnt alterā. 7 III. pot fieri. ptū. II. car. Vat 7 ualuit
sēp. xx. sol. Hanc trā tenuit Almar hō Brictrici.
non potuit uende pter ej licentiā.
In Holendone ten Nigell de Milone. I. uirg. Tra est
dim car. 7 ibi. ē cū. I. uitto. Vat 7 ualuit. III. sol. T.R.E:
IIII. sol. Ille q hanc trā tenuit. n potuit dare t uende. T.R.E.
In Withungraue ten Nigell de Milone. v. hid
p uno m. Tra. ē. v. car. Ibi. VII. uitti cū. II. bord hnt
.II. car 7 dim. 7 totid possunt fieri. Ibi. I. seruus. ptū
v. car. Vat. XL. sol. Qdo recep: c. sol. 7 tntd. T.R.E.
Hoc m tenuit Brictric hō regine Eddid. 7 uende pot.

Land for 28 ploughs; in lordship 10 hides; 8 ploughs there. 150 b
50 villagers with 10 smallholders have 20 ploughs.
17 slaves; 1 mill at 12s; meadow for 28 ploughs; woodland, 150 pigs.
Total value £30; when acquired £16; before 1066 £30.
Brictric, Queen Edith's man, held this manor.

5 In (East) CLAYDON 2 Englishmen hold 2 hides from Miles.
Land for 1 plough; it is there, with
3 smallholders.
Meadow for 1 plough.
The value is and always was 20s.
They also held it before 1066; they were Haming's men; they could sell.

6 In (East) CLAYDON Geoffrey holds 7 hides and 3 virgates from Miles as one manor. Land for 5 ploughs; in lordship 2.
4 villagers with 3 smallholders have 3 ploughs.
3 slaves; meadow for 2 ploughs; woodland, 100 pigs.
In total, value £4; when acquired 20s; before 1066 £4.

7 In (North?) MARSTON Seric holds 1 hide from Miles.
Land for 1 plough; it is there, with
1 smallholder.
Meadow for 1 plough.
The value is and always was 20s.
He also held it before 1066; he was Brictric's man; he could sell.

In COTTESLOE Hundred

8 In SOULBURY Roger holds 1 hide and 1½ virgates from Miles.
Land for 3 ploughs; in lordship 1.
2 villagers have another; a third possible.
Meadow for 2 ploughs.
The value is and always was 20s.
Aelmer, Brictric's man, held this land; he could not sell except with his permission.

9 In HOLLINGDON Nigel holds 1 virgate from Miles.
Land for ½ plough. It is there, with
1 villager.
The value is and was 3s; before 1066, 4s.
The holder of this land could not grant or sell before 1066.

0 In WINGRAVE Nigel holds 5 hides from Miles as one manor.
Land for 5 ploughs.
7 villagers with 2 smallholders have 2½ ploughs; as many possible.
1 slave; meadow for 5 ploughs.
Value 40s; when acquired 100s; as much before 1066.
Brictric, Queen Edith's man, held this manor; he could sell.

In eađ uilla ten̄ Turſtin̄ pb̄r de Milone dim̄ hiđ. Tra
ē dim̄ car̄. Ibi. I. uitts. p̄tū dim̄ car̄. Vat̄ 7 ualuit sēp
. x. ſot̄. Hanc trā tenuit Lemar hō Brictric, 7 uende pot.
In eađ uilla ten̄ Almar de Milone. II. hiđ. p uno ꝸ.
Tra. ē. III. car̄. In dn̄io. ē una. 7 VII. uitti hn̄t. II. car.
p̄tū. III. car̄. Vat̄ 7 ualuit sēp. XL. ſot̄. Hoc ꝸ tenuit
Almar hō Brictrici. 7 uende potuit.
In Litecote ten̄ Robt̄ de Milone. I. hiđ. Tra. ē. I. car̄,
7 ibi. ē cū. I. uitto. P̄tū. I. car̄. Vat̄ xv. ſot̄. Q̄do
recep̄: v. ſot̄. T.R.E: xxv. ſot̄. Hanc trā tenuit Herch
hō Brictrici, 7 uende potuit.
In Harduich ten̄ Witts de milone. I. hiđ. Tra. ē. I. car̄,
7 ibi. ē cū. II. borđ. p̄tū. I. car̄. Vat̄ xx. ſot̄. Q̄do recep̄:
x. ſot̄. T.R.E: xx. ſot̄. Hanc trā tenuit Oſulf 7 uende pot.
In Bricſtoch ten̄ Witts de Milone, III. uirḡ. Tra. ē. I. car̄.
Ibi. III. uitti. P̄tū. I. car̄. Vat̄ 7 ualuit xv. ſot̄. T.R.E: xx. ſot̄,
Hanc trā tenuit Oſulf hō Brictrici. 7 uende potuit.
ꝸ In Pinceleſtorne ten̄ Rog̃ de Milone *IN ERLAI HVND*,
v. hiđ p uno ꝸ. Tra. ē. II. car̄. In dn̄io. ē una, 7 III. uitti
cū. I. borđ hn̄t dim̄ car̄, 7 dim̄ pot̄ fieri. Silua XL. porc.
Vat̄. xxx. ſot̄. Q̄do recep̄: xx. ſot̄. T.R.E: XL. ſot̄. Hoc ꝸ
tenuit Lepſi hō Brictrici. 7 uende potuit.
In eađ uilla ten̄ Suerting de Milone. II. hiđ. Tra. ē
. I. car̄. 7 ibi. ē cū. I. borđ. 7 II. ſeruis. Silua. xx.v. porc,
Vat̄ 7 ualuit. x. ſot̄, T.R.E: xx. ſot̄. Hanc trā tenuit
Lepſi hō Brictrici. 7 uende potuit.

21 In the same village Thurstan the priest holds ½ hide from Miles.
Land for ½ plough.
1 villager.
Meadow for ½ plough.
The value is and always was 10s.
Leofmer, Brictric's man, held this land; he could sell.

22 In the same village Aelmer holds 2 hides from Miles as one manor.
Land for 3 ploughs; in lordship 1.
7 villagers have 2 ploughs.
Meadow for 3 ploughs.
The value is and always was 40s.
Aelmer, Brictric's man, held this manor; he could sell.

23 In LITTLECOTE Robert holds 1 hide from Miles. Land for 1 plough; it is there, with
1 villager.
Meadow for 1 plough.
Value 15s; when acquired 5s; before 1066, 25s.
Herch, Brictric's man, held this land; he could sell.

24 In HARDWICK William holds 1 hide from Miles.
Land for 1 plough; it is there, with
2 smallholders.
Meadow for 1 plough.
Value 20s; when acquired 10s; before 1066, 20s.
Oswulf held this land; he could sell.

25 In BURSTON William holds 3 virgates from Miles. Land for 1 plough.
3 villagers.
Meadow for 1 plough.
The value is and was 15s; before 1066, 20s.
Oswulf, Brictric's man, held this land; he could sell.

In YARDLEY Hundred

26 M. In PITSTONE Roger holds 5 hides from Miles as one manor.
Land for 2 ploughs; in lordship 1.
3 villagers with 1 smallholder have ½ plough; [another] ½ possible.
Woodland, 40 pigs.
Value 30s; when acquired 20s; before 1066, 40s.
Leofsi, Brictric's man, held this manor; he could sell.

27 In the same village Swarting holds 2 hides from Miles.
Land for 1 plough; it is there, with
1 smallholder and 2 slaves.
Woodland, 25 pigs.
The value is and was 10s; before 1066, 20s.
Leofsi, Brictric's man, held this land; he could sell.

In Hortone ten Suerting de Milone . I . hid . Tra . ē
dim car.

150 c

Ibi . ē car cū . I . uitto 7 II . seruis . P̃tū dim car . Vat 7 ua
luit sep̃ . XIII . sot 7 IIII . den . Lepsi ten hō Brict . 7 uende pot.

In Stiuelai ten Nigellus de Milone *IN MVSELAI HD.*
III . hid 7 dim p uno M . Tra . ē . IX . car . In dnio . ē una.
7 II . poss fieri . Ibi . IX . uitti cū . II . bord hnt . III . car
7 dim . 7 II . 7 dim adhuc poss fieri . P̃tū . IX . car . Vat
7 ualuit . IIII . lib . Hoc M tenuit Brictric teign . R . E . 7 uende

In Eddintone ten Eddulf *IN LAMVA HVND.* pot.
dim hid . Tra . ē dim car . 7 ibi . ē . Vat . x . sot . Qdo recep:
v . sot . T.R.E: x . sot . Hanc trā tenuit Leuui hō Eduui.

In Brodeuuelle ten *IN SIGELAI HVND.* 7 uende pot.
Witts de Milone . II . hid . 7 III . uirg . Tra . ē . III . car . In
dnio . II . car . 7 ibi . v . uitti . poss habe . I . car . Ibi . II . serui.
p̃tū . II . car . Vat XL . sot . Qdo recep: XX . sot . T . R . E:
LX . sot . Hoc M tenuer . II . teigni . Sibi 7 Goduin . hoēs
Alrici filij Goding . 7 uende potuer.

M Radulf ten Stantone de Milone . p v . hid se defd.
Tra . ē . v . car 7 dim . In dnio sunt . II . 7 VII . uitti cū . III .
bord hnt . III . car . 7 adhuc dim pot fieri . Ibi . IIII . serui.
7 I . molin de . x . sot 7 VIII . den . 7 L . anguitt . p̃tū . IIII .
car . In totis ualent uat . VI . lib . Qdo recep: C . sot . T.R.E:
VI . lib . Hoc M tenuit Bisi teign . R . E . 7 uende potuit.

Almar de odona ten . I . hid de Milone. *IN MOSLAI HD.*
Tra . ē . I . car . 7 ibi . ē cū . III . uittis 7 II . bord . p̃tū . I . car.
Vat 7 ualuit sep . x . sot . Hanc trā tenuit Orduui hō Wigot
de Walingeford . 7 uende potuit.

28 In HORTON Swarting holds 1 hide from Miles. Land for ½ plough; a plough there, with 150 c
1 villager and 2 slaves.
Meadow for ½ plough.
The value is and always was 13s 4d.
Leofsi, Brictric's man, held it; he could sell.

In MURSLEY Hundred

29 In STEWKLEY Nigel holds 3½ hides from Miles as one manor.
Land for 9 ploughs; in lordship 1; 2 possible.
9 villagers with 2 smallholders have 3½ ploughs; a further 2½ possible.
Meadow for 9 ploughs.
The value is and was £4.
Brictric, a thane of King Edward's, held this manor; he could sell.

In LAMUA Hundred

30 In ADDINGTON Edwulf holds ½ hide. Land for ½ plough; it is there.
Value 10s; when acquired 5s; before 1066, 10s.
Leofwin, Edwin's man, held this land; he could sell.

In SECKLOE Hundred

31 In BRADWELL William holds 2 hides and 3 virgates from Miles.
Land for 3 ploughs; in lordship 2 ploughs.
5 villagers can have 1 plough.
2 slaves; meadow for 2 ploughs.
Value 40s; when acquired 20s; before 1066, 60s.
Two thanes, Sibbi and Godwin, Alric son of Goding's men, held this manor; they could sell.

32 M. Ralph holds STANTON(BURY) from Miles. It answers for 5 hides.
Land for 5½ ploughs; in lordship 2.
7 villagers with 3 smallholders have 3 ploughs; a further ½ possible.
4 slaves; 1 mill at 10s 8d and 50 eels; meadow for 4 ploughs.
Total value £6; when acquired 100s; before 1066 £6.
Bisi, a thane of King Edward's, held this manor; he could sell.

In MOULSOE Hundred

33 Aelmer of Wootton holds 1 hide from Miles. Land for 1 plough; it is there, with
3 villagers and 2 smallholders.
Meadow for 1 plough.
The value is and always was 10s.
Ordwy, Wigot of Wallingford's man, held this land; he could sell.

.XXII. TERRA EDWARDI SARISBER. *IN ELESBERIE HVND.*

EDWARDVS Saresbiensis ten *ESTONE* . p xx . hid se desd . Tra . ē xvii . car . In dnio . ix . hidæ 7 i . uirg 7 ibi sunt . vi . car . 7 xxviii . uitti cū . iiii . bord . hnt xi . car . 7 adhuc xii . pot fieri . Ibi . xiii . serui . 7 i . molin de . v . oris argenti . ptū . xvii . car . Silua . ccc . porc . 7 ferra carucis dnicis . In totis ualent uat xviii . lib . Qdo recep : x . lib . T.R.E : xx . lib . Hoc m tenuit Wluuen hō regis . E . 7 uende potuit. *IN VOTESDVNE HVND.*

Rannulf ten de Edwardo . i . hid 7 i . uirg 7 dimid . Tra . ē . i . car . 7 ibi . ē cū . i . uitto 7 i . bord . 7 iiii . seruis . ptū . i . car . Vat 7 ualuit . x . sol . T.R.E. xx . sol . hanc tram tenuit Almar de Wluuene de Cresselai . 7 uende potuit.

Isd Rannulf ten *CRESSELAI* . p . v . hid se desd . Tra . ē . vi . car . In dnio sunt . iiii . 7 vi . uitti cū . i . bord hnt . ii . car . Ibi . v . serui . ptū . v . car . In totis ualent uat . c . sol . Qdo recep : iiii . lib . T.R.E : vi . lib . Hoc m tenuit Wluuen qdā femina T.R.E . 7 uende potuit.

.XXV. TERRA HVGONIS DE BELCAMP. *IN CORTESHALA HVND.*

HVGO de belcamp ten *LINCELADA* . p xv . hid se desd . Tra . ē . xvi . car . In dnio . v . hidæ . 7 ibi sunt . ii . car . 7 adhuc . iii . poss fieri . Ibi . xxii . uitti cū . vi . bord hnt . xi . car . Ibi . v . serui . 7 i . molin de . xx . sol . ptū . ii . car . Int tot uat . x . lib . Qdo recep : c . sol . T.R.E : x . lib . Hoc m tenuit Aluuin hō Eddid regine . 7 uende pot.

In Soleberie ten Hugo . ii . part uni uirg . Tra . ē . iiii . bob . Vat 7 ualuit . iii . sol . T.R.E : iiii . sol . Hanc tram tenuit Dot hō dei . potuit uende cui uoluit.

24 LAND OF EDWARD OF SALISBURY

In AYLESBURY Hundred

1 M. Edward of Salisbury holds ASTON (Clinton). It answers for 20 hides.
Land for 17 ploughs; in lordship 9 hides and 1 virgate; 6 ploughs there.
28 villagers with 4 smallholders have 11 ploughs;
a further twelfth possible.
13 slaves; 1 mill at 5 *ora* of silver; meadow for 17 ploughs;
woodland, 300 pigs; shares for the lord's ploughs.
Total value £18; when acquired £10; before 1066 £20.
Wulfwen, King Edward's man, held this manor; she could sell.

In WADDESDON Hundred

2 Ranulf holds 1 hide and 1½ virgates from Edward. Land for 1 plough;
it is there, with
1 villager, 1 smallholder and 4 slaves.
Meadow for 1 plough.
The value is and was 10s; before 1066, 20s.
Aelmer held this land from Wulfwen of Creslow; he could sell.

3 Ranulf also holds CRESLOW. It answers for 5 hides.
Land for 6 ploughs; in lordship 4.
6 villagers with 1 smallholder have 2 ploughs.
5 slaves; meadow for 5 ploughs.
Total value 100s; when acquired £4; before 1066 £6.
Wulfwen, a woman, held this manor before 1066; she could sell.

25 LAND OF HUGH OF BEAUCHAMP

In COTTESLOE Hundred

1 M. Hugh of Beauchamp holds LINSLADE. It answers for 15 hides.
Land for 16 ploughs; in lordship 5 hides; 2 ploughs there;
a further 3 possible.
22 villagers with 6 smallholders have 11 ploughs.
5 slaves; 1 mill at 20s; meadow for 2 ploughs.
Total value £10; when acquired 100s; before 1066 £10.
Alwin, Queen Edith's man, held this manor; he could sell.

2 In SOULBURY Hugh holds 2 parts of one virgate. Land for 4 oxen.
The value is and was 3s; before 1066, 4s.
Dot, a man of God (?), held this land; he could sell to whom
he would.

In Lateberie ten. W. de Orenge *IN BONESTOV HD.*
iiii. hid de Hugone. p uno M. Tra. e. iii. car. In
dnio sunt. ii. 7 iiii. uitti cu. iiii. bord hnt. i. car.
Ibi. iii. serui. Ptu. iii. car. Silua, c. porc. Vat. iiii. lib.
Qdo recep: xx. sol. T.R.E: lx. sol. Hoc M tenuer
ii. teigni Leuric 7 Oluiet p. ii. M. 7 uende potuer.

.XXVI. TERRA HVGON DE BOLEBECH. *IN STANES HVND.*

HVGO de Bolebech ten Vluiet de eo In Missedene.
dim hid. Tra. e. i. car. 7 ibi. e. cu. i. bord. ptu. i. car.
Silua. xxx. porc. Vat 7 ualuit sep x. sol. Istemet
tenuit T.R.E. ho Wluui epi fuit. 7 uende potuit.
In Elmodesha ten Vluiet de Hugone *IN BVRNEHA HD.*
dimid hid. Tra. e ii. car. 7 ibi sunt cu. ii. uittis 7 iii. bord
Ibi. i. molin de. v. sol. Silua. xx. porc. Vat 7 ualuit
sep. xx. sol. Istemet tenuit T.R.E. 7 uende potuit.
Ipse hugo ten in *CESTREHA*. viii. hid 7 dim. Tra. e
xvi. car. In dnio. i. hida 7 dim. 7 ibi sunt. ii. car. 7 xvi.
uitti cu. vi. bord hnt. xii. car. 7 adhuc. ii. poss fieri.
Ibi. vi. serui. 7 i. molin de. x. sol. ptu. xvi. car. Silua
octingent porc. 7 ferru car. In totis ualent uat. x. lib.
.iii. sol min. T.R.E: xii. lib. Hoc M tenuit Brictric ho
Eddid reginæ. 7 ibi. ii. sochi tenuer. iiii. hid. hoes Bric
trici fuer. 7 uende potuer. *IN DVSTENBERG HVND.*
M Ipse Hugo ten *MEDEMEHA*. p x. hid se desd. Tra. e
x. car. In dnio. iiii. hidæ. 7 ibi sunt. ii. car. 7 x. uitti
cu. viii. bord hnt. viii. car. Ibi. iiii. serui. de piscar
mille anguitt. ptu car omibz. Silua. L. porc. Int
totu uat 7 ualuit. c. sol. T.R.E: viii. lib. Hoc M
tenuit Wlstan teign. R.E. 7 cui uoluit uende pot.

In BUNSTY Hundred 150 d

3 In LATHBURY William of Orange holds 4 hides from Hugh as one manor.
Land for 3 ploughs; in lordship 2.
4 villagers with 4 smallholders have 1 plough.
3 slaves. Meadow for 3 ploughs; woodland, 100 pigs.
Value £4; when acquired 20s; before 1066, 60s.
Two thanes, Leofric and Wulfgeat, held this manor as two manors; they could sell.

26 LAND OF HUGH OF BOLBEC

In STONE Hundred

1 Hugh of Bolbec holds ½ hide in (Little) MISSENDEN; Wulfgeat from him.
Land for 1 plough; it is there, with
1 smallholder.
Meadow for 1 plough; woodland, 30 pigs.
The value is and always was 10s.
He also held it before 1066; he was Bishop Wulfwy's man; he could sell.

In BURNHAM Hundred

2 In AMERSHAM Wulfgeat holds ½ hide from Hugh. Land for 2 ploughs; they are there, with
2 villagers and 3 smallholders.
1 mill at 5s; woodland, 20 pigs.
The value is and always was 20s.
He also held it before 1066; he could sell.

3 Hugh holds 8½ hides in CHESHAM himself. Land for 16 ploughs; in lordship 1½ hides; 2 ploughs there.
16 villagers with 6 smallholders have 12 ploughs; a further 2 possible.
6 slaves; 1 mill at 10s; meadow for 16 ploughs; woodland, 800 pigs and plough-shares.
Total value £10 less 3s; before 1066 £12.
Brictric, Queen Edith's man, held this manor. There 2 Freemen held 4 hides; they were Brictric's men; they could sell.

In DESBOROUGH Hundred

4 M. Hugh holds MEDMENHAM himself. It answers for 10 hides.
Land for 10 ploughs; in lordship 4 hides; 2 ploughs there.
10 villagers with 8 smallholders have 8 ploughs.
4 slaves; from the fishery 1,000 eels; meadow for all the ploughs; woodland, 50 pigs.
The total value is and was 100s; before 1066 £8.
Wulfstan, a thane of King Edward's, held this manor; he could sell to whom he would.

Ipse hugo ten Broch p una hida. Tra. ē. I. car. 7 ibi
est cū. I. uitto 7 II. bord. Vat 7 ualuit sep. x. sot. Hanc
trā tenuit Odo hō Brictrici fuit. 7 uende potuit.

In Cetedone ten Hugo dim hid. *IN ERLAI HVND.*
sed wastata. ē. Hanc trā tenuit Vluuin de Wadone.

In Wadone ten ten Hugo. I. hid. 7 uende pot.
Tra. ē. I. car. 7 ibi. ē cū uno uitto. pt̄u. I. car. Valet
7 ualuit. x. sot. T.R.E. xx. sot. Hanc trā tenuer. II.
hoēs Brictrici 7 uende potuer. *IN SIGELAI HVND.*

M Ipse Hugo ten CALVRETONE. p x. hid se defd. Tra
ē. x. car. In dnio. III. hidæ. 7 ibi sunt. III. car. 7 XVIII.
uitti cū. VIII. bord hnt. VII. car. 7 IX^{na}. pot fieri. Ibi
IX. serui. 7 I. molin de XIII. sot 7 IIII. den. Ptū. v. car.
In totis ualent uat 7 ualuit. x. lib. T.R.E. XII. lib.
Hoc M tenuit Bisi teign. R.E. 7 ibi. I. hō Eddid reginæ
II. hid habuit p uno M. 7 uende potuit.

M In Linforde ten Hugo. II. hid 7 I. uirg 7 dim p uno
M. Tra. ē. II. car. In dnio. ē una. 7 v. uitti cū. II. bord
hnt. I. car. pt̄u ibi. I. car. Vat 7 ualuit. xx. sot. T.R.E.
XL. sot. Hoc M tenuer. III. teigni. 7 dare 7 uende pot.

In Herulfmede ten Hugo dim uirḡ. Tra. ē. II. bou.
pt̄u. II. bob. Silua. v. porc. Vat 7 ualuit. II. solid.
Hanc trā tenuit Vlgrim hō Leuuini comitis. 7 uende pot.

In Wauuendone ten Ansel de Hugone. III. hid. una
uirg min p uno M. Tra. ē. III. car. Ibi sunt. IIII. boues.

151 a

cū. II. uittis 7 III. bord. Ptū. III. car. Vat 7 ualuit XL.
sot. T.R.E. LX. sot. Hanc trā tenuit Suen hō Heraldi comitis.
7 uende potuit.

VII XX. TERRA HENRICI DE FEIRERES *IN ESSEDENE HVND.*

M HENRICVS de Ferreres ten Grennedone. p. II.

5 Hugh holds *BROCH* himself for 1 hide.
Land for 1 plough; it is there, with
1 villager and 2 smallholders.
The value is and always was 10s.
Odo held this land; he was Brictric's man; he could sell.

In YARDLEY Hundred

6. In CHEDDINGTON Hugh holds ½ hide, but it is laid waste.
Wulfwin of Whaddon held this land; he could sell.

7 In WHADDON Hugh holds 1 hide. Land for 1 plough; it is there, with
1 villager.
Meadow for 1 plough.
The value is and was 10s; before 1066, 20s.
Two of Brictric's men held this land; they could sell.

In SECKLOE Hundred

8 M. Hugh holds CALVERTON himself. It answers for 10 hides.
Land for 10 ploughs; in lordship 3 hides; 3 ploughs there.
18 villagers with 8 smallholders have 7 ploughs; a ninth possible.
9 slaves. 1 mill at 13s 4d; meadow for 5 ploughs.
The total value is and was £10; before 1066 £12.
Bisi, a thane of King Edward's, held this manor.
There a man of Queen Edith's had 2 hides as one manor;
he could sell.

9 M. In (Great) LINFORD Hugh holds 2 hides and 1½ virgates as one manor.
Land for 2 ploughs; in lordship 1.
5 villagers with 2 smallholders have 1 plough.
Meadow there for 1 plough.
The value is and was 20s; before 1066, 40s.
Three thanes held this manor; they could grant and sell.

[In MOULSOE Hundred]

10 In HARDMEAD Hugh holds ½ virgate. Land for 2 oxen.
Meadow for 2 oxen; woodland, 5 pigs.
The value is and was 2s.
Ulfgrim, Earl Leofwin's man, held this land; he could sell.

11 In WAVENDON Ansel(m) holds 3 hides less 1 virgate from Hugh as
one manor. Land for 3 ploughs. 4 oxen there, with 151 a
2 villagers and 3 smallholders.
Meadow for 3 ploughs.
The value is and was 40s; before 1066, 60s.
Swein, Earl Harold's man, held this land; he could sell.

27 LAND OF HENRY OF FERRERS

In ASHENDON Hundred

1 Henry of Ferrers holds GRENDON (Underwood). It answers for 2 hides.

hiđ ſe defđ. Tra. ē. VIII. car. In dnio. I. hida. 7 ibi
ſunt. III. car. 7 XII. uitti cū. II. borđ hnt. V. car. Ibi
★ IIII. ſerui. Ptū. II. car. Silua qngent porc. In totis
ualent uat 7 ualuit. VI. lib. T. R. E.: VII. lib. Hoc M
tenuit Boding conſtabulari T. R. E. 7 uende pot.

M In Sibdone ten Henricus. VII. hiđ. Tra. ē. VII. car.
In dnio. III. hidæ. 7 ibi ſunt. II. car. 7 aliæ. II. poſs. ee.
Ibi. IIII. uitti cū. I. borđ hnt. II. car. 7 III[cia]. pot fieri.
Ibi. I. ſeruus. ptū. I. car. Vat 7 ualuit. LX. ſot. T. R. E.:
C. ſot. Hoc M tenuit Boding conſtabulari. T. R. E.

XXVIII. TERRA WALTERIJ DE VERNON. *IN STANES HVND.*

WALTERIVS de Vernon. ten in In Herdeuuelle
dim hiđ. Tra. ē dim car. ſed n̄ eſt ibi car. Vat 7 ualuit
sēp. X. ſot. Hanc trā tenuit Turgot teign R. E. 7 uende pot.
In Berlaue ten Walter. VI. hiđ 7 I. uirg 7 dim.
Tra. ē. VI. car. In dnio. III. hiđ 7 dim. 7 ibi ſunt. II. car.
7 VIII. uitti cū. VI. borđ hnt. II. car 7 dim. 7 adhuc
una car 7 dim pot fieri. Ibi. I. ſeruus. 7 ptū. II. car.
Vat 7 ualuit. C. ſot. T. R. E.: IIII. lib. Hanc trā tenuit
Godric hō Aſgari ſtalre. 7 uende pot. *IN VOTESDONE HD*

M Ipſe Walterius ten *MERSTONE*. p. III. hiđ ſe defđ.
Tra. ē. VI. car. In dnio. ē una hida. 7 ibi. ē. I. car. 7 alia
pot fieri. Ibi. VI. uitti cū. V. borđ. hnt. III. car. 7 IIII[ta].
pot fieri. Ibi. I. ſeruus. ptū. II. car. Vat. XL. ſot. Qdo
recep: C. ſot. 7 tntđ T. R. E. Hoc M tenuit Turgot
hō [comitis] Leuuini. 7 uende potuit.

XXIX. TERRA WALTERIJ FILIJ OTHER *IN STOCHES HVND.*

★ M WALTERIVS filius Otheri. ten *STOCHES* [HORTVNE]. p X. hiđ
ſe defđ. Tra. ē. IX. car. In dnio. II. hide. 7 ibi ſunt
II. car. 7 XV. uitti cū. V. borđ. hnt. VI. car. 7 VII[ma]. pot
fieri. Ibi. IIII. ſerui. 7 I. molin de. XX. ſot. ptū. III. car.

Land for 8 ploughs; in lordship 1 hide; 3 ploughs there.
12 villagers with 2 smallholders have 5 ploughs.
4 slaves; meadow for 2 ploughs; woodland, 500 pigs.
The total value is and was £6; before 1066 £7.
Boding the Constable held this manor before 1066; he could sell.

2 M. In SHIPTON (Lee) Henry holds 7 hides. Land for 7 ploughs;
in lordship 3 hides; 2 ploughs there; another 2 possible.
4 villagers with 1 smallholder have 2 ploughs; a third possible.
1 slave; meadow for 1 plough.
The value is and was 60s; before 1066, 100s.
Boding the Constable held this manor before 1066.

28 LAND OF WALTER OF VERNON

In STONE Hundred

1 Walter of Vernon holds ½ hide in HARTWELL. Land for ½ plough;
but there is no plough there.
The value is and always was 10s.
Thorgot, a thane of King Edward's, held this land; he could sell.

[In DESBOROUGH Hundred]

2 In MARLOW Walter holds 6 hides and 1½ virgates. Land for 6 ploughs;
in lordship 3½ hides; 2 ploughs there.
8 villagers with 6 smallholders have 2½ ploughs;
a further 1½ ploughs possible.
1 slave; meadow for 2 ploughs.
The value is and was 100s; before 1066 £4.
Godric, Asgar the Constable's man, held this land; he could sell.

In WADDESDON Hundred

3 M. Walter holds (Fleet?) MARSTON himself. It answers for 3 hides.
Land for 6 ploughs; in lordship 1 hide; 1 plough there; another possible.
6 villagers with 5 smallholders have 3 ploughs; a fourth possible.
1 slave; meadow for 2 ploughs.
Value 40s; when acquired 100s; as much before 1066.
Thorgot, Earl Leofwin's man, held this manor; he could sell.

29 LAND OF WALTER SON OF OTHERE

In STOKE Hundred

1 M. Walter son of Othere holds HORTON. It answers for 10 hides.
Land for 9 ploughs; in lordship 2 hides; 2 ploughs there.
15 villagers with 5 smallholders have 6 ploughs; a seventh possible.
4 slaves; 1 mill at 20s; meadow for 3 ploughs.

In totis ualent uał.vi.lib. Q̃do recep̃: L.sol.T.R.E: vi.lib.
Hoc ϖ tenuit Eldred hō Stig archiepi.7 uende pot.
ϖ Ipse Walter ten *ETTONE*.p xii.hid. *IN BVRNEHÃ HD.*
se defd. Tra.ē.viii.car. In dnio.iii.hide.7 ibi sunt.ii.car.
7 xv.uitti cū.iiii.bord hnt.vi.car. Ibi.iiii.serui.7 ii.
molend de.xx.sol.ptū.ii.car.Silua.cc.porc. De pis
car.mille anguitt. In totis ualent uał.vi.lib. Q̃do
recep: c.sol.T.R.E: vi.lib. Hoc ϖ tenuit Eddid regina.
ϖ Ipse Walter ten *BVRNEHÃ*.p xviii.hid se defd.
Tra.ē.xv.car. In dnio.iii.hidæ.7 ibi sunt.iii.car.
7 xxviii.uitti cū vii.bord hnt.xii.car. Ibi.ii.serui.
ptū.iii.car.Silua sexcent porc.7 ferrū carucis.
In totis ualent uał.x.lib.Q̃do recep: vi.lib.T.R.E:
x.lib.Hoc ϖ tenuit Elmar teign regis.E.

151 b

Radulf ten de Walterio.iiii.hid *IN MOSELAI HVND.*
p uno ϖ.Tra.ē.vi.car. In dnio sunt.ii.7 ix.uitti cū
vii.bord hnt.iiii.car. Ibi.ii.serui.ptū.ii.car. Silua
c.porc. Int tot uał.lx.sol.Q̃do recep: c.sol.T.R.E:
iiii.lib. Hoc ϖ tenuit Osuui.hō Alrici.7 uende pot.

.XXX W TERRA WALTERIJ FLANDRENS *IN MOSELAI HVND.*

WALTERIVS Flandrensis ten 7 Fulcuin de eo
.i.hid 7 i.uirg p uno ϖ.Tra.ē.i.car. Ibi.i.uitts
ptū.i.car. Vał.x.sol.Q̃do recep: xx.sol.7 tntd.T.R.E.
Hanc trā tenuit Suenine hō Heraldi comitis.7 uende pot.

.XXXI. W TERRA WILLI DE FELGERES. *IN STODFALT HVND.*

WILLELM de Felgeres ten *TVRVESTONE*.p v.hid
se defd. Tra.ē.viii.car. pter has.v.hidas. In dnio
sunt.iii.carucatæ træ.7 ibi una car.7 adhuc.ii.pois
esse.7 vi.uitti cū.iiii.bord hnt.v.car. Ibi.iiii.serui.
7 unū molend de vii.sol 7 vi.den. Ptū.viii.car.

Total value £6; when acquired 50s; before 1066 £6.
Aldred, Archbishop Stigand's man, held this manor; he could sell.

In BURNHAM [STOKE] Hundred

2 M. Walter holds ETON himself. It answers for 12 hides.
Land for 8 ploughs; in lordship 3 hides; 2 ploughs there.
15 villagers with 4 smallholders have 6 ploughs.
4 slaves; 2 mills at 20s; meadow for 2 ploughs;
woodland, 200 pigs; from fisheries, 1,000 eels.
Total value £6; when acquired 100s; before 1066 £6.
Queen Edith held this manor.

3 M. Walter holds BURNHAM himself. It answers for 18 hides.
Land for 15 ploughs; in lordship 3 hides; 3 ploughs there.
28 villagers with 7 smallholders have 12 ploughs.
2 slaves; meadow for 3 ploughs; woodland, 600 pigs and plough-shares.
Total value £10; when acquired £6; before 1066 £10.
Aelmer, a thane of King Edward's, held this manor.

In MOULSOE Hundred

151 b

4 Ralph holds 4 hides from Walter as one manor. Land for 6 ploughs;
in lordship 2.
9 villagers with 7 smallholders have 4 ploughs.
2 slaves; meadow for 2 ploughs; woodland, 100 pigs.
Total value 60s; when acquired 100s; before 1066 £4.
Oswy, Alric's man, held this manor; he could sell.

30 LAND OF WALTER OF FLANDERS

In MOULSOE Hundred

1 Walter of Flanders holds 1 hide and 1 virgate as one manor,
and Fulkwin from him. Land for 1 plough.
1 villager.
Meadow for 1 plough.
Value 10s; when acquired 20s; as much before 1066.
Swening, Earl Harold's man, held this land; he could sell.

31 LAND OF WILLIAM OF FEUGERES

In STOTFOLD Hundred

1 William of Feugères holds TURWESTON. It answers for 5 hides.
Land for 8 ploughs besides these 5 hides; in lordship 3
carucates of land; 1 plough there; a further 2 possible.
6 villagers with 4 smallholders have 5 ploughs.
4 slaves; 1 mill at 7s 6d; meadow for 8 ploughs.

In totis ualent uat 7 ualuit .IIII. lib. T.R.E. c. sol.
Hoc m tenuit Wenesi camerari R.E. 7 uende pot.

.XXXII. TERRA WILLI CAMERARIJ. *IN STANES HVND.*

WILLELM camerarius ten 7 Robt de eo .II. hid
in Herdeuuelle. Tra. e .II. car. In dnio. e una. 7 II. uilli
cu .IIII. bord hnt .I. car. Vat 7 ualuit sep .XXX. sol.
Hanc tra tenuit Wlmar pbr. R.E. 7 uende potuit.

.XXXIII. TERRA WILLI FILIJ CONSTANTINI. *IN STANES HVND.*

WILLELM fili constantini ten 7 Suetin de eo
in Sudcote .I. uirg trae 7 VI. acs. Tra. e dim car. Vat
7 ualuit sep. VI. sol. Hanc tra tenuit Vluricus ho
Stigandi archiepi. 7 uende potuit.

.XXXIIII. TERRA WILLI FILIJ MANNE. *IN ESSEDENE HVND.*

WILLELM filius Manne ten in Lotegarser .II. hid
Tra. e .II. car. In dnio .I. hida 7 I. uirg. 7 ibi. e una car.
7 III. uilli hnt .I. car. ptu .I. car. Vat 7 ualuit sep. xx.
sol. Hoc m tenuit Aluric camerarius R.E. 7 uende pot.

.XXXV. TERRA TVRSTINI FILIJ ROLF. *IN STANES HVND.*

TVRSTINVS Filius Rolfi ten 7 Albert de eo parua
CHENEBELLE. p x. hid se defd. Tra. e. x. car. In dnio
sunt .II. 7 aliae .II. poss fieri. Ibi .x. uilli cu uno bord
hnt .III. car. 7 alie .III. poss. ee. Ibi .II. serui. 7 un molin
de .XVI. sol. ptu .x. car. In totis ualent uat 7 ualuit
.c. sol. T.R.E. VI. lib. Hoc m tenuit Brictric teign. R.E.

m In HARDVIC ten Turstin .XIX. hid. *IN COTESLAI HVND.*
Tra. e .XIX. car. In dnio .IX. hidae 7 dim. 7 ibi sunt
.III. car. 7 IIII. pot fieri. Ibi .XXIIII. uilli cu .IIII. bord
hnt .XIIII. car 7 dim. 7 adhuc dim pot fieri. Ibi
VIII. serui. Ptu .x. car. In totis ualent uat .XV.
lib. Qdo recep. x. lib. T.R.E. XVI. lib. Hoc m te
nuit Saxi teign. R.E.

The total value is and was £4; before 1066, 100s.
Wynsi, King Edward's chamberlain, held this manor; he could sell.

32 LAND OF WILLIAM THE CHAMBERLAIN

In STONE Hundred

1 William the Chamberlain holds 2 hides in HARTWELL and Robert from him. Land for 2 ploughs; in lordship 1.
2 villagers with 4 smallholders have 1 plough.
The value is and always was 30s.
Wulfmer, King Edward's priest, held this land; he could sell.

33 LAND OF WILLIAM SON OF CONSTANTINE

In STONE Hundred

1 William son of Constantine holds 1 virgate of land and 6 acres in SOUTHCOTE and Sweeting from him. Land for ½ plough.
The value is and always was 6s.
Wulfric, Archbishop Stigand's man, held this land; he could sell.

34 LAND OF WILLIAM SON OF MANN

In ASHENDON Hundred

1 William son of Mann holds 2 hides in LUDGERSHALL. Land for 2 ploughs; in lordship 1 hide and 1 virgate; 1 plough there.
3 villagers have 1 plough.
Meadow for 1 plough.
The value is and always was 20s.
Aelfric, King Edward's chamberlain, held this manor; he could sell.

35 LAND OF THURSTAN SON OF ROLF

In STONE Hundred

1 Thurstan son of Rolf holds LITTLE KIMBLE and Albert from him. It answers for 10 hides. Land for 10 ploughs; in lordship 2; another 2 possible.
10 villagers with 1 smallholder have 3 ploughs; another 3 possible.
2 slaves; 1 mill at 16s; meadow for 10 ploughs.
The total value is and was 100s; before 1066 £6.
Brictric, a thane of King Edward's, held this manor.

In COTTESLOE Hundred

2 M. In HARDWICK Thurstan holds 19 hides. Land for 19 ploughs; in lordship 9½ hides; 3 ploughs there; a fourth possible.
24 villagers with 4 smallholders have 14½ ploughs; a further ½ possible.
8 slaves; meadow for 10 ploughs.
Total value £15; when acquired £10; before 1066 £16.
Saxi, a thane of King Edward's, held this manor.

~~In Briestoch ten Rainald de Turstino. I. hid. Tra. ē. I. car.~~
~~7 ibi. ē cū. II. bord. 7 I. seruo. ꝑtū. I. car. Val. xx. sol.~~
~~Qdo recep: x. sol. T.R.E. xx. sol. Hanc trā tenuit Aluene quædā femina Siuuardi. 7 potuit dare cui uoluit.~~

151 c

XXXVI. TERRA TVRTINI MANTEL.

TVRSTINVS Mantel ten dim hid *IN STANES HD.*
in Missedene. Tra. ē. II. car. In dnio. ē una. 7 II. uitti
cū uno bord hnt. I. car. ꝑtū. II. car. Silua. xxx. porc.
Val 7 ualuit xx. sol. T.R.E. xxx. sol. Hanc trā tenuit
Seric hō Sired. 7 uende potuit. *IN BVRNEHĀ HVND.*
In Elmodeshā ten Turstin dim hid. Tra. ē. II. car. Ibi
est una. 7 alia pot fieri. Ibi. II. uitti cū uno bord. ꝑtū
II. car. Silua. xxx. porc. Val 7 ualuit. XIII. sol 7 IIII.
den. T.R.E. xx. sol. Hanc trā tenuit Turchil hō. R.E.
In Cestrehā ten Turstin dim hid. 7 uende pot.
Tra. ē. I. car. sed wastata. ē. Val 7 ualuit sēp. v. sol.
Hanc trā tenuit Epy hō Brictric. 7 uende potuit.

XXXVII TERRA RADVLFI DE FELGERES. *IN LĀMVA HVND.*

M RADVLFVS de Felgeres ten *TVEVERDE*. p XVII. hid
se defd. Tra. ē. XVIII. car. In dnio. VI. hidæ. 7 ibi sunt
III. car. 7 adhuc. II. possunt. ee. Ibi. XV. uitti cū. x. bord
hnt. XI. car. 7 adhuc poss. II. fieri. Ibi. IX. serui. ꝑtū
III. car. Silua. c. porc. In totis ualent ual. x. lib.
Qdo recep: VIII. lib. T.R.E. XII. lib. Hoc M tenuit
Goda comitissa. 7 ibi qdā hō Heraldi comitis habuit. III. hid p uno M.
M Ipse Radulf ten *CREDENDONE*. p. x. hid. 7 uende pot.
se defd. Tra. ē. x. car. In dnio. II. hidæ. 7 ibi sunt. II. car.

3 *In BURSTON Reginald holds 1 hide from Thurstan. Land for 1 plough; it is there, with*
2 smallholders and 1 slave.
Meadow for 1 plough.
Value 20s; when acquired 10s; before 1066, 20s.
Aelfwen, a woman of Siward's, held this land; she could grant to whom she would.

36 LAND OF THURSTAN MANTLE

151 c

In STONE Hundred

1 Thurstan Mantle holds ½ hide in (Little) MISSENDEN.
Land for 2 ploughs; in lordship 1.
2 villagers with 1 smallholder have 1 plough.
Meadow for 2 ploughs; woodland, 30 pigs.
The value is and was 20s; before 1066, 30s.
Seric, Sired's man, held this land; he could sell.

In BURNHAM Hundred

2 In AMERSHAM Thurstan holds ½ hide. Land for 2 ploughs; 1 there; another possible.
2 villagers with 1 smallholder.
Meadow for 2 ploughs; woodland, 30 pigs.
The value is and was 13s 4d; before 1066, 20s.
Thorkell, King Edward's man, held this land; he could sell.

3 In CHESHAM Thurstan holds ½ hide. Land for 1 plough, but it is laid waste.
The value is and always was 5s.
Oepi, Brictric's man, held this land; he could sell.

37 LAND OF RALPH OF FEUGERES

In LAMUA Hundred

1 M. Ralph of Feugeres holds TWYFORD. It answers for 17 hides.
Land for 18 ploughs; in lordship 6 hides. 3 ploughs there; a further 2 possible.
15 villagers with 10 smallholders have 11 ploughs; a further 2 possible.
9 slaves; meadow for 3 ploughs; woodland, 100 pigs.
Total value £10; when acquired £8; before 1066 £12.
Countess Goda held this land; there a man of Earl Harold's had 3 hides as one manor; he could sell.

3 M. Ralph holds CHARNDON himself. It answers for 10 hides.
Land for 10 ploughs; in lordship 2 hides; 2 ploughs there.

7 xviii . uitti cū . xi . bord hnt . viii . car . Ibi . iiii . serui.
ptū . ii . car . Int totū uat 7 ualuit . viii . lib . T . R . E : ix . lib.
Hoc m̄ tenuit Eingar hō Heraldi [comitis] . 7 uende potuit.

.VIII.
.XXX — TERRA BERTRANNI DE VERDVN. *IN STOCHES HVND.*

m̄ BERTRANVS de Verduno ten *FERNEHĀ* . p x . hid se desd . Tra . ē . viii . car . In dnio . v . hidæ . 7 ibi sunt . ii . car . 7 v . uitti cū . iii . bord hnt . iiii . car . 7 adhuc . ii . poss . ee . Ibi . ii . serui . ptū . ii . car . Silua | [sexcent'] dc . porc . Int tot uat c . sol . Qdo recep : iiii . lib . 7 tntd T . R . E . Hoc m̄ tenuit Goda comitissa . De hoc m̄ ten Goisfrid de mãneuile dim hid in Elmodeshā . de qua desaisiuit pdictū Bertrãnū dū eet transmare in seruitio regis . Hoc attestat HVNDRET.
7 Radulf tailgebosc fecit sup trā Bertrãni . unū molin . qui non fuit ibi . T . R . E . ut hund testatur.

.XXXIX. — TERRA NIGEL DE ALBINGI. *IN DVSTENBERG HD.*

m̄ NIGELLVS de Albingi ten 7 Rogeri de eo *TILLEBERIE* . p . v . hid se desd . Tra . ē . xi . car . In dnio sunt . iii . 7 xiii . uitti cū . i . bord hnt . vii . car . 7 viii [ua] . pot fieri . Silua . xx [ti] . porc . Int tot uat . vii . lib . Qdo recep : c . sol . T . R . E : vii . lib . Hoc m̄ tenuit Turbt hō Algari [com] . 7 uende potuit.

m̄ In *EIE* . ten Nigell [Wast] de Nigello . ix . hid . *IN TICHESHELE HVND.* 7 unã uirg . Tra . ē . vii . car . In dnio . sunt . iii . 7 x . uitti hnt . iiii . car . Ibi . iiii . serui . ptū . vii . car . In totis ualent uat . vii . lib . Qdo recep : c . sol . T . R . E : viii . lib . Hoc m̄ tenuer . vii . teigni hoēs . R . E . 7 uende potuer.

.XL. — TERRA NIGELLI DE BEREVILE. *IN MVSELAI HVND.*

NIGELLVS de Bereuile ten in Draintone . ii . hid 7 i . uirg p uno m̄ . Tra . ē . viii . car . In dnio . ē una . 7 adhuc ii . poss[æ]unt fieri . Ibi . viii . uitti cū . ii . bord hnt . iiii . car 7 dim . 7 adhuc dim pot fieri . Ibi . iii . serui . ptū . viii . car.

18 villagers with 11 smallholders have 8 ploughs.
4 slaves; meadow for 2 ploughs.
The total value is and was £8; before 1066 £9.
Eingar, Earl Harold's man, held this manor; he could sell.

38 LAND OF BERTRAM OF VERDUN

In STOKE Hundred

1 M. Bertram of Verdun holds FARNHAM (Royal). It answers for 10 hides.
Land for 8 ploughs; in lordship 5 hides; 2 ploughs there.
5 villagers with 3 smallholders have 4 ploughs; a further 2 possible.
2 slaves; meadow for 2 ploughs; woodland, 600 pigs.
Total value 100s; when acquired £4; as much before 1066.
Countess Goda held this manor. Geoffrey de Mandeville held ½ hide of this manor in Amersham, of which he dispossessed the said Bertram while he was overseas on the King's service. The Hundred confirms this. Ralph Tallboys built a mill on Bertram's land which was not there before 1066, as the Hundred testifies.

39 LAND OF NIGEL OF AUBIGNY

In DESBOROUGH Hundred

1 M. Nigel of Aubigny holds TURVILLE and Roger from him.
It answers for 5 hides. Land for 11 ploughs; in lordship 3.
13 villagers with 1 smallholder have 7 ploughs; an eighth possible.
Woodland, 20 pigs.
Total value £7; when acquired 100s; before 1066 £7.
Thorbert, Earl Algar's man, held this manor; he could sell.

In IXHILL Hundred

2 M. In KINGSEY Nigel of le Vast holds 9 hides and 1 virgate from Nigel.
Land for 7 ploughs; in lordship 3.
10 villagers have 4 ploughs.
4 slaves; meadow for 7 ploughs.
Total value £7; when acquired 100s; before 1066 £8.
Seven thanes, King Edward's men, held this manor; they could sell.

40 LAND OF NIGEL OF BERVILLE

In MURSLEY Hundred

1 Nigel of Berville holds 2 hides and 1 virgate in DRAYTON (Parslow) as one manor. Land for 8 ploughs; in lordship 1; a further 2 possible.
8 villagers with 2 smallholders have 4½ ploughs; a further ½ possible.
3 slaves; meadow for 8 ploughs.

Vał.xl.sol.Qdo recep:c.sol.7 tntđ T.R.R.Hoc ϖ
tenuit Leuuin de Neuhā.de rege.7 postea.T.R W.

151 d

de eodē Leuuino tenuit Radulf passaquā.7 inuc
niebat.ii.Loricatos in custodiā de Windesores.
Hunc Radulfū desaisiuit eps constantiensis.7 libauit
Nigello supdicto.

.XLI. TERRA ROGERIJ DE IVERI. *IN TICHESELE HVND.*

ROGERIVS de Iueri ten 7 Picot de eo *LESA*.p.ii.
hid se defđ.Tra.ē.iiii.car.In dnio sunt.ii.7 iiii.
uitti.cū.ii.bord hnt.ii.car.Ibi.ii.serui.ptū.i.car.
Silua.cc.porc.In totis ualent uał.xl.sol.Qdo re
cep:xxx.sol.T.R.E:l.sol.Hoc ϖ tenuit Azorius
filius Toti.hō reginæ Eddid.7 uende potuit.
In Westberie ten Pagan de Rogerio *IN MVSELAI HD.*
ii.hid 7 dim p uno ϖ.Tra.ē.vii.car.In dnio sunt.ii.
car 7 dim.7 viii.uitti cū.ii.bord hnt.iiii.car 7 dim.
Ibi.i.seruus.7 ii.molini de.xviii.sol.ptū.v.car.
Silua.ccL.porc.In totis ualent uał.lx.sol.Qdo recep:
.l.sol.T.R.E:lx.sol.Hoc ϖ tenuit Aluuin fr epi Wluui.
In Dodeforde ten Haimard de Rogerio 7 uende potuit.
ii.hid p uno ϖ.Tra.ē.iiii.car.Ibi.ē una.7 iii.adhuc
poss fieri.Ibi.iiii.bord 7 i.seruus.ptū.iiii.car.Silua
cc.porc.Int totū uał.xx.sol 7 ualuit.T.R.E:xxx.sol.
Hoc ϖ tenuit Leuuin hō Burgeredi.7 dare 7 uende pot.
ϖ Fulco ten de Rogerio *RADECLIVE*.p v.hid se defđ.
Tra.ē.viii.car.In dnio sunt.iii.7 vi.uitti cū.iiii.bord
hnt.iii.car.7 adhuc.ii.poss fieri.Ibi.iii.serui.7.i.mot
de.v.sol.ptū.viii.car.Int totū uał.c.sol.Qdo

Value 40s; when acquired 100s; as much before 1066.

Leofwin of Nuneham held this manor from the King; later, in King William's time, Ralph Passwater held from the same Leofwin; he found 2 mail-clad men for the guard of Windsor. The Bishop of Coutances dispossessed Ralph and delivered (the manor) to the said Nigel. 151d

41 LAND OF ROGER OF IVRY

In IXHILL Hundred

1 Roger of Ivry holds NASHWAY and Picot from him.
It answers for 2 hides. Land for 4 ploughs; in lordship 2.
4 villagers with 2 smallholders have 2 ploughs.
2 slaves. Meadow for 1 plough; woodland, 200 pigs.
Total value 40s; when acquired 30s; before 1066, 50s.
Azor son of Toti, Queen Edith's man, held this manor; he could sell.

In MURSLEY Hundred

2 In WESTBURY Payne holds 2½ hides from Roger as one manor.
Land for 7 ploughs; in lordship 2½ ploughs.
8 villagers with 2 smallholders have 4½ ploughs.
1 slave; 2 mills at 18s; meadow for 5 ploughs; woodland, 250 pigs.
Total value 60s; when acquired 50s; before 1066, 60s.
Alwin, Bishop Wulfwy's brother, held this manor; he could sell.

[In STOTFOLD Hundred]

3 In DADFORD Haimard holds 2 hides from Roger as one manor.
Land for 4 ploughs. 1 there; a further 3 possible.
4 smallholders and 1 slave.
Meadow for 4 ploughs; woodland, 200 pigs.
In total, the value is and was 20s; before 1066, 30s.
Leofwin, Burgred's man, held this manor; he could grant and sell.

4 M. Fulk holds RADCLIVE from Roger. It answers for 5 hides.
Land for 8 ploughs; in lordship 3.
6 villagers with 4 smallholders have 3 ploughs; a further 2 possible.
3 slaves; 1 mill at 5s; meadow for 8 ploughs.

recep̄: IIII. lib̄. T.R.E: VI. lib̄. Hoc ꝫ tenuit Azor Toti filius. 7 uende potuit. *IN ROVELAI HVND.*

In Bechentone ten Leuuin de Rogerio. I. hid. Tra ē. I. car. 7 ibi. ē cū. II. uitt̄is. p̄tū. I. car. Vał 7 ualuit sep. x. sol. Hanc trā tenuit Leuric hō Azor. 7 uende potuit.

ꝫ Godefrid ten de Rogerio *TERNITONE*. p. VIII. hid se defd. Tra. ē. x. car. In dn̄io sunt. III. 7 IIII. pot fieri. Ibi. XII. uitt̄i cū. v. bord hn̄t. v. car. 7 VI. pot fieri. Ibi. III. serui. 7 I. mol de. x. oris. p̄tū VI. car. In totis ualent uał 7 ualuit. VI. lib̄. T.R.E: VIII. lib̄. Hoc ꝫ tenuit Azor toti filius. 7 uende pot.

Fulco ten de Rogerio Hasceleie. p una hid. Tra. ē. I. car 7 dim. Ibi. ē una car. 7 dim pot fieri. Ibi. I. bord. 7 I. seruus. p̄tū. I. car 7 dim. Vał. xxx. sol 7 ualuit. T.R.E: xl. sol. Hoc ꝫ tenuit Thori hō regis. E. 7 uende pot.

.XLII. TERRA RICARDI INGANIA. *IN MVSELAI HD.*

RICARDVS Ingania ten in *SENELAI*. II. hid 7 dim p uno ꝫ. Tra. ē. II. car. 7 ibi sunt. cū. VIII. uitt̄is 7 II. seruis. p̄tū. II. car. Silua. L. porc. Vał 7 ualuit sep. XL. sol. Hoc ꝫ tenuit Wluuard teign. R.E.

★. XLIII. TRA MANNON BRITON. *IN ELESBERIE HVND.*

ꝫ MAIGNO Brito ten in *ESENBERGA*. XIIII. hid 7 dim. Tra. ē. XI. car. In dn̄io. v. hidæ. 7 ibi sunt. III. car. 7 VIII. uitt̄i cū. x. bord hn̄t. VIII. car. Ibi. IIII. serui. P̄tū. III. car. Silua. c. porc. In totis ualent uał. VI. lib̄. Q̄do recep̄: IIII. lib̄. T.R.E: x. lib̄. Hoc ꝫ tenuit Leuenot hō regis. E. *IN BVRNEHĀ HD.*

In Celfunte. ten Maigno. IIII. hid 7 III. uirg. Tra. ē. xv. car.

In total, value 100s; when acquired £4; before 1066 £6.
Azor son of Toti held this manor; he could sell.

In ROWLEY Hundred

5 In BEACHAMPTON Leofwin holds 1 hide from Roger.
Land for 1 plough; it is there, with
2 villagers.
Meadow for 1 plough.
The value is and always was 10s.
Leofric, Azor's man, held this land; he could sell.

6 M. Godfrey holds THORNTON from Roger. It answers for 8 hides.
Land for 10 ploughs; in lordship 3; a fourth possible.
12 villagers with 5 smallholders have 5 ploughs;
a sixth possible.
3 slaves; 1 mill at 10 *ora*; meadow for 6 ploughs.
The total value is and was £6; before 1066 £8.
Azor son of Toti held this manor; he could sell.

7 Fulk holds 'HASELEY' from Roger for 1 hide.
Land for 1½ ploughs; 1 plough there; [another] ½ possible.
1 smallholder and 1 slave.
Meadow for 1½ ploughs.
The value is and was 30s; before 1066, 40s.
Thori, King Edward's man, held this manor; he could sell.

42 LAND OF RICHARD THE ARTIFICER

In MURSLEY Hundred

1 Richard the Artificer holds 2½ hides in SHENLEY (Brook End)
as one manor. Land for 2 ploughs; they are there, with
8 villagers and 2 slaves.
Meadow for 2 ploughs; woodland, 50 pigs.
The value is and always was 40s.
Wulfward, a thane of King Edward's, held this manor.

43 LAND OF MAINOU THE BRETON

In AYLESBURY Hundred

1 M. Mainou the Breton holds 14½ hides in ELLESBOROUGH.
Land for 11 ploughs; in lordship 5 hides; 3 ploughs there.
8 villagers with 10 smallholders have 8 ploughs.
4 slaves; meadow for 3 ploughs; woodland, 100 pigs.
Total value £6; when acquired £4; before 1066 £10.
Leofnoth, King Edward's man, held this manor.

In BURNHAM Hundred

2 In CHALFONT (St. Giles) Mainou holds 4 hides and 3 virgates.

In dnio.i.hida.7 ibi sunt.iii.car.7 xiii.uitti 7 viii.bord
hnt.xii.car.Ibi.iiii.serui.7 iii.molend.Vn redd.v.orcs.
7 alij.ii.nil reddun.ptu.i.car.Silua sexcent porc.
7 in ead silua una Area Accipitris.In totis ualent uat
vi.lib 7 x.sol.Qdo recep: c.sol.T.R.E: vi.lib 7 x.sol.
Hoc m tenuit Toui teign.R.E.7 ibi Aluuard ho ej
dimid hid habuit.7 uendere potuit.
In Estone ten Odo de Maignone.iiii.hid 7 dimid.Tra
est.iiii.car 7 dim.In dnio sunt.iii.7 iii.uitti cu.iiii.bord
hnt.i.car 7 dim.Ibi.vi.serui.ptu.ii.car.Int totu
uat.c.sol.Qdo recep: iiii.lib.T.R.E: c.sol.Hoc m te
nuit Sotinz ho Tosti comitis.7 uende potuit. *IN COTESLAI HVND.*
In Helpestrope ten Helgot de Maignone
iiii.hid 7 una uirg p uno m.Tra.e.iii.car.In dnio.ii.car.
7 ii.uitti cu.i.car.Ibi.ii.serui.Ptu.iii.car.Vat.xl.sol.
Qdo recep: xx.sol.T.R.E: iiii.lib.Hoc m tenuer.iiii.
teigni.Vn ho Leuuini comitis.alt ho Wluuen.7 iii.ho Leuuini cius
de Mentemore.7 iiii.ho Brictrici tus.Oms u uende potuer.
In Draitone ten Helgot de Maignone *IN ERLAI HVND.*
vi.hid 7 iii.uirg p uno m.7 iii.acras.Tra.e.iiii.car.
In dnio est una.7 xiii.uitti hnt.iii.car.Ibi.ii.serui.
Ptu.iii.car.Silua.cc.porc.Int totu uat 7 ualuit.iiii.
lib.T.R.E: c.sol.Hoc m tenuit Aluric teign R.E.7 uende pot.
In Landport ten Girard de *IN STODFALD HVND.*
Maignone.ii.hid 7 dim.Tra.e.iii.car.In dnio.e una.
7 unus uitts cu.iii.bord hnt.i.car.7 alia pot fieri.Ibi un
seruus.ptu.i.car.Silua.xl.porc.Int totu uat.xxx.sol.
Qdo recep: xvi.sol.T.R.E: xxx.sol.Hanc tra tenuit
Rauuen ho Wluui epi.7 uende potuit. *IN LAMVA HVND.*
In Torneberge ten Berner de Maignone xiiii.hid 7 i.uirg
p uno m.Tra.e.xi.car.In dnio sunt.iii.7 xiiii.uitti

Land for 15 ploughs; in lordship 1 hide; 3 ploughs there. 152 a
13 villagers and 8 smallholders have 12 ploughs.
4 slaves; 3 mills; one of them pays 5 *ora* and the other two pay nothing; meadow for 1 plough; woodland, 600 pigs; in this woodland, a hawk's eyrie.
Total value £6 10s; when acquired 100s; before 1066 £6 10s.
Tovi, a thane of King Edward's, held this manor; his man, Alfward, had ½ hide there; he could sell.

[In IXHILL Hundred]

3 In ASTON (Sandford) Odo holds 4½ hides from Mainou.
Land for 4½ ploughs; in lordship 3.
3 villagers with 4 smallholders have 1½ ploughs.
6 slaves; meadow for 2 ploughs.
In total, value 100s; when acquired £4; before 1066, 100s.
Soting, Earl Tosti's man, held this manor; he could sell.

In COTTESLOE Hundred

4 In HELSTHORPE Helgot holds 4 hides and 1 virgate from Mainou as one manor. Land for 3 ploughs; in lordship 2 ploughs.
2 villagers with 1 plough.
2 slaves; meadow for 3 ploughs.
Value 40s; when acquired 20s; before 1066 £4.
Four thanes held this manor; one was Earl Leofwin's man, the second Wulfwen's man, the third, Leofwin of Mentmore's man, the fourth, Brictric's man; they could all sell.

In YARDLEY Hundred

5 In DRAYTON (Beauchamp) Helgot holds 6 hides and 3 virgates and 3 acres from Mainou as one manor. Land for 4 ploughs; in lordship 1.
13 villagers have 3 ploughs.
2 slaves; meadow for 3 ploughs; woodland, 200 pigs.
In total, the value is and was £4; before 1066, 100s.
Aelfric, a thane of King Edward's, held this manor; he could sell.

In STOTFOLD Hundred

6 In LAMPORT Gerard holds 2½ hides from Mainou.
Land for 3 ploughs; in lordship 1.
1 villager with 3 smallholders has 1 plough; another possible.
1 slave; meadow for 1 plough; woodland, 40 pigs.
In total, value 30s; when acquired 16s; before 1066, 30s.
Raven, Bishop Wulfwy's man, held this land; he could sell.

In LAMAU Hundred

7 In THORNBOROUGH Berner holds 14 hides and 1 virgate from Mainou as one manor. Land for 11 ploughs; in lordship 3.

cu̅.viii.borđ hn̅t.viii.car̃.Ibi.iii.serui.7 i.molin̄ de.xx.ti
sot.p̃tu̅.iiii.car̃.In totis ualent̃ uat.viii.lib.Qdo recep̃:
vi.lib.T.R.E:viii.lib.Hoc M̄ tenuit Thori teign̄.R.E.

M̄ Ipse Maigno ten̄ PATEBERIE.p xx.hiđ se defđ.Tra.ē
.xiiii.car̃.In dn̄io sunt.iii.7 iiii.pot̃ fieri.Ibi xv.uilli
cu̅.vi.borđ.hn̅t.viii.car̃.7 adhuc.iii.poss̄ fieri.Ibi.viii.
serui.7 i.molin̄ de.xv.sot.Silua.xxx.porc̃.In totis ua
lentijs uat.xii.lib.Qdo recep̃:vii.lib.T.R.E:xii.lib.

M̄ Ipse Maigno ten̄ STOCHES.p.x.hiđ *IN SIGELAI HVND.*
se defđ.Tra.ē.x.car̃.In dn̄io.iii.hide.7 ibi sunt.iii.car̃.
7 xii.uilli cu̅.iiii.borđ hn̅t.vi.car̃.7 vii.ma pot̃ fieri.Ibi
vi.serui.7 i.molin̄ de.viii.sot.P̃tu̅.vi.car̃.In totis
ualent̃ uat 7 ualuit sep̄.x.lib.Hoc M̄ tenuer̄.viii.
teigni.Vn̄ eoꝝ.vi.hiđ dim̃ uirg̃ min̄ tenuit p uno M̄.
7 ipse 7 om̄s alij.vii.potuer̄ uende tr̄a sua̅ cui uoluer̄.

In Lochintone ten̄.ii.milites de Maignone.v.hiđ
p uno M̄.Tra.ē.v.car̃.In dn̄io sunt.ii.7 vi.uilli cu̅.ii.
borđ hn̅t.i.car̃ 7 dim̃.7 dim̃ pot̃ fieri.Ibi.i.seruus.
p̃tu̅.v.car̃.In totis ualent̃ uat 7 ualuit.iii.lib.T.R.E:iiii.lib.
Hoc M̄ tenuit Aluric teign̄.R.E.7 uende potuit.

M̄ Ipse Maigno ten̄ Wluerintone.p xx.ti hiđ se defđ.
152 b
Tra.ē.xx.car̃.In dn̄io.ix.hide.7 ibi sunt.v.car̃.
7 xxxii.uilli cu̅.viii.borđ hn̅t.x.car̃.7 adhuc.v.
possunt fieri.Ibi.x.serui.7 ii.molini de.xxxii.sot.
7 viii.den̄.P̃tu̅.ix.car̃.In totis ualent̃ uat.xx.lib.
Qdo recep̃:xv.lib.T.R.E:xx.ti lib.Hoc M̄ tenuer̄
iii.teigni.Hoꝝ un̄ Goduin̄ ho̅ Heraldi com̄.x.hiđ ha
buit.7 alt̃ Tori Huscarle.R.E.habuit.vii.hiđ
7 dim̃.7 iii.cius Aluric ho̅ Eddid reginæ.ii.hiđ 7 dim̃
habuit.Ipsi om̄s cui uoluer̄ uendere potuerũt.

14 villagers with 8 smallholders have 8 ploughs.
3 slaves; 1 mill at 20s; meadow for 4 ploughs.
Total value £8; when acquired £6; before 1066 £8.
Thori, a thane of King Edward's, held this manor.

8 M. Mainou holds PADBURY himself. It answers for 20 hides.
Land for 14 ploughs; in lordship 3; a fourth possible.
15 villagers with 6 smallholders have 8 ploughs;
a further 3 possible.
8 slaves; 1 mill at 15s; woodland, 30 pigs.
Total value £12; when acquired £7; before 1066 £12.

In SECKLOE Hundred

9 M. Mainou holds STOKE (Hammond) himself. It answers for 10 hides.
Land for 10 ploughs; in lordship 3 hides; 3 ploughs there.
12 villagers with 4 smallholders have 6 ploughs;
a seventh possible.
6 slaves; 1 mill at 8s; meadow for 6 ploughs.
The value is and always was £10.
Eight thanes held this manor. One of them held 6 hides less ½ virgate as one manor; he himself and all the other seven could sell their land to whom they would.

10 In LOUGHTON 2 men-at-arms held 5 hides from Mainou as one manor.
Land for 5 ploughs; in lordship 2.
6 villagers with 2 smallholders have 1½ ploughs;[another] ½ possible.
1 slave; meadow for 5 ploughs.
The total value is and was £3; before 1066 £4.
Aelfric, a thane of King Edward's, held this manor; he could sell.

11 Mainou holds WOLVERTON himself. It answers for 20 hides.
Land for 20 ploughs; in lordship 9 hides; 5 ploughs there. 152b
32 villagers with 8 smallholders have 10 ploughs;
a further 5 possible.
10 slaves; 2 mills at 32s 8d; meadow for 9 ploughs.
Total value £20; when acquired £15; before 1066 £20.
Three thanes held this manor. One of them, Godwin, Earl Harold's man, had 10 hides; the second, Thori, one of King Edward's Guards, had 7½ hides; the third, Aelfric, Queen Edith's man, had 2½ hides; they could all sell to whom they would.

.XLIIII. TERRA GOZELINI BRITONIS. *IN BVRNEHĀ HVND.*

M GOZELINVS Brito ten In Elmodesham dim hid.

Tra.ē.I.car.7 ibi.ē cū.v.bord.7 I.molin de.IIII.sol.
ptū.I.car. Val 7 ualuit sēp.xx.sol. Hanc trā tenuit
Aluric hō Godric uicecom.7 uende pot. *IN COTESLAI HD.*
In Soleberie ten Gozelin.I.hid 7 dim.7 III.partē
uni uirg.p uno M.Tra.ē.IIII.car. In dnio dim hida
7 ibi.ē una car.7 IIII.uitti cū.II.bord hnt.III.car.
Ibi.III.serui.7 I.molin de.XVI.sol.ptū.I.car.Val
7 ualuit sēp.XL.sol. Hoc M tenuit Aluuin hō Eddeue
pulchræ.7 uende potuit.

M Ipse Gozelin ten *COBLINGOTE*.p x.hid se defd.
Tra.ē.IX.car. In dnio.VI.hide.7 ibi sunt.IIII.car.
7 VIII.uitti cū.VIII.bord hnt.v.car.Ibi.v.serui.
ptū.IIII.car. Int totū ual.VI.lib. Qdo recep.III.lib.
T.R.E.VI.lib. Hoc M tenuer.II.hoēs R.E.p.II.M.
Goduin.II.hid 7 Torchill.VIII.hid.7 uende potuer.
In Langraue ten Robt de Gozelino.II.hid 7 dim.
Tra.ē.II.car. In dnio.ē una.7 II.uitti hnt alterā car.
Val 7 ualuit.xx.sol.T.R.E.XXVII.sol. Hoc M te
nuer.II.frs.7 uende potuer. *IN ERLAI HVND.*
Radulf ten de Gozelino.I.hid 7 dim.
Tra.ē.I.car.7 ibi.ē cū.I.uitto 7 II.bord.Ptū.I.car.
Val 7 ualuit.xv.sol.T.R.E.xx.sol. Hanc trā
tenuit Aluuin hō Eddeuæ pulchræ 7 uende pot.

.XLV. TERRA VRSON DE BERSERS. *IN MVSELAI HVND.*

VRSO de Berseres.ten in *SENLAI*.II.hid 7 dim.
p uno M.Tra.ē.II.car. In dnio.I.hida 7 dim.
7 ibi.ē una car.7 uitti hnt.I.car.

44 LAND OF JOCELYN THE BRETON

In BURNHAM Hundred

1 M. Jocelyn the Breton holds ½ hide in AMERSHAM.
Land for 1 plough; it is there, with
5 smallholders.
1 mill at 4s; meadow for 1 plough.
The value is and always was 20s.
Aelfric, Godric the Sheriff's man, held this land; he could sell.

In COTTLESLOE Hundred

2 In SOULBURY Jocelyn holds 1½ hides and the third part of 1 virgate as one manor. Land for 4 ploughs; in lordship ½ hide; 1 plough there.
4 villagers with 2 smallholders have 3 ploughs.
3 slaves; 1 mill at 16s; meadow for 1 plough.
The value is and always was 40s.
Alwin, Edeva the Fair's man, held this manor; he could sell.

3 M. Jocelyn holds CUBLINGTON himself. It answers for 10 hides.
Land for 9 ploughs; in lordship 6 hides; 4 ploughs there.
8 villagers with 8 smallholders have 5 ploughs.
5 slaves; meadow for 4 ploughs.
In total, value £6; when acquired £3; before 1066 £6.
Two men of King Edward's held this manor as 2 manors, Godwin, 2 hides and Thorkell, 8 hides; they could sell.

4 In GROVE Robert holds 2½ hides from Jocelyn. Land for 2 ploughs; in lordship 1.
2 villagers have another plough.
The value is and was 20s; before 1066, 27s.
Two brothers held this manor; they could sell.

In YARDLEY Hundred

5 Ralph holds 1½ hides from Jocelyn. Land for 1 plough; it is there, with
1 villager and 2 smallholders.
Meadow for 1 plough.
The value is and was 15s; before 1066, 20s.
Alwin, Edeva the Fair's man, held this land; he could sell.

45 LAND OF URSO OF BERCHERES

In MURSLEY Hundred

1 Urso of Bercheres holds 2½ hides in SHENLEY (Brook End) as one manor.
Land for 2 ploughs; in lordship 1½ hides; 1 plough there.
The villagers have 1 plough.

Silua . L . porc . Vat 7 ualuit xxx . sot . T.R.E. xL . sot.
Hoc m̃ tenuit Morcar hõ com Heraldi . 7 uende potuit.

.XLVI. TERRA WINEMARI FLANDR. *IN BONESTOV HVND.*

m̃ WINEMARVS ten *HAMESCLE* . p x . hid se defd.
Tra . ẽ . xxvi . car . In dñio sunt . v . hide . 7 p̃t has
v . carucatæ tre . 7 ibi sunt . II . car̃ . 7 adhuc . IIII . poss
fieri . Ibi . xxx.vi . uitti cũ . xi . bord hñt . xviii . car̃.
7 adhuc . II . car poss . ee . Ibi . VIII . serui . 7 I . molin̄ de
xII . sot . Ptũ . xi . car . Silua mille porc . In totis ualent
uat . xxiiii . lib . Qdo recep: xx . lib . T.R.E: xxiiii . lib.
Hoc m̃ tenuit Aldene Huscarl . R.E. 7 uende pot.

.XLVII. TERRA MARTINI. *IN SIGELAI HVND.*

MARTINVS ten In Vlchetone . v . hid 7 dim
p uno m̃ . Tra . ẽ . v . car . In dñio . ẽ una 7 dimidia.

152 c

7 dimid pot fieri . Ibi . vi . uitti cũ . III . bord hñt . III . car.
Ptũ . II . car . Ibi . IIII . serui . Int totũ uat 7 ualuit . c . sot.
T.R.E: vi . lib . Hoc m̃ tenuit Azor filius Toti teign . R.E.
7 alt teign hõ ej tenuit . I . hid . 7 uende potuit.

XLVIII TERRA HERVEI. *IN DVSTENBERG HVND.*

HERVEVS Legat ten in Hibestanes . II . hid de rege.
Tra . ẽ . v . car . In dñio dim hidæ . 7 ibi sunt . II . car . 7 vII.
uitti hñt . II . car . 7 III . pot fieri . Ibi un faber . 7 IIII . serui.
Silua . c . porc . In totis ualent uat 7 ualuit . IIII . lib . T.R.E:
.c . sot . Hoc m̃ tenuit Toui teign . R.E . 7 uende potuit.

.XLIX TERRA HASCOIT MVSARD

HAISCOIT musard ten 7 Eudo de eo In Chentone . II . hid
7 dim p uno m̃ . Tra . ẽ . IIII . car . In dñio . II . car . 7 IIII . uitti
cũ . III . bord hñt . I . car . 7 alia pot fieri . Ibi . II . serui . ptũ
.II . car . Silua . c . porc . Int totũ uat 7 ualuit sep . L . sot.
Hoc m̃ tenuit Azor Toti filius Huscarle . R.E . 7 uende pot.

Woodland, 50 pigs.
The value is and always was 30s; before 1066, 40s.
Morcar, Earl Harold's man, held this manor; he could sell.

46 LAND OF WINEMAR THE FLEMING

In BUNSTY Hundred

1 M. Winemar holds HANSLOPE. It answers for 10 hides. Land for 26 ploughs; in lordship 5 hides and besides them 5 carucates of land; 2 ploughs there; a further 4 possible.
36 villagers with 11 smallholders have 18 ploughs; a further 2 ploughs possible.
8 slaves; 1 mill at 12s; meadow for 11 ploughs; woodland, 1,000 pigs.
Total value £24; when acquired £20; before 1066 £24.
Haldane, one of King Edward's Guards, held this manor; he could sell.

47 LAND OF MARTIN

In SECKLOE Hundred

1 Martin holds 5½ hides in WOUGHTON as one manor.
Land for 5 ploughs; in lordship 1½; [another] ½ possible.
6 villagers with 3 smallholders have 3 ploughs. 152 c
Meadow for 2 ploughs. 4 slaves.
In total, the value is and was 100s; before 1066 £6.
Azor son of Toti, a thane of King Edward's, held this manor; a second thane, his man, held 1 hide; he could sell.

48 LAND OF HERVEY

In DESBOROUGH Hundred

1 Hervey the Commissioner holds 2 hides in IBSTONE from the King. Land for 5 ploughs; in lordship ½ hide; 2 ploughs there.
7 villagers have 2 ploughs; a third possible.
A smith; 4 slaves; woodland, 100 pigs.
The total value is and was £4; before 1066, 100s.
Tovi, a thane of King Edward's, held this manor; he could sell.

49 LAND OF HASCOIT MUSARD

[In ASHENDON Hundred]

1 Hascoit Musard holds 2½ hides in QUAINTON as one manor and Eudo from him. Land for 4 ploughs; in lordship 2 ploughs.
4 villagers with 3 smallholders have 1 plough; another possible.
2 slaves; meadow for 2 ploughs; woodland, 100 pigs.
In total, the value is and always was 50s.
Azor son of Toti, one of King Edward's Guards, held this manor; he could sell.

.L. TERRA GVNFRIDI DE CIOCHES. *IN COTESHALA HVND.*

GVNFRID de Cioches ten̄ 7 Wibald de eo IN Witun graue . vi . hid̄ p̄ uno m̄ . Tra . ē . v . car̄ . In dn̄io sunt . iii . 7 viii . uilli cū . iii . bord̄ hn̄t . ii . car̄ . Ibi . i . seruus . p̄tū . v . car̄ . In totis ualent̄ uat̄ 7 ualuit . c . sol̄ . T.R.E. vi . lib̄ . Hoc m̄ tenuit Suen teign̄ . R.E. 7 uende potuit.

.LI. TERRA GILONIS FR̄IS ANSCVLF *IN STOCHES HVND.*

GILO fr̄ Ansculfi ten̄ *DACETA* . p̄ xiii . hid̄ 7 dim̄ . Tra . ē . xii . car̄ . In dn̄io . v . hidæ . 7 ibi . ē . i . car̄ . 7 iiii . car̄ poss̄ fieri . Ibi . xvi . uilli cū . vi . bord̄ hn̄t . vii . car̄ . Ibi iii . serui . p̄tū . v . car̄ . Silua . ccc . porc̄ . 7 ii . piscariæ . ii . mil̄ anguill̄ . In totis ualent̄ uat̄ 7 ualuit . vi . lib̄ . T.R.E. xii . lib̄ . De hoc m̄ tenuit Seulf . vi . hid̄ 7 iii . uirḡ p̄ uno m̄ . hō Leuuini com̄ . 7 Siuuard fr̄ . vi . hid̄ 7 iii . uirḡ . hō Heraldi com̄ . 7 ipsi uende potuer̄ . *IN BVRNEHĀ HVND.*

In Bouenie ten̄ Girard de Gilone . iii . hid̄ . Tra . ē . ii . car̄ 7 dim̄ . Ibi . ē dimidia . 7 ii . car̄ poss̄ fieri . p̄tū . ii . car̄ . Silua . lx . porc̄ . Vat̄ 7 ualuit . xx . sol̄ . T.R.E. lx . sol̄ . Hoc m̄ tenuit Siuuard hō Heraldi com̄ . 7 uende potuit.

Aluered de Tame ten̄ de Gilone *IN TICHESHELE HD̄.* . i . hid̄ 7 iii . uirḡ . Tra . ē . ii . car̄ . 7 ibi sunt cū . ii . uillis 7 i . seruo . p̄tū . ii . car̄ . Vat̄ . xxx . sol̄ . Q̄do recep̄ . x . sol̄ . T.R.E. xl . sol̄ . Hoc m̄ tenuit Seulf hō Radulfi com̄ . 7 uende

.LII. TERRA MATHILDIS REGINE. *IN DVSTENBERG HD̄*

m̄ MATHILDIS regina ten̄ *MERLAVE* . p̄ xv . hid̄ se defd̄ . Tra . ē . xxvi . car̄ . In dn̄io . v . hidæ . 7 ibi sunt . ii . car̄ . 7 xxxv . uilli cū . xxiii . bord̄ hn̄t . xxiiii . car̄ . Ibi un seruus . 7 i . molin̄ de . xx . sol̄ . P̄tū . xxvi . car̄ . Silua mille porc̄ . 7 de . i . piscar̄ mille Anguill̄ . In totis ualent̄ uat̄ . xxv . lib̄ . Q̄do recep̄ . x . lib̄ . 7 tntd̄ T.R.E. Hoc m̄ tenuit Algarus comes.

50 LAND OF GUNFRID OF CHOCQUES

In COTTESLOE Hundred

1 Gunfrid of Chocques holds 6 hides in WINGRAVE as one manor and Wibald from him. Land for 5 ploughs; in lordship 3.
8 villagers with 3 smallholders have 2 ploughs.
1 slave; meadow for 5 ploughs.
The total value is and was 100s; before 1066 £6.
Swein, a thane of King Edward's, held this manor; he could sell.

51 LAND OF GILES BROTHER OF ANSCULF

In STOKE Hundred

1 Giles brother of Ansculf holds DATCHET for 13½ hides. Land for 12 ploughs; in lordship 5 hides; 1 plough there; 4 ploughs possible.
16 villagers with 6 smallholders have 7 ploughs.
3 slaves; meadow for 5 ploughs; woodland, 300 pigs;
2 fisheries 2,000 eels.
The total value is and was £6; before 1066 £12.
Saewulf, Earl Leofwin's man, held 6 hides and 3 virgates of this manor as one manor; his brother Siward, Earl Harold's man, 6 hides and 3 virgates; they could sell.

In BURNHAM Hundred

2 In BOVENEY Gerard holds 3 hides from Giles.
Land for 2½ ploughs; ½ there; 2 ploughs possible.
Meadow for 2 ploughs; woodland, 60 pigs.
The value is and was 20s; before 1066, 60s.
Siward, Earl Harold's man, held this manor; he could sell.

In IXHILL Hundred

3 Alfred of Thame holds 1 hide and 3 virgates from Giles.
Land for 2 ploughs; they are there, with
2 villagers and 1 slave.
Meadow for 2 ploughs.
Value 30s; when acquired 10s; before 1066, 40s.
Saewulf, Earl Ralph's man, held this manor; he could sell.

52 LAND OF QUEEN MATILDA

In DESBOROUGH Hundred

1 M. Queen Matilda holds MARLOW. It answers for 15 hides.
Land for 26 ploughs; in lordship 5 hides; 2 ploughs there.
35 villagers with 23 smallholders have 24 ploughs.
1 slave; 1 mill at 20s; meadow for 26 ploughs;
woodland, 1,000 pigs; from 1 fishery 1,000 eels.
Total value £25; when acquired £10; as much before 1066.
Earl Algar held this manor.

M Ipsa regina ten HANBLEDENE . p xx . hid se defd.
Tra . ē . xxx . car . In dnio sunt . v . 7 ibi . III . car . 7 L . uitti
cū . IX . bord hnt . XXVII . car . Ibi . IX . serui . 7 I . molin de
. xx . sol . 7 de . I . piscar mille anguitt . ptū . VIII . car . Silua
septingent porc . In totis redditionibz p annū redd . xxxv .
lib . 7 ad numerū . Qdo uiuebat regina: xv . lib . T.R.E: xvi . lib .
Hoc M tenuit Algar comes.

TERRA JUDITÆ COMITISSÆ. *IN COTESLAU HUND.*

.LIII JUDITA comitissa ten in Holedene . I . hid 7 III . uirg 7 dim .
Torchill ten de ea . Tra . ē . II . car . In dnio . ē una . 7 I . uitts
cū . III . bord ht . I . car . Val 7 ualuit xx . sol . T.R.E: xxx . sol .
Istemet tenuit T.R.E . 7 uende potuit. *IN BONESTOU HUND.*
In Westone ten Anschitill de Jud comit . III . uirg . Tra . ē
dim car . 7 ibi est . ptū . IIII . boū . Silua . xx . porc . Val 7 ua
luit . x . sol . T.R.E: xx . sol . Hanc trā tenuit Vluric hō Wallef com'.
In Lauendene ten Roger de comitissa 7 uende pot.
II . hid 7 I . uirg . 7 IIII . partē uni uirg . Tra . ē . II . car . In dnio
est una . 7 III . uitti cū . II . bord hnt . I . car . Ptū . II . car .
Silua . xxx . porc . Val . xxx . sol . Qdo recep: x . sol . T.R.E:
XL . sol . Hoc M tenuit Hūman hō Alli . 7 uende pot .
In ead uilla ten Gislebt de blosseuile ten de comitissa
II . hid 7 I . uirg . Tra . ē . III . car . sed n̄ sunt ibi . nisi . IIII . bord .
ptū . III . car . Silua . xx . porc . Val 7 ualuit sēp . xx . sol .
Hoc M tenuit Alli Huscarl . R.E . 7 uende potuit.
In ead uilla ten Radulf de comitissa . I . hid . Tra . ē
. I . car 7 dimid . Ibi . I . uitts 7 III . bord . Ptū . I . car 7 dim .
Silua . xv . porc . Val 7 ualuit . x . sol . T.R.E: xx . sol .
Hoc M tenuit Turbt hō Godæ comitissæ . 7 uende pot .

2 M. The Queen holds HAMBLEDEN herself. It answers for 20 hides. 152 d
Land for 30 ploughs; in lordship 5 [hides]; 3 ploughs there.
50 villagers with 9 smallholders have 27 ploughs.
9 slaves; 1 mill at 20s; from 1 fishery, 1,000 eels;
meadow for 8 ploughs; woodland, 700 pigs.
In all its payments it pays £35 a year at face value;
when the Queen was alive £15; before 1066 £16.
Earl Algar held this manor.

53 LAND OF COUNTESS JUDITH

In COTTESLOE Hundred

1 Countess Judith holds 1 hide and 3½ virgates in HOLLINGDON;
Thorkell holds from her. Land for 2 ploughs; in lordship 1.
1 villager with 3 smallholders has 1 plough.
The value is and was 20s; before 1066, 30s.
He also held before 1066; he could sell.

In BUNSTY Hundred

2 In WESTON (Underwood) Ansketel holds 3 virgates from
Countess Judith. Land for ½ plough; it is there.
Meadow for 4 oxen; woodland, 20 pigs.
The value is and was 10s; before 1066, 20s.
Wulfric, Earl Waltheof's man, held this land; he could sell.

3 In LAVENDON Roger holds 2 hides, 1 virgate and the fourth part
of 1 virgate from the Countess. Land for 2 ploughs; in lordship 1.
3 villagers with 2 smallholders have 1 plough.
Meadow for 2 ploughs; woodland, 30 pigs.
Value 30s; when acquired 10s; before 1066, 40s.
Hunman, Alli's man, held this manor; he could sell.

4 In the same village Gilbert of Blosseville holds 2 hides and 1 virgate
from the Countess. Land for 3 ploughs; but they are not there; only
4 smallholders.
Meadow for 3 ploughs; woodland, 20 pigs.
The value is and always was 20s.
Alli, one of King Edward's Guards, held this manor; he could sell.

5 In the same village Ralph holds 1 hide from the Countess.
Land for 1½ ploughs.
1 villager and 3 smallholders.
Meadow for 1½ ploughs; woodland, 15 pigs.
The value is and was 10s; before 1066, 20s.
Thorbert, Countess Goda's man, held this manor; he could sell.

IN MOSLAI HD̄ In Cliftone ten̄ Rogeri de Olnei . I . hid 7 dim̄ uirg.
Tra . ē . I . car̄ . sed n̄ ē ibi . Ibi . II . bord . Ptū . I . car̄ . Silua
x . porc̄ . Vał 7 ualuit sep̄ . x . sol . Hanc trā tenuer̄ . II.
teigni hoēs Alrici filij Goding . 7 uende potuit.
In ead ten̄ Nigellus de comitissa . I . hid 7 dim̄ . Tra . ē . II . car̄.
7 ibi sunt cū . II . uillis . 7 IIII . bord . Ibi . I . seruus . 7 dim̄ molin̄
de . XI . sol . Ptū . II . car̄ . Silua . xx . porc̄ . De piscar̄ . c 7 xxv.
anguill . Vał 7 ualuit . xxx . sol . T.R.E . xl . sol . Hoc m̄
tenuit Aluric hō Wluui epi . 7 uende potuit.
In Ambritone ten̄ Roger de comitissa . III . hid p uno m̄.
Tra . ē . III . car̄ . In dn̄io sunt . II . 7 VI . uilli cū . III . bord hn̄t
pot . . I . car̄ . ptū . II . car̄ . Silua . LX . porc̄ . Vał . LX . sol . Qdo
recep̄ . XL . sol . T.R.E . LX . sol . Hoc m̄ tenuit Alric hō Wluui epi.
In Herulfmede ten̄ Morcar . I . hid 7 I . uirg de comitissa.
Tra . ē . I . car̄ 7 ibi . ē . cū . III . uillis 7 I . bord . Ptū . I . car̄.
Silua . L . porc̄ . Vał 7 ualuit . x . sol . T.R.E . xx . sol.
Istemet tenuit T.R.E . 7 uende potuit absq; lictia dn̄i sui.
In Brotone ten̄ Morcar de comitissa . I . hid p uno m̄.
Tra . ē . I . car̄ . 7 ibi . ē cū . I . uillo 7 I . bord . Ptū . I . car̄.
Vał 7 ualuit . x . sol . T.R.E . xx . sol . Istemet tenuit T.R.E . 7 uende pot.

153 a

★ .LIIII. AZELINA uxor Rad tailgebosch *IN COTESHALE HVND.*
ten̄ de rege dim̄ hid in Soleberie . Tra . ē . I . car̄.

In MOULSOE Hundred

6 In CLIFTON (Reynes) Roger of Olney holds 1 hide and ½ virgate.
Land for 1 plough; but it is not there.
2 smallholders.
Meadow for 1 plough; woodland, 10 pigs.
The value is and always was 10s.
Two thanes, Alric son of Goding's men, held this land; they could sell.

7 In the same [village] Nigel holds 1½ hides from the Countess.
Land for 2 ploughs; they are there, with
2 villagers and 4 smallholders.
1 slave; ½ mill at 11s; meadow for 2 ploughs; woodland, 20 pigs; from the fishery 125 eels.
The value is and was 30s; before 1066, 40s.
Aelfric, Bishop Wulfwy's man, held this manor; he could sell.

8 In EMBERTON Roger holds 3 hides from the Countess as one manor.
Land for 3 ploughs; in lordship 2.
6 villagers with 3 smallholders have 1 plough.
Meadow for 2 ploughs; woodland, 60 pigs.
Value 60s; when acquired 40s; before 1066, 60s.
Alric, Bishop Wulfwy's man, held this manor.

9 In HARDMEAD Morcar holds 1 hide and 1 virgate from the Countess.
Land for 1 plough; it is there, with
3 villagers and 1 smallholder.
Meadow for 1 plough; woodland, 50 pigs.
The value is and was 10s; before 1066, 20s.
He also held before 1066; he could sell without his lord's permission.

10 In BROUGHTON Morcar holds 1 hide from the Countess as one manor.
Land for 1 plough; it is there, with
1 villager and 1 smallholder.
Meadow for 1 plough.
The value is and was 10s; before 1066, 20s.
He also held before 1066; he could sell.

54 [LAND OF AZELINA] 153 a

In COTTESLOE Hundred

1 Azelina wife of Ralph Tallboys holds ½ hide in SOULBURY from the King.
Land for 1 plough; it is there.
Meadow for 1 plough.

7 ibi.ẽ.p̃tũ.I.car. Vał 7 ualuit sẽp.x.sot.Duo angli

.LV. teneñ.7 ipsi tenuer̃.T.R.E. *In Lãmva hvnd.*

M̃ Alricvs coquus ten de rege *Claindone.*

p.xx.hid se defd.Tra.ẽ.xxIIII.car.In dñio.v.hide.

7 ibi sunt.v.car.7 L.uitti cũ.III.bord hñt.xIx.car.

Ibi.vII.serui.P̃tũ.IIII.car.Silua.c.porc.In totis

ualent uał xvI.lib.Q̃do recep̃:xI.lib.7 tntđ

T.R.E. Hoc M̃ tenuit Eddid regina.

.LVI. Terra Alsi *In Bvrnehã hvnd.*

M̃ Alsi ten de rege in *Cestrehã*.IIII.hid.Tra.ẽ.Ix.car.

In dñio.I.hida 7 dim.7 ibi sunt.II.car.7 x.uitti cũ.v.bord

hñt.vII.car.Ibi.vI.serui.7 p̃tũ.II.car.Silua octingent

porc.7 I.moliñ de.vI.sot 7 vIII.den.Vał 7 ualuit.IIII.lib.

T.R.E:c.sot.Hoc M̃ tenuit Eddid regina.7 ipsa dedit

eidẽ Alsi post aduentũ regis.W. *In Essedene hđ.*

In Sortelai ten Alsi.IIII.hid p uno.M̃.Tra.ẽ.vI.car.

In dñio.II.hidæ.7 ibi sunt.II.car.7 v.uitti cũ.IIII.bord

hñt.III.car.Ibi.II.serui.p̃tũ.II.car.Silua.cccc.porc.

In totis ualent uał 7 ualuit sẽp III.lib.Hoc M̃ tenuit

Wluuard hõ reginæ Eddid.T.R.E.7 ipsa dedit huic

Alsi.cũ filia Wluuardi.

In Sibdone ten Alsi.II.hid de rege.Tra.ẽ.I.car.Ibi.ẽ

dim car.7 dim pot fieri.P̃tũ.I.car.Vał 7 ualuit.x.

sot.T.R.E:xx.sot.7 hanc trã sũpsit cũ uxore sua.

.LVII Terra Lewini de Neweham. *In Mvselai hvnd.*

Lewinvs de Neuhã ten de rege in Sceldene.II.hid

7 III.uirg 7 dim p uno M̃.Tra.ẽ.III.car.In dñio.I.car.

The value is and always was 10s.
Two Englishmen hold it and held it themselves before 1066.

55 [LAND OF ALRIC COOK]

In LAMUA Hundred

1 M. Alric Cook holds (Steeple) CLAYDON from the King. It answers for 20 hides. Land for 24 ploughs; in lordship 5 hides; 5 ploughs there.
50 villagers with 3 smallholders have 19 ploughs.
7 slaves; meadow for 4 ploughs; woodland, 100 pigs.
Total value £16; when acquired £11; as much before 1066.
Queen Edith held this manor.

56 LAND OF ALFSI

In BURNHAM Hundred

1 M. Alfsi holds 4 hides in CHESHAM from the King.
Land for 9 ploughs; in lordship 1½ hides; 2 ploughs there.
10 villagers with 5 smallholders have 7 ploughs.
6 slaves; meadow for 2 ploughs; woodland, 800 pigs; 1 mill at 6s 8d.
The value is and was £4; before 1066, 100s.
Queen Edith held this manor; she gave it to Alfsi after King William's arrival.

In ASHENDON Hundred

2 In 'SHORTLEY' Alfsi holds 4 hides as one manor. Land for 6 ploughs; in lordship 2 hides; 2 ploughs there.
5 villagers with 4 smallholders have 3 ploughs.
2 slaves; meadow for 2 ploughs; woodland, 400 pigs.
The total value is and always was £3.
Wulfward, Queen Edith's man, held this manor before 1066; she gave it to Alfsi with Wulfward's daughter.

3 In SHIPTON (Lee) Alfsi holds 2 hides from the King.
Land for 1 plough; ½ plough there; [another] ½ possible.
Meadow for 1 plough.
The value is and was 10s; before 1066, 20s.
He took this land with his wife.

57 LAND OF LEOFWIN OF NUNEHAM [AND OTHERS]

In MURSLEY Hundred

1 Leofwin of Nuneham holds 2 hides and 3½ virgates in SALDEN from the King as one manor. Land for 3 ploughs; in lordship 1 plough.

7 vi . uitti cū . iii . borđ hnt . ii . car . Ibi . ii . serui . ptū . iii .
car . Vat 7 ualuit xxx . sot . Qdo recep: xl . sot . Hoc m
tenuit istemet . T.R.E . 7 uende potuit.

In Muselai ten Leuuin . iiii . hid . Tra . ē . iii . car . Ibi
sunt . ii . 7 tcia pot fieri . Ibi . iiii . uitti cū . ii . borđ . ptū
i . car . Vat 7 ualuit . xx . sot . T.R.E: xxx . sot . Hoc m
tenuit istemet . T.R.E . 7 uende potuit. *In STODFALD HD.*

In Mortone ten Leuuin . v . hid p uno m . Tra . ē . v .
car . In dnio . ii . hidæ . 7 ibi . ē dimid car . 7 alia 7 dim
pot fieri . Ibi . iii . uitti cū . ii . borđ hnt . i . car 7 dim.
7 adhuc dim pot fieri . Ibi . v . serui . 7 i . molin de . x .
sot . ptū . ii . car . In totis ualent uat 7 ualuit sep . xl .
sot . Hoc m tenuit istemet . T.R.E . 7 uende potuit.

In Bechentone ten Leuuin . iiii . hid *In ROVELAI HD.*
p uno m . Tra . ē . iiii . car . In dnio . i . hida . 7 ibi sunt . ii .
car . 7 v . uitti cū . vi . borđ hnt . ii . car . Ibi . ii . serui .
Ptū . iii . car . Vat 7 ualuit . xl . sot . T.R.E: l . sot .
Hoc m tenuit isđ Leuuin T.R.E . 7 uende potuit.

In Wauendone ten Goduin pbr de Leuuino *In MOSLAI HD*
. i . uirg . Tra . ē . iiii . bob . Ibi . iii . borđ . 7 ptū . iiii . bob.
Vat 7 ualuit . ii . sot . T.R.E . v . sot . Istemet tenuit T.R.E.
7 uende potuit. *In STODFALD HVND.*

Quidā Loripes ten In elemosina de rege Euresel . p una hida . Tra . ē . ii . car .
7 ibi sunt cū . ii . uittis . Vat 7 ualuit sep . xx . sot . Istemet tenuit . T.R.E.

153 b

HVGO Gozeri filius in Dodeforde *In STODFALD HD.*
ten de rege . ii . hid in elemosina . Tra . ē . iiii . car .
Ibi . ē una . 7 iii . poss fieri . Ibi . iii . borđ . ptū . iiii .

6 villagers with 3 smallholders have 2 ploughs.
2 slaves; meadow for 3 ploughs.
The value is and was 30s; when acquired 40s.
He also held this manor before 1066; he could sell.

2 In MURSLEY Leofwin holds 4 hides. Land for 3 ploughs; 2 there; a third possible.
4 villagers with 2 smallholders.
Meadow for 1 plough.
The value is and was 20s; before 1066, 30s.
He also held this manor before 1066; he could sell.

In STOTFOLD Hundred

3 In (Maids) MORETON Leofwin holds 5 hides as one manor. Land for 5 ploughs; in lordship 2 hides; ½ plough there; another 1½ possible.
3 villagers with 2 smallholders have 1½ ploughs; a further ½ possible.
5 slaves; 1 mill at 10s; meadow for 2 ploughs.
The total value is and always was 40s.
He also held this manor before 1066; he could sell.

In ROWLEY Hundred

4 In BEACHAMPTON Leofwin holds 4 hides as one manor. Land for 4 ploughs; in lordship 1 hide; 2 ploughs there.
5 villagers with 6 smallholders have 2 ploughs.
2 slaves; meadow for 3 ploughs.
The value is and was 40s; before 1066, 50s.
Leofwin also held this manor before 1066; he could sell.

In MOULSOE Hundred

5 In WAVENDON Godwin the priest holds 1 virgate from Leofwin. Land for 4 oxen.
3 smallholders.
Meadow for 4 oxen.
The value is and was 2s; before 1066, 5s.
He also held before 1066; he could sell.

In STOTFOLD Hundred

6 A cripple holds EVERSHAW from the King in alms for 1 hide. Land for 2 ploughs; they are there, with
2 villagers.
The value is and always was 20s.
He also held before 1066.

In STOTFOLD Hundred 153 b

7 Hugh son of Gozhere holds 2 hides in DADFORD from the King in alms. Land for 4 ploughs; 1 there; 3 possible.
3 smallholders.

car̄ . Silua . cc . porc̄ . Val 7 ualuit . xx . sol . T.R.E.⁄
xl . sol . Hanc trā tenuer̄ . ii . teigni . Rauaius
7 Vluuard . 7 uende potuer̄. *In Moslai hund.*
Leuuin Chaua ten̄ de rege . i . hid in Wauen
done . Tra . ē . i . car . 7 ibi . ē cū . iii . uilłis 7 v . bord.
Ibi . i . seruus . 7 pt̄ū . i . car̄ . Silua . l . porc . Val
7 ualuit sēp . x . sol . Hanc trā tenuit ipse Leuuin
p̄fect regis . 7 uende potuit. *In Sigelai hund.*
Leuuin ten de rege . i . hid 7 i . uirg . in Suiui
nestone . Tra . ē . i . car . 7 ibi . ē cū . ii . uilłis 7 ii .
bord . pt̄ū . i . car̄ . Val 7 ualuit sēp . x . sol . Iste
met tenuit T.R.E . 7 uende potuit. *In Elesberie hd.*
Leuuin ten de rege dim hid in Wandene.
Tra . ē . i . car̄ . Ibi . ē dimidia . 7 dimid pot fieri.
Ibi . i . bord . Silua . xxx . porc . 7 x . sol redd.
Val 7 ualuit sēp . x . sol . Istemet tenuit . T.R.E.
7 uende potuit . Hanc trā apposuit Radulf
in Wandoure . sz n̄ fuit ibi . T.R.E.
In Wandoure ten . iii . hoēs . i . hid de rege . Tra . ē
. i . car̄ . 7 ibi . ē cū . i . bord . Val 7 ualuit . xx . sol.
T.R.E.⁄ xl . sol . Istimet tenuer̄ T.R.E . 7 uende
potuer̄ . m̄ sunt in firma regis in Wandoure . ubi
non fuer̄ . T.R.E. *In Bonestov hund.*
Chetel ten̄ de rege dim hid in Lauuedene.
Tra . ē dim̄ car̄ . 7 ibi . ē cū . i . bord . pt̄ū . i . car.
Silua . x . porc̄ . Val 7 ualuit . vii . sol . T.R.E.⁄ x . sol.
Istemet tenuit T.R.E . 7 uende potuit. *In Moslai hd.*
Godricus cratel ten̄ de rege . viii . hid 7 dimid
p uno m̄ in Middeltone . Tra . ē . x . car̄ . In
dn̄io . ii . car 7 dim . 7 dim pot fieri . Ibi . xviii .

Meadow for 4 ploughs; woodland, 200 pigs.
The value is and was 20s; before 1066, 40s.
Two thanes, Raven and Wulfward, held this land; they could sell.

In MOULSOE Hundred

8 Leofwin Cave holds 1 hide in WAVENDON from the King.
Land for 1 plough; it is there, with
3 villagers and 5 smallholders.
1 slave; meadow for 1 plough; woodland, 50 pigs.
The value is and always was 10s.
Leofwin, the King's reeve, held this land himself; he could sell.

In SECKLOE Hundred

9 Leofwin Wavre holds 1 hide and 1 virgate in SIMPSON from the King.
Land for 1 plough; it is there, with
2 villagers and 2 smallholders.
Meadow for 1 plough.
The value is and always was 10s.
He also held before 1066; he could sell.

In AYLESBURY Hundred

10 Leofwin holds ½ hide in 'WANDEN' from the King.
Land for 1 plough; ½ there; [another] ½ possible.
1 smallholder.
Woodland, 30 pigs, and it pays 10s.
The value is and always was 10s.
He also held before 1066; he could sell. Ralph put this land in Wendover; but it was not there before 1066.

11 In WENDOVER 3 men held 1 hide from the King.
Land for 1 plough; it is there, with
1 smallholder.
The value is and was 20s; before 1066, 40s.
They held it themselves before 1066; they could sell. Now they are in the King's revenue in Wendover, where they were not before 1066.

In BUNSTY Hundred

12 Ketel holds ½ hide in LAVENDON from the King. Land for ½ plough; it is there, with
1 smallholder.
Meadow for 1 plough; woodland, 10 pigs.
The value is and was 7s; before 1066, 10s.
He also held before 1066; he could sell.

In MOULSOE Hundred

13 Godric Cratel holds 8½ hides from the King as one manor in MILTON (Keynes). Land for 10 ploughs; in lordship 2½ ploughs; ½ possible.

uitti cũ . vi . bord hñt . viii . car̃ . Ibi . vi . serui.
7 i . moliñ de . vi . sol 7 viii . den . p̃tũ . viii . car̃.
Int totũ ual 7 ualuit . c . sol . T . R . E . viii . lib.
Hoc m̃ tenuit Eddid regina. *IN RISBERG HVND.*
Harding ten de rege . i . hid 7 dim in Horsedune.
Tra . ẽ . i . car . 7 ibi . ẽ cũ . ii . bord . Val 7 ualuit . x . sol.
T . R . E . xx . sol . Hanc trã tenuit Vluured . 7 uende pot.
Suarting 7 Herding ten de rege *IN DVSTENBERG HD̃.*
Bradehã . p . ii . hid . Tra . ẽ . ii . car . 7 ibi sunt cũ . ii . uittis.
Val 7 ualuit sẽp . xx . sol . Duo frs hões . R . E . tenuer̃ . 7 uende pot.
In Cetendone ten Suerting de rege . ii . hid *IN ERLAI HD̃.*
7 i . uirg . Tra . ẽ . i . car̃ . 7 ibi . ẽ cũ . i . uitto 7 ii . seruis . p̃tũ . i.
car̃ . Val 7 ualuit sẽp . xx . sol . Fin dan tenuit . 7 uende pot.
In Caldecote ten Suerting . ii . hid 7 dim *IN SIGELAI HVND.*
Tra . ẽ . i . car̃ . Ibi . ẽ una . 7 alia pot fieri . In dñio . i . hida 7 dim.
Ibi . ii . bord . 7 p̃tũ . i . car . Val 7 ualuit sẽp . xx . sol . Hanc trã
tenuit Gonni hõ Aluric filij Goding . 7 uende potuit.
In Soleberie ten Goduin bedellus de rege dim hid. *IN COTESHALE HD̃.*
Tra . ẽ . i . car̃ . 7 ibi . ẽ cũ . i . bord . p̃tũ . i . car̃ . Val 7 ualuit sẽp . vii.
sol . 7 dim . Alric bolest tenuit . T . R . E . 7 hoc dic̃ iste q̃ nc̃ tenet.
qd p aduentũ . R . W . fuit forisfacta.

18 villagers with 6 smallholders have 8 ploughs.
6 slaves; 1 mill at 6s 8d; meadow for 8 ploughs.
In total the value is and was 100s; before 1066 £8.
Queen Edith held this manor.

In RISBOROUGH Hundred
14 Harding holds 1½ hides in HORSENDEN from the King.
Land for 1 plough; it is there, with
2 smallholders.
The value is and was 10s; before 1066, 20s.
Wilfred held this land; he could sell.

In DESBOROUGH Hundred
15 Swarting and Harding hold BRADENHAM from the King for 2 hides.
Land for 2 ploughs; they are there, with
2 villagers.
The value is and always was 20s.
Two brothers, King Edward's men, held it; they could sell.

In YARDLEY Hundred
16 In CHEDDINGTON Swarting holds 2 hides and 1 virgate from the King.
Land for 1 plough; it is there, with
1 villager and 2 slaves.
Meadow for 1 plough.
The value is and always was 20s.
Fin the Dane held it; he could sell.

In SECKLOE Hundred
17 In CALDECOTE Swarting holds 2½ hides. Land for 1 plough; 1 there; another possible; in lordship 1½ hides.
2 smallholders.
Meadow for 1 plough.
The value is and always was 20s.
Gunni, Aelfric son of Goding's man, held this land; he could sell.

In COTTESLOE Hundred
18 In SOULBURY Godwin the Beadle holds ½ hide from the King.
Land for 1 plough; it is there, with
1 smallholder.
Meadow for 1 plough.
The value is and always was 7½s.
Alric Bolest held before 1066. The present holder says this, that after King William's arrival it was forfeited.

153 c, d blank page

BUCKINGHAMSHIRE HOLDINGS ENTERED ELSEWHERE IN THE SURVEY

The Latin text of these entries is given in the county volumes concerned.

In BEDFORDSHIRE

27 LAND OF GILBERT OF GHENT 215 b

In the Half-Hundred of STANBRIDGE

E1 1 Gilbert of Ghent holds EDLESBOROUGH. It answers for 10 hides. Land for 7 ploughs. In lordship 5 hides; 4 ploughs there.
10 villagers have 4 ploughs.
Total value 100s 10[d]; when acquired the same; before 1066 £10.
Ulf, a thane of King Edward's, held this manor; he could do what he would with it.

In OXFORDSHIRE

7 LAND OF THE BISHOP OF BAYEUX 155 c

In LEWKNOR Hundred

E2 5 Ilbert of Lacy holds 2½ hides in TYTHORP from the Bishop of Bayeux. Land for 3 ploughs. Now in lordship 1 plough; 155 d
4 villagers have the others.
Meadow, 10 acres.
The value was 60s; now 40s.

E3 6 Wadard holds 2½ hides and 12 acres of land in the same village. Land for 3 ploughs. Now in lordship 1 plough; 2 slaves.
2 villagers have another (plough).
Meadow, 10 acres.
The value was 60s; now 40s.

49 LAND OF REINBALD 160 b

E4 1 Reinbald holds 1 hide in BOYCOTT from the King. Land for 3 ploughs. Now in lordship 1 plough, with
1 villager.
Woodland 4 furlongs long and 2 wide.
The value was 40s; now 20s. Blackman held it freely.

52 LAND OF BENZELIN 160 b

E5 1 Benzelin holds LILLINGSTONE (Lovell) from the King. 2½ hides. Land for 2 ploughs. Now in lordship 1 plough.
3 villagers with 1 smallholder have 1 plough.
Woodland 10 furlongs long and 5 furlongs wide.
The value is and was 40s. Azor held it freely before 1066.

58 LAND OF RICHARD AND OTHERS OF THE KING'S OFFICERS 160 c

E6 1 Richard the Artificer holds 2½ hides in LILLINGSTONE (Lovell) from the King. Land for 2 ploughs. 1 hide and 1 virgate of this land is in lordship.
5 villagers with 1 smallnolder and 1 slave have 2 ploughs.
Woodland 10 furlongs long and 5 furlongs wide.
The value was 40s; now 60s.

E7 11 Hervey holds 1 hide in IBSTONE from the King. Land for 1 plough.
1 villager.
Meadow, 3 acres.
The value is and was 20s. This land does not pay tax.

E8 13 Hervey also holds IBSTONE. 1 hide. Land for 1 plough.
Value 10s. Ulf held it.

Notes on the Text and Translation

NOTES

ABBREVIATIONS used in the notes. DB... Domesday Book. DG... H.C. Darby and G.R. Versey *Domesday Gazetteer* Cambridge 1975. EPNS... English Place-Name Society Survey, (Buckinghamshire), 1925. MS... Manuscript. OEB... G. Tengvik *Old English Bynames* Uppsala 1938. OE... Old English. OG... Old German. PNDB... O. von Feilitzen *Pre-Conquest Personal Names of Domesday Book* Uppsala 1937. VCH... Victoria County History (Bucks., vol. 1).

The editor is grateful to Mr. J.D. Foy for collating the place identifications with the Lay Subsidy Rolls, (LSR).

The manuscript is written on leaves, or folios, of parchment (sheepskin), measuring about 15 in. by 11 in. (38 by 28 cm), on both sides. On each side, or page, are two columns, making four to each folio. The folios were numbered in the 17th century, and the four columns of each are here lettered a,b,c,d. The manuscript emphasises words and usually distinguishes chapters and sections by the use of red ink. Underlining here indicates deletion.

BUCKINGHAMSHIRE. *BOCHINGHA(M)SCIRE* in red across both columns on folios 143 ab,cd; *BOCHINGH(AM)SCIRE* across every other folio except the last two, 152 cd, 153 ab where there is no title.

The Text

Generally a very neat MS; there is one deletion at the foot of column 151 b but there are no cramped entries or marginal inserts. The numbering of the Landholders List and chapter headings does not correspond. The Bishop of Lincoln entry has no number in the text; this has been corrected in the English translation by the insertion of number 3a. The List of Landholders omits XXXIX thereby being out of phase by two numbers, finally agreeing with the text numbering by the last chapter, the text having omitted to number the two previous entries, Alric Cook and Alfsi, which the List of Landholders omits to name.

4,18 MARLOW. MS has *Berlaue* for *Merlaue*. See also 28,2 and compare 14,1.

4,24 LAND FOR... Space left for number of ploughs to be added.

5,21 1 HIDE. MS figure 1 blotted. (VCH, 241, has 4 hides.)

7,1 THE THANE WULFSTAN. Farley does not reproduce *steign* of MS.

12,12 OF WHOM ONE WAS. Farley reproduces peculiar form *Vhorum* in MS, probably for *quorum (vhorum* for *hvorum* for *quorum* by [hw] [kw] assimilation).

12,31 MEN. *cho(min)es* for *homines*.

12,37 A FURTHER ½ possible. *Facere* for *fieri*.

14,1 BOLBEC. MS in error has *Molebec*. Compare *Berlaue* for *Merlaue* 4,18 and 28,2.

14,33 LENBOROUGH. MS has *EDINGEBERGE* for *LEDINGEBERGE*.

17,29 2 OR... TRE value *ii.vel* followed by a gap, perhaps for *sol.*, or entry awaiting revision.

19,3 £6...8 HIDES... MS is blotted, probably as the clerk wrote the number of pounds, but the numerals are legible and Farley shows them correctly.

21,7 ...VILLAGERS. Gap left for number to be added.

26,7 HOLDS. MS and Farley repeat *ten'*.

27,1 4 SLAVES. Number is unclear in MS. The first stroke is smaller than the others in the group and could be a badly blotched dot. Farley is probably right to read it as 4, although the reading 3 cannot be ruled out.

28,2 MARLOW. See 4,18 note.

29 Chapter NUMBER. MS has XXXIX in error. Farley numbers in sequence.

29,1 HORTON. *STOCHES* deleted by underlining and *HORTUNE* written above.

36 THURSTAN. *TURTINI* for *TURSTINI*.

40,1 BEFORE 1066. *T.R.R.* for *T.R.E.*

43 LAND OF... Farley in error has *TR A*. MS shows TERRA clearly.

54-55 HOLES in the MS, now filled in with repair parchment. Farley does not reproduce the holes. There are three, one to the left of chapter 54 title, one in chapter 54 and one in chapter 55. The writing goes round the holes.

57,9 LEOFWIN. *Wavre* MS *oaura* interlined. The 'o' is clear in the MS. See notes to translation 57,8 and 57,9.

The Translation

B 1 MEADOW FOR ... PLOUGHS. Grazing for the oxen which pulled the plough, reckoned at eight. See 1,1 note.

B 3 BISHOP OF COUTANCES. Geoffrey of Mowbray, a principal minister of King William. 6s. 6d. DB uses the old English currency system which endured for a thousand years until 1971. The pound contained 20 shillings, each of 12 pence, abbreviated as £*(ibrae)*, s*(olidi)*, d*(enarii)*.

B 13 LEOFWIN OF NUNEHAM. Nuneham Courtenay in Oxfordshire, PNDB 318. See also 12,25 Alwin of Nuneham.

L Numbering. For inconsistencies in numbering see introduction to the notes on the Text above.

1,1 HUNDRED. As in some other Shires, the Buckinghamshire Hundreds are normally entered in the same order in each chapter, with the exception of Chapter 1, the King's Land. The order is : Stone, Risborough, Aylesbury, Stoke, Burnham, Desborough, Ixhill, Ashendon, Waddesdon, Cottesloe, Yardley, Mursley, Stotfold, Rowley, Lamua, Seckloe, Bunsty, Moulsoe. In chapter 57 entries occur in this relative order within the separate holdings listed. Square brackets show where DB appears to have omitted a Hundred heading. Places where a Hundred heading seems out of 'order' are noted.
LAND FOR ... PLOUGHS. The number of ploughs entered here is the total of lordship ploughs, villagers' ploughs and ploughs 'possible'. The figures generally tally throughout the county with a few exceptions, see for example 8,2. 21,4. 24,1. 43,8. Meadow for the plough oxen is not always sufficient for the total number of ploughs, see for example 5,7. 13,2.

1,3 SALT-BOILER. The inland salt workings centred on Nantwich in Cheshire and Droitwich in Worcestershire used boilers for the preparation of salt, in contrast to the coastal salt-pans where the salt evaporated naturally. See Warwicks. 28,16 note.

1,5 UPTON. In Stone Hundred near Slough. Many Hundred headings are omitted in the first chapter of the county, and the Hundred 'order' does not apply. See 1,1 note.

2,2 HALTON. Mapped here in Aylesbury Hundred, its geographical position. Hundred 'order' (see 1,1 note) suggests it to be in Stone and EPNS 162 places it in a detached portion of Stone. Later it appears in Feudal Aids in Aylesbury. Compare 4,5, Weston Turville.

3a,1 EIGHT HUNDREDS. *In circuitu* probably means no more than the VCH translation 'which lie round Aylesbury' (VCH 233) and not a Circuit or District of Aylesbury in a formal sense. Eight Hundreds, including Aylesbury Hundred do in fact encircle Aylesbury.

4,1-3 HELTO. VCH (234) notes that Helto held from the Bishop of Bayeux in Kent and was probably the Bishop's steward.

4,5 WESTON TURVILLE. Mapped in Aylesbury Hundred although with Halton (2,2) may have been in detached Stone Hundred.
LISIEUX. Gilbert Maminot, Bishop of Lisieux, the King's doctor and chaplain.

4,6 VARUS. Not as PNDB 160 '? of Ware, Herts.' See also Aelfric Varus, 12,31 and PNDB 179. Compare Edsige Ware, 'the Wary' OEB 357.

4,14 'DILEHURST'. Lost in Taplow, DG and EPNS 232. Round (VCH 235) favours identifying *Dileherst* with Tyler's Green in Penn; *Tygelhurst* in 1316 (Feudal Aids i 48) becoming Tilehurst and by corruption Tyler's; but *tygel-* is from OE *tigel* 'a tile' and *dile-* is OE *dile* 'dill, vetch', so the two place-names are not identical.

4,18 MARLOW. The four entries for *MERLAVE,* here and at 23,4. 28,2 and 52,1 have a total of 35 hides. Great and Little Marlow have both been mapped but not differentiated. For confusion of initial *M* with *B* see note on the text 4,18 above.

4,19 SAUNDERTON. Geographically in Risborough Hundred, but Hundred 'order' (see 1,1 note) suggests Desborough Hundred here and at 23,5. The LSR and EPNS 192 have Saunderton in Desborough Hundred.

4,20 *HANECHEDENE*. Unidentified. DG has Radnage, but see EPNS 203, note 1, which mentions an identification with Winchbottom in Chipping Wycombe. The form *Hanechedene* probably represents *Hauechedene* from OE *hafoca-dene* 'at the valley of the hawks'.

4,23 ASTON SANDFORD. In detached portion of Ixhill Hundred, EPNS 114.

4,25 MARSTON. A total of 9¾ hides for entries here, at 5,4. 17,7-8 and 23,17 suggests this is North Marston, identification at 17,7 confirmed by Feudal Aids i 84 (VCH 254). The smaller holding, 3 hides, is probably Fleet Marston. Both are in Waddesdon Hundred, though later North Marston is sometimes in Ashendon, sometimes in Waddesdon, EPNS 107.

5,1 QUEEN EDITH. Wife of King Edward, daughter of Earl Godwin.

5,10 BLEADON. *Bledone*. The only place named in DB with the same or similar spelling (OE *bleo dun,* 'blue' or coloured hill) is Bleadon in Somerset, with which VCH identifies it, followed by DG. But perhaps this is a variant spelling for Blewbury or Blewburton (EPNS Berks. 151-2) or a lost place. See Beds. 3,8 note and also 5,18 Bucks.

5,17 GOD (?). The phrase *hō di·* here and at 5,19, *hō dei* at 25,2 is unusual. VCH 241 translates 'a man of Deus'. 'Man of God' suggests perhaps an itinerant priest or hermit.

7,2 *ORA*. Literally an ounce. A unit of currency still in use in Scandinavia. Reckoned at either 16d, as here, or at 20d.

12,1 THE MISSENDENS. The entries for Great and Little Missenden are clearly in Stone Hundred. They were later in Aylesbury Hundred, EPNS 152 and LSR. This detached part of DB Stone Hundred may have been linked with Kimble to the NW. Since the neighboruing parishes are all long, thin strips running SE up the combes, part of what was later Great Hampden may have been included, joining Missenden to the main part of the Hundred. See Hampden, 17,4.

12,3 PLOUGH-SHARES, or plough iron, from the woodland where the fuel was; iron was forged more easily there than by hauling timber to the village.

12,25 ALWIN of Nuneham Courtenay. See note B 13.

12,30 VAVASSORS. Undertenants. Obsolete form retained here. It has been observed only in DB Hants. and Suffolk.

12,31 EIGHT THANES. Ten are mentioned in fact.
VARUS. See 4,6 note.

14,3 MISSENDEN. See note 12,1 above.

14,17 LITTLECOTE. Clearly in Cotteslow Hundred in DB. Now in Stewkley parish in Mursley Hundred.

14,18 BURSTON. Entry repeated and deleted at 35,3.

14,26 800 PIGS and 6. Probably shillings omitted, though perhaps 806 pigs was meant.

14,37 LA COUTURE. St. Pierre de la Couture at Le Mans (VCH 251).

14,38 NEWTON LONGVILLE. The Priory of St. Faith at Longueville, Walter's Norman lordship, was afterwards endowed with lands here (Round, VCH 251).

15,2 FISH POND. *Vivarium piscium,* an artificial pond or 'stew' for keeping live fish and eels for domestic consumption.

16,7 VCH 253 suggests that *non* has been omitted before *potuit* in last line, but see 17,26.

17,4 HAMPDEN. Aylesbury Hundred here, later Stone, (LSR). See 12,1 note.

17,7 NORTH MARSTON. See 4,25 note.

17,9 HOGGESTON. Mursley Hundred geographically, though inserted Hundred heading is not in usual Hundred 'order', see 1,1 note.

17,16 ALRIC. An unusual note of sympathy for his condition?

17,17 THE OTHER MEN. The meaning of this passage is not clear. It could be translated 'The Burgesses have 6½ ploughs, and [the] other man's, working outside the 5 hides.', *laborantes = burgenses* or *carucae.* VCH 255 suggests the MS may be defective and the sentence incomplete. The 6½ ploughs are additional to the manorial ploughs.
CARUCATES. Equivalent to the hide in Danish areas, but here probably equivalent to 'land for 1 plough', or *inland,* land exempt from tax, see VCH 225. See also Beds. 10,1 note. For use of 'carucate' elsewhere in Bucks. cf. 17,27. 31,1. 46,1.

17,30 SILVER MARK. 13s 4d making 3 marks to £2.

18,3 BOSC-LE-HARD (?) *Boscroard.* Tengvik 74 s.n., and 73 s.n. *de Bosc,* discusses a suggestion for surname from Bosc-le-hard, Seine Inferieure, Normandy (Tengvik, Map I, p.64). But an alternative and more satisfactory analysis of the form *Boscroard* should be suggested — a French place-name (unidentified as yet) from *bosc* 'bois, wood' and the Old French personal name *Roart, Ruard* = (OG) *Hrodard* (see Forssner 220, s.n. *Rothard).*

19,1 PADBURY. Held by Mainou the Breton, 43,8 but no mention is made of this exchange there.

20,1 CATTLE. *Animalia.* Horses, and other domestic animals kept for the use of the court. See also 19,2.

21,8 VARUS. See 4,6 note.

23,11 'SHORTLEY'. Lost in Quainton, DG and EPNS 111.

23,28 A PLOUGH. Perhaps an error for 'It (the half plough) is there.'

25,2 GOD(?). See 5,17 note.

26,5 *BROCH.* It is probable that Brooks's Copse (grid. ref 81 86 on 2½ in. OS map) is the last trace of this DB manor of *Broch,* EPNS 191.

28,3 MARSTON. Probably Fleet Marston. See 4,25 note, EPNS 136.

29,2 ETON. Mapped in Stone Hundred, as Burnham is probably here misplaced in mistake for the next entry. Eton was in Stoke in LSR, see EPNS 236.

29,4 UNNAMED manor certainly Hardmead, VCH 266.

30,1 UNNAMED manor probably at Bow Brickhill, VCH 266.

35,3 BURSTON. Repeat of 14,18 deleted by underlining.

39,2 KINGSEY. From its size *EIE* included both Kingsey and Towersey (now in Oxon.). The two villages are now divided by the county boundary, but Kingsey, before 1894 partly in Oxon., Towersey at that time being in Bucks. By an order of 1932 the two parishes were exchanged between the two counties. The County Archivist of

Buckinghamshire kindly provided this information.

40,1 PARSLOW. It would seem that, thanks to DB, Ralph Passwater (Passe l'eau) regained this manor as the place still retains his name.

41,7 'HASELEY'. Now lost in Thornton, DG and EPNS 64.

42 ARTIFICER. *Inganie* has the double meaning of 'engineer' and in ingenious or crafty person, (Hunts. 19,15; 26). OEB 347.

43,6 1 VILLAGER HAS... *Habent* a plural verb with singular subject, but *unus villanus cum iii bordariis* is a sort of collective.

48,1 IBSTONE. On the Oxfordshire border. Until 1895 the boundary ran through the main living room of the manor house, EPNS 185.

56 ALFSI. See VCH p. 216 on Wulfward White, his wife and Alfsi, his son-in-law.

57,8 LEOFWIN CAVE. 'Quick, active', see OEB 343.

57,9 LEOFWIN WAVRE. 'Restless, wavering', see OEB 352.

57,10 'WANDEN'. VCH 276 has ?Wendover Dean for *Wandene*. DG also but not EPNS 157.

E Princes Risborough and Twyford are mentioned briefly in DB Oxfordshire in the Borough of Oxford entry, see Oxon. B 5.

Index of Persons

Index of Places

Maps and Map Keys

Systems of Reference

Technical Terms

INDEX OF PERSONS

Familiar modern spellings are given when they exist. Unfamiliar names are usually given in an approximate late 11th century form, avoiding variants that were already obsolescent or pedantic. Spellings that mislead the modern eye are avoided where possible. Two, however, cannot be avoided: they are combined in the name of 'Leofgeat', pronounced 'Leffyet,' or 'Levyet.' The definite article is omitted before bynames, except where there is reason to suppose that they described the individual. The chapter numbers of listed landholders are printed in italics.

Secular Titles and Occupational Names. Artificer *(ingania)* ... Richard. Beadle *(bedellus)* ... Godwin. Chamberlain *(camerarius)*... Aelfric, William, Wynsi. Commissioner *(legatus)*... Hervey. Constable *(stalre, constabularius)*... Asgar, Boding, Bondi. Count *(comes)*... of Mortain. Countess *(comitissa)*... Goda, Gytha, Judith. Earl *(comes)*... Algar, Aubrey, Edwin, Harold, Hugh, Leofwin, Morcar, Ralph, Tosti. Guard *(huscarl)*... Alli, Azor, Burghard, Godnir, Haldane, Thori, Ulf. Queen *(regina)*... Edith, Matilda. Reeve *(prefectus)*... Leofwin. Sheriff *(vicecomes)*... Ansculf, Godric, and 1,1; 3. Young *(cilt)*... Alfward, Alnoth, Edward, Godwin, Wulfward.

INDEX OF PLACES

The name of each place is followed by (i) the initial of its Hundred and its location on the Map in this volume; (ii) its National Grid reference; (iii) chapter and section reference in DB. Bracketed figures denote mention in sections dealing with a different place. Unless otherwise stated, the identifications of EPNS and the spellings of the Ordnance Survey are followed for places in England, of OEB for places abroad. Inverted commas mark lost places with known modern spelling; unidentifiable places are given in DB spelling, in italics. The National Grid reference system is explained on all Ordnance Survey maps, and in the Automobile Association Handbooks; the figures reading from left to right are given before those reading from bottom to top of the map. Places marked with an (*) are in the 100 kilometre grid square lettered SU; those marked (†) in square TQ; all others are in square SP. The Buckinghamshire Hundreds are Ashendon (As); Aylesbury (Ay); Burnham (Bh); Bunsty (Bn); Cottesloe (C); Desborough (D); Ixhill (I); Lamua (L); Moulsoe (Mo); Mursley (Mu); Risborough (Ri); Rowley (Ro); Seckloe (Se); Stoke (Sk); Stone (Sn); Stotfold (Sf); Waddesdon (W); Yardley (Y).

	Map	*Grid*	*Text*
Addingrove	I 5	66 11	14,6
Addington	L 4	74 28	4,40. 23,30
Adstock	L 3	73 30	16,8
Akeley	Sf 8	70 37	14,26
Amersham	Bh 2	*96 97	4,11. 12,4. 21,1. 26,2. 36,2. (38,1). 44,1
Ashendon	As 8	70 14	14,11. 23,9
Aston Abbots	C 10	84 20	8,2
Aston Clinton	Ay 4	87 12	24,1
Ivinghoe Aston	Y 6	95 18	12,20. 21,5
Aston Sandford	I 12	75 07	4,23. 23,6. 43,3
Aylesbury	Ay 2	81 13	1,1. (3a,1)
Barton Hartshorn	Ro 4	64 31	4,37
Beachampton	Ro 10	77 37	14,31. 41,5. 57,4
Beachendon	As 10	75 13	4,24. 23,13
Bedgrove	Ay 6	84 12	4,6
Biddlesden	Sf 1	63 40	1,7. 12,27
Bierton	Ay 1	84 15	4,7
Bleadon			(5,10;18) note
Bledlow	Ri 4	77 02	12,3
Bourton	Ro 2	70 33	B 1. 14,32
Boveney	Bh 10	*93 77	11,1. 51,2
Boycott	Sf B	65 37	E 4
Bradenham	D 2	*82 97	57,15
Bradwell	Se 7	83 39	14,40. 17,20. 23,31
(Bow) Brickhill	Mo 12	90 34	6,2. 14,48-9
Great Brickhill	Mo 14	90 30	13,4
Little Brickhill	Mo 13	90 32	4,43
Brill	I 1	65 13	1,6
Broch (Brooks's Copse)	D 12	*81 86	26,5 see note
Broughton	Ay 3	84 13	15,1
Broughton	Mo 9	89 40	14,46. 53,10
Buckingham	Ro 1	69 34	B 1-13
Buckland	Ay 5	88 12	3a,2
Burnham	Bh 8	*93 82	29,3
East Burnham	Bh 5	*95 84	7,2
Burston	C 12	83 18	12,12-13. 14,18. 23.25. 35,3
Caldecote	Se 4	87 42	12,30. 17,18. 57,17
Calverton	Se 6	79 39	26,8
Caversfield (Oxon.)	Ro 12	58 25	15,2
Chalfont St. Giles	Bh 3	*98 93	43,2
Chalfont St. Peter	Bh 4	†00 91	4,10
Charndon	L 8	67 24	37,2
Chearsley	As 13	71 10	14,12. 23,10
Cheddington	Y 5	92 17	12,21-22. 17,13. 18,2. 19,5. 26,6. 57,16
Chesham	Bh 1	95 01	4,12-13. 26,3. 36,3. 56,1
Chetwode	Ro 7	64 29	4,36
Chicheley	Mo 5	90 45	17,24-26
Chilton	I 6	68 11	14,7
East Claydon	W 2	73 25	16,7. 21,3. 23,15-16
Middle Claydon	W 1	72 25	16,5

	Map	Grid	Text
Medmenham	D 15	*80 84	26,4
Mentmore	C 15	90 19	13,1
Milton Keynes	Mo 10	89 39	14,47. 17,31. 57,13
Great Missenden	Sn 9	89 01	14,3
Little Missenden	Sn 10	*92 98	12,1. 26,1. 36,1
Monks Risborough, see Risborough			
Maids Moreton	Sf 13	70 35	14,28-29. 57,3
Moulsoe	Mo 8	91 42	14,45
Mursley	Mu 8	81 28	12,26. 14,24. 57,2
Nashway	I 3	64 13	41,1
Newport Pagnell	Se 1	87 43	17,17
Newton Longville	Se 15	84 31	14,38
Oakley	I 4	64 12	19,3
Olney	Bs 4	88 51	5,13
Oving	As 1	78 21	5,3
Oxford			(1,3)
Padbury	L 2	72 30	(19,1.) 43,8
Pitstone	Y 9	94 15	12,16-19. 14,19. 23,26-27
Pollicot	As 11	70 13	14,10
Preston Bissett	Ro 8	65 29	4,35
Quainton	As 3	74 20	23,12. 49,1
Quarrendon	W 8	80 15	21,4
Radclive	Sf 15	67 33	41,4
Ravenstone	Bs 2	85 50	14,42
Monks Risborough	Ri 1	80 04	2,3
Princes Risborough	Ri 2	80 03	1,3. (17,2) E (note)
Salden	Mu 6	82 29	12,25. 57,1
Saunderton	D 1	79 01	4,19. 23,5
Shabbington	I 11	66 06	23,7
Shalstone	Sf 11	64 36	4,30. 19,6
Shenley Brook End	Mu 2	83 35	42,1. 45,1
Shenley Church End	Se 12	83 36	13,2-3
Sherington	Mo 4	88 46	5,20
Shipton Lee	As 2	73 21	16,4. 27,2. 56,3
'Shortley'	As	- -	23,11. 56,2
Simpson	Se 13	88 36	5,6. 57,9
Singleborough	Mu 4	77 32	14,22
Slapton	Y 2	93 20	9,1
Soulbury	C 2	88 27	17,10. 23,18. 25,2. 44, 2. 54,1. 57,18
Southcote	Sn 5	79 11	33,1
Staines (Middx.)			(7,2)
Stantonbury	Se 2	84 42	23,32
Stewkley	Mu 11	85 26	5,5. 23,29

	Map	Grid	Text
Stoke Goldington	Bs 5	83 48	5,11. 16,10
Stoke Hammond	Se 16	88 29	43,9
Stoke Mandeville	Ay 7	83 10	3a,1
Stoke Poges	Sk 2	*98 84	17,6
Stone	Sn 1	78 12	4,1. 18,1
Stowe	Sf 6	67 37	4,31
Water Stratford	Sf 12	65 34	19,7
Swanbourne	Mu 10	80 27	1,4. 12,24. 14,20. 17,14. 21,6
Taplow	Bh 7	*91 82	4,15
Tetchwick	As 5	68 19	16,3
Thornborough	L 1	74 33	43,7
Thornton	Ro 11	75 35	41,6
Tickford	Mo 7	90 42	17,27
Tingewick	Ro 3	65 32	4,38
Towersey, see Kingsey			39,2(note)
Turville	D 7	*76 91	39,1
Turweston	Sf 2	60 37	31,1
Twyford	L 5	66 26	37,1.E(note)
Tyringham	Bs 8	85 46	5,10. 17,22
Tythorp	Sn T	73 07	E 2-3
Upton	Sn 3	77 11	1,5. 16,2. 23,1
Waddesdon	W 6	74 17	23,14
Waldridge	I 13	78 07	4,22. 21,2
'Wanden'	Ay	- -	57,10
Water Eaton, see Eaton			
Water Stratford, see Stratford			
Wavendon	Mo 11	91 37	12,36-38. 26,11. 57,5;8
Wendover	Ay 10	86 07	1,2. 57,(10)-11
Westbury	Sf 10	62 35	4,29
Westbury (by Shenley)	Mu 1	82 35	41,2
Weston Turville	Ay 8	85 11	4,5
Weston Underwood	Bs 3	86 50	5,12. 12,34. 53,2
Whaddon	Mu 3	80 34	14,23
Whaddon (in Slapton)	Y 1	92 21	4,26. 26,7
Whitchurch	C 5	80 20	14,16
Lower Winchendon	As 12	73 12	14,13
Upper Winchendon	As 9	74 14	10,1
Windsor (Berks.)		*96 76	(40,1)
Wing	C 8	88 22	12,7
Wingrave	C 13	87 19	12,9. 23,20-22. 50,1
Winslow	Mu 7	76 27	8,3
Wolverton	Se 5	81 41	43,11
Wooburn	D 14	*90 87	3a,4

Places not named

Places not in Buckinghamshire

References are to entries in the Indices of Persons and Places.

Elsewhere in Britain

See also Index of Churches and Clergy.

Outside Britain

BUCKINGHAMSHIRE NORTHERN HUNDREDS

Ashendon (As)
1 Oving
2 Shipton Lee
3 Quainton
4 Grendon Underwood
5 Tetchwick
6 Ludgershall
7 Wotton Underwood
8 Ashendon
9 Upper Winchendon
10 Beachendon
11 Pollicot
12 Lower Winchendon
13 Chearsley

Bunsty (Bs)
1 Lavendon
2 Ravenstone
3 Weston Underwood
4 Olney
5 Stoke Goldington
6 Hanslope
7 Gayhurst
8 Tyringham
9 Lathbury
10 Little Linford
11 Haversham

Cottesloe (C)
1 Hollingdon
2 Soulbury
3 Littlecote
4 Linslade
5 Whitchurch
6 Creslow
7 Cublington
8 Wing
9 Grove
10 Aston Abbots
11 Hardwick
12 Burston
13 Wingrave
14 Crafton
15 Mentmore
16 Helsthorpe

Lamua (L)
1 Thornborough
2 Padbury
3 Adstock
4 Addington
5 Twyford
6 Steeple Claydon
7 Marsh Gibbon
8 Charndon
9 Edgcott

Moulsoe (Mo)
1 Clifton Reynes
2 Emberton
3 Hardmead
4 Sherington
5 Chicheley
6 North Crawley
7 Tickford
8 Moulsoe
9 Broughton
10 Milton Keynes
11 Wavendon
12 Bow Brickhill
13 Little Brickhill
14 Great Brickhill

Mursley (Mu)
1 Westbury
2 Shenley Brook End
3 Whaddon
4 Singleborough
5 Great Horwood
6 Salden
7 Winslow
8 Mursley
9 Drayton Parslow
10 Swanbourne
11 Stewkley
12 Hoggeston
13 Dunton

Rowley (Ro)
1 Buckingham
2 Bourton
3 Tingewick
4 Barton Hartshorn
5 Gawcott
6 Lenborough
7 Chetwode
8 Preston Bissett
9 Hillesden
10 Beachampton
11 Thornton
12 Caversfield

Seckloe (Se)
1 Newport Pagnell
2 Stantonbury
3 Great Linford
4 Caldecote
5 Wolverton
6 Calverton
7 Bradwell
8 Little Woolstone
9 Great Woolstone
10 Loughton
11 Woughton on the Green
12 Shenley Church End
13 Simpson
14 Water Eaton
15 Newton Longville
16 Stoke Hammond

Stotfold (Sf)
1 Biddlesden
2 Turweston
3 Evershaw
4 Dadford
5 Lillingstone Dayrell
6 Stowe
7 Lamport
8 Akeley
9 Leckhampstead
10 Westbury
11 Shalstone
12 Water Stratford
13 Maids Moreton
14 Foxcote
15 Radclive
B Boycott
L Lillingstone Lovell

Waddesdon (W)
1 Middle Claydon
2 East Claydon
3 Granborough
4 Hogshaw
5 North Marston
6 Waddesdon
7 Fleet Marston
8 Quarrendon

Yardley (Y)
1 Whaddon
2 Slapton
3 Horton
4 Edlesborough
5 Cheddington
6 Ivinghoe Aston
7 Ivinghoe
8 Marsworth
9 Pitstone
10 Drayton Beauchamp

Not Mapped
'Shortley' (As)
'Haseley' (Ro)

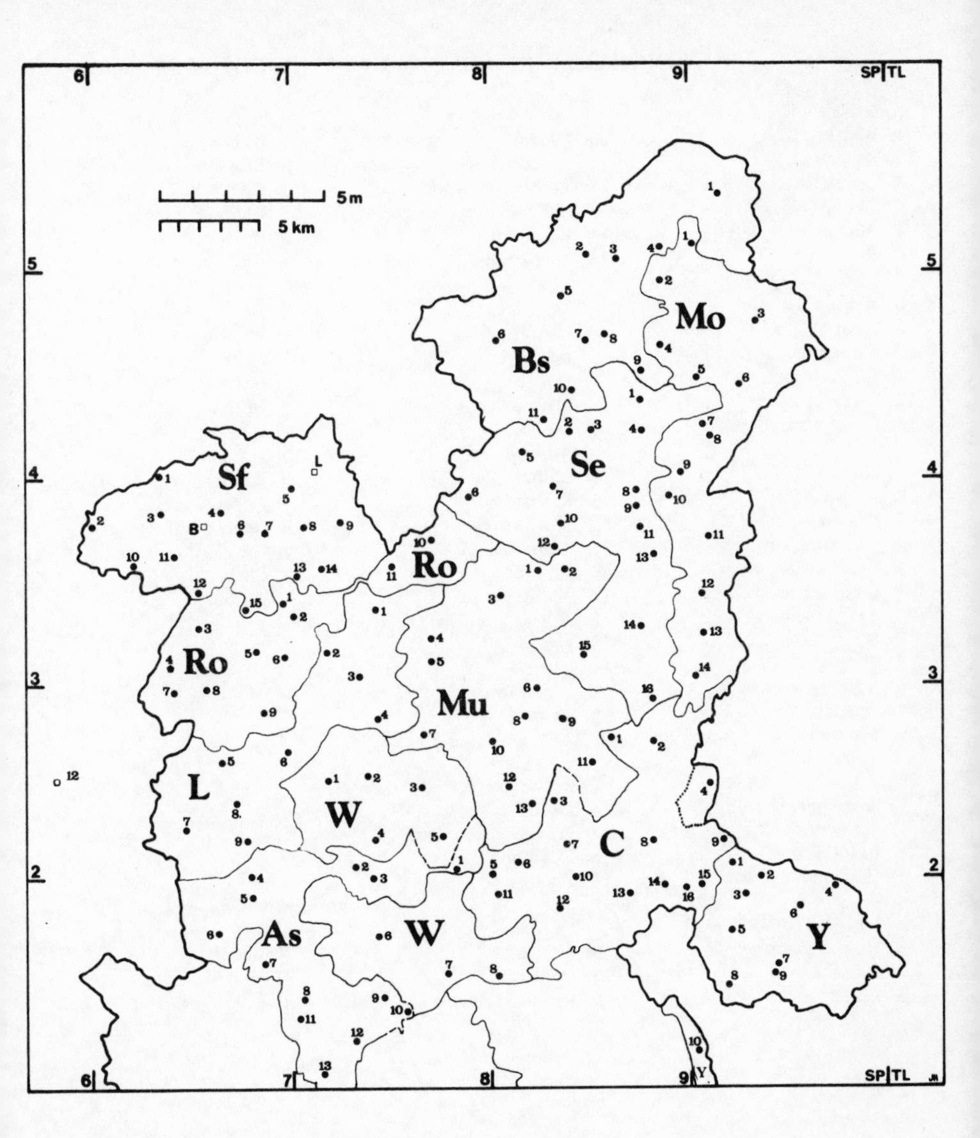

BUCKINGHAMSHIRE NORTHERN HUNDREDS

The County Boundary is marked by thick lines, continuous for 1086, broken where uncertain, dotted for modern boundary; Hundred boundaries (1086) by thin lines, broken where uncertain. An open square denotes a place entered elsewhere in the Survey; an open circle for a place entered in Bucks. but in Oxfordshire.

National Grid 10-kilometre squares are shown on the map border.

Each four-figure square covers one square kilometre, or 247 acres, approximately 2 hides, at 120 acres to the hide.

BUCKINGHAMSHIRE SOUTHERN HUNDREDS

Aylesbury (Ay)

1 Bierton
2 Aylesbury
3 Broughton
4 Aston Clinton
5 Buckland
6 Bedgrove
7 Stoke Mandeville
8 Weston Turville
9 Halton
10 Wendover
11 Ellesborough
12 Little Hampden
13 Great Hampden

Burnham (Bh)

1 Chesham
2 Amersham
3 Chalfont St. Giles
4 Chalfont St. Peter
5 East Burnham
6 Hitcham
7 Taplow
8 Burnham
9 Dorney
10 Boveney

Desborough (D)

1 Saunderton
2 Bradenham
3 Hughenden
4 Ibstone
5 West Wycombe
6 High Wycombe
7 Turville
8 Lude
9 Little Marlow
10 Fawley
11 Hambleden
12 Brooks's Copse
13 Marlow
14 Wooburn
15 Medmenham

Ixhill (I)

1 Brill
2 Dorton
3 Nashway
4 Oakley
5 Addingrove
6 Chilton
7 Easington
8 Long Crendon
9 Worminghall
10 Ickford
11 Shabbington
12 Aston Sandford
13 Waldridge
14 Kingsey and Towersey
15 Ilmer

Risborough (R)

1 Monks Risborough
2 Princes Risborough
3 Horsenden
4 Bledlow

Stoke (Sk)

1 Denham
2 Stoke Poges
3 Farnham Royal
4 Iver
5 Eton
6 Ditton
7 Datchet
8 Horton
9 Wraysbury

Stone (Sn)

1 Stone
2 Hartwell
3 Upton
4 Dinton
5 Southcote
6 Haddenham
7 Little Kimble
8 Great Kimble
9 Great Missenden
10 Little Missenden
T Tythorp

Not Mapped

'Wanden' (Ay)
'Dilehurst' (Bh)
Hanechedene (D)

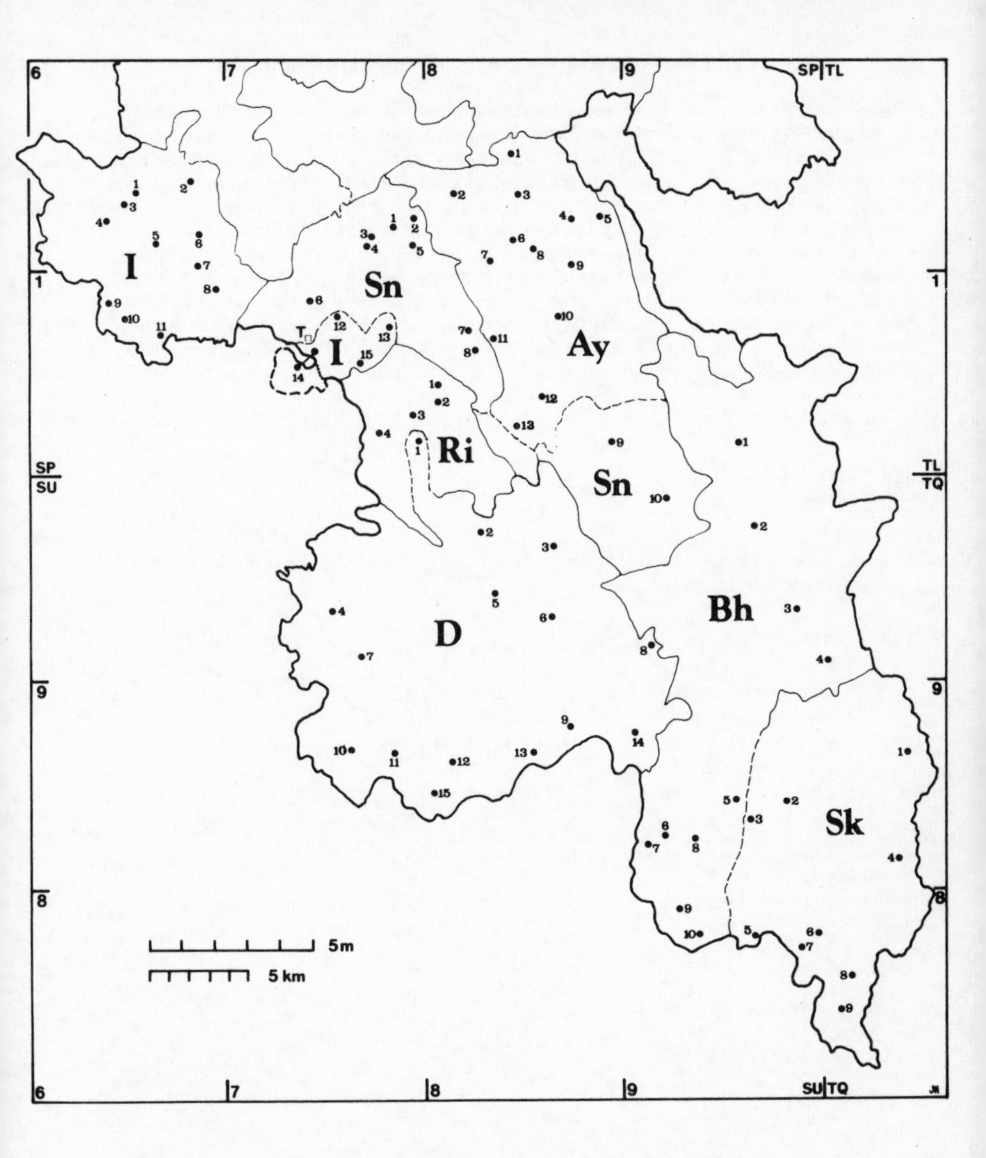

BUCKINGHAMSHIRE SOUTHERN HUNDREDS

The County Boundary is marked by thick lines, continuous for 1086, broken where uncertain, dotted for modern boundary; Hundred boundaries (1086) by thin lines, broken where uncertain. An open square denotes a place entered elsewhere in the Survey.

National Grid 10-kilometre squares are shown on the map border.

Each four-figure square covers one square kilometre, or 247 acres, approximately 2 hides, at 120 acres to the hide.

SYSTEMS OF REFERENCE TO DOMESDAY BOOK

The manuscript is divided into numbered chapters, and the chapters into sections, usually marked by large initials and red ink. Farley however did not number the sections. References have therefore been inexact, by folio numbers, which cannot be closer than an entire page or column. Moreover, half a dozen different ways of referring to the same column have been devised. In 1816 Ellis used three separate systems in his indices; (i) on pages i-cvii; 435-518; 537-570; (ii) on pages 1-144; (iii) on pages 145-433 and 519-535. Other systems have since come into use, notably that used by Vinogradoff, here followed. This edition numbers the sections, the normal practicable form of close reference; but since all discussion of Domesday for three hundred years has been obliged to refer to page or column, a comparative table will help to locate references given. The five columns below give Vinogradoff's notation, Ellis' three systems, and that employed by Welldon Finn and others. Maitland, Stenton, Darby and others have usually followed Ellis (i).

Vinogradoff	*Ellis (i)*	*Ellis (ii)*	*Ellis (iii)*	*Finn*
152 a	152	152 a	152	152ai
152 b	152	152 a	152.2	152a2
152 c	152 b	152 b	152 b	152bi
152 d	152 b	152 b	152b2	152b2

In Buckinghamshire, the relation between the Vinogradoff column notation, here followed, and the chapters and sections is

143a	B 1 - B 13	147a	13,3 - 14,9	151a	26,11 - 29,3
b	L - 1,1	b	14,9 - 14,20	b	29,4 - 35,3
c	1,2 - 1,7	c	14,20 - 14,30	c	36,1 - 40,1
d	2,1 - 3a,1	d	14,30 - 14,39	d	40,1 - 43,2
144a	3a,2 - 4,5	148a	14,40 - 14,49	152a	43,2 - 43,11
b	4,5 - 4,15	b	15,1 - 16,10	b	43,11 - 47,1
c	4,16 - 4,26	c	17,1 - 17,10	c	47,1 - 52,1
d	4,27 - 4,35	d	17,11 - 17,22	d	52,2 - 53,10
145a	4,36 - 4,43	149a	17,22 - 17,31	153a	54,1 - 57,6
b	5,1 - 5,10	b	18,1 - 19,3	b	57,7 - 57,18
c	5,10 - 5,19	c	19,4 - 21,4	c	blank column
d	5,20 - 8,2	d	- 21,4 - 23,3	d	blank column
146a	8,3 - 12,5	150a	23,3 - 23,14		
b	12,6 - 12,18	b	23,14 - 23,28		
c	12,19 - 12,31	c	23,28 - 25,2		
d	12,31 - 13,2	d	25,3 - 26,11		

TECHNICAL TERMS

Many words meaning measurements have to be transliterated. But translation may not dodge other problems by the use of obsolete or made-up words which do not exist in modern English. The translations here used are given in italics. They cannot be exact; they aim at the nearest modern equivalent.

ARPENT. A measure of extent, usually of vineyards. *arpent*
BORDARIUS. Cultivator of inferior status, usually with a little land. *smallholder*
CARUCA. A plough, with the oxen which pulled it, usually reckoned as 8. *plough*
CARUCATA. See note 17,17. *carucate*
COTARIUS. Inhabitant of a *cote*, cottage, often without land. *cottager*
DOMINICUS. Belonging to a lord or lordship. *the lord's* or *household*
DOMINIUM. The mastery or dominion of a lord (*dominus*); including ploughs, land, men, villages, etc., reserved for the lord's use; often concentrated in a *home farm* or *demesne*, a 'Manor Farm' or 'Lordship Farm'. *lordship*
FEUDUM. Continental variant of *feuum*, not used in England before 1066; either a landholder's total holding, or land held by special grant. *Holding*
FIRMA. Old English *feorm*, provisions due to the King or lord; a fixed sum paid in place of these and of other miscellaneous dues. *revenue*
HIDE. A unit of measurement, reckoned at 120 acres. See Sussex, Appendix. *hide*
HUNDRED. A district within a shire, whose assembly of notables and village representatives usually met about once a month. *Hundred*
M. Marginal abbreviation for *manerium*, manor. *M.*
PRAEPOSITUS. Old English *gerefa*, a royal officer. *reeve*
SOCHEMANNUS. 'Soke man', exercising or subject to jurisdiction; free from many villagers' burdens; before 1066 often with more land and higher status than villagers (see e.g.Bedfordshire, Middlesex Appendices); bracketed in the Commissioners' brief with the *liber homo* (free man). *Freeman*
TEIGNUS. Person holding land from the King by special grant; formerly used of the King's ministers and military companions. *thane*
T.R.E. *Tempore regis Edwardi*, in King Edward's time. *before 1066*
VILLA. Translating Old English *tun*, town. The later distinction between a small *village* and large *town* was not yet in use in 1086. *village* or *town*
VILLANUS. Member of a *villa*, usually with more land than a *bordarius*. *villager*
VIRGATA. A quarter of a hide, reckoned at 30 acres. *virgate*